COLLECTED WHEEL PUBLICATIONS

VOLUME 23

NUMBERS 345 – 361

BPS PARIYATTI EDITIONS

BPS Pariyatti Editions
An imprint of Pariyatti Publishing
www.pariyatti.org

© Buddhist Publication Society, 2008

All rights reserved. No part of this book may be used or reproduced in any manner whatsoever without the written permission of BPS Pariyatti Editions, except in the case of brief quotations embodied in critical articles and reviews.

Copies of this book for sale in the Americas only. Although this is an American edition, we have left any British spelling of words unchanged.

First BPS Pariyatti Edition, 2026
ISBN: 978-1-68172-212-2 (Print)
ISBN: 978-1-68172-213-9 (PDF)
ISBN: 978-1-68172-214-6 (ePub)
ISBN: 978-1-68172-215-3 (Mobi)
LCCN: 2018940050

Contents

WH 345   Mahā Kassapa
              Hellmuth Hecker 1

WH 346   Buddhist Perspectives on the Ecocrisis
to 348   *Klas Sandell* 33

WH 349   Inspiration from Enlightened Nuns
& 350   *Susan Elbaum Jootla* 99

WH 351   The Jhānas
to 353   *Henepola Gunaratana Mahāthera* 139

WH 354   Buddhist Stories (From the Dhammapada Commentary, Part IV)
to 356   *Eugene Watson Burlingame/Bhikkhu Khantipālo* 205

WH 357   A Taste of Freedom
to 359   *Ven. Ajahn Chah* 257

WH 360   Mātṛceṭa's Hymn to the Buddha
& 361   *Ven. S. Dhammika* 321

Key to Abbreviations

A	Aṅguttara Nikāya	Paṭis	Paṭisambhidāmagga
Ap	Apadāna	Peṭ	Peṭakopadesa
Bv	Buddhavaṃsa	S	Saṃyutta Nikāya
Cp	Cariyāpiṭaka	Sn	Suttanipātā
D	Dīgha Nikāya	Th	Theragāthā
Dhp	Dhammapada	Thī	Therigātha
Dhs	Dhammasaṅgaṇī	Ud	Udāna
It	Itivuttaka	Vibh	Vibhaṅga
Ja	Jātaka verses and commentary	Vin	Vinayapiṭaka
Khp	Khuddakapāṭha	Vism	Visuddhimagga
M	Majjhima Nikāya	Vism-mhṭ	Visuddhimagga Sub-commentary
Mil	Milindapañha	Vv	Vimānavatthu
Nett	Nettipakaraṇa	Nidd	Niddesa

The above is the abbreviation scheme of the Pali Text Society (PTS) as given in the *A Dictionary of Pali* by Margaret Cone.

The commentaries, *aṭṭhakathā*, are abbreviated by using a hyphen and an "a" ("-a") following the abbreviation of the text, e.g., *Dīgha Nikāya Aṭṭhakathā* = D-a. Likewise the sub-commentaries are abbreviated by a "ṭ" ("-ṭ") following the abbreviation of the text.

The sutta reference abbreviation system for the four Nikāyas, as is used in Bhikkhu Bodhi's translations is:

AN	Aṅguttara Nikāya	DN	Dīgha Nikāya
MN	Majjhima Nikāya	Sn	Saṃyutta Nikāya
J	Jātaka story	Mv	Mahāvagga (Vinaya Piṭaka)
Cv	Cullavagga (Vinaya Piṭaka)	SVibh	Suttavibhaṅga (Vinaya Piṭaka)

Mahā Kassapa

Father of the Saṅgha

by
Hellmuth Hecker

Revised and enlarged translation from the German by
Nyanaponika Thera

Copyright © Kandy; Buddhist Publication Society, (1987)

1. Kassapa's Early Years

Among those of the Buddha's disciples who were closest to him, there were two friends, Sāriputta and Mahā Moggallāna, who were the chief disciples of the Buddha, the exemplary pair of disciples. There were also two brothers, Ānanda and Anuruddha, who were likewise eminent "Fathers of the Order." In between these two pairs stands a great solitary figure, Pipphali Kassapa, who later was called Mahā Kassapa, Kassapa the Great, to distinguish him from the others of the Kassapa clan, such as Kumara Kassapa and Uruvela Kassapa.

After Sāriputta and Mahā Moggallāna had passed away, predeceasing the Buddha, it was Mahā Kassapa who was held in greatest respect and reverence in the Order. But even after the Buddha's passing away, Mahā Kassapa did not become the elected head of the Order of Monks, as it had been the Buddha's express wish that there should not be a supreme authoritative head of the Saṅgha. Shortly before his passing away, the Buddha had said: "That which I have proclaimed and made known, Ānanda, as the Teaching and the Discipline (Dhamma-Vinaya), that shall be your Master when I am gone" (D 16).

Yet the natural authority emanating from Mahā Kassapa made him particularly honoured and venerated in the Saṅgha. There were many factors that contributed to his pre-eminent position after the death of the Master. He had been praised by the Buddha as being equal to him in many respects[1] and he shared with the Master seven of the thirty-two "Marks of a Great Man." He had been the only monk with whom the Buddha had exchanged robes. Mahā Kassapa possessed to the highest degree the ten "qualities that inspire confidence."[2] He was also a model of a disciplined

---

1. He had in common with the Buddha the attainment of the eight meditative absorptions and the six supernormal knowledges (*abhiññā*), which include Arahatship.

2. According to the Gopaka-Moggallāna Sutta (M.108), the ten qualities of a monk that inspire confidence (*pasādaniya-dhamma*) are: he is (1) virtuous, (2) learned, (3) content with his requisites, (4) can easily obtain the four jhānas; he possesses (5) the supernormal powers, (6) the divine ear, (7) penetration of

and austere life devoted to meditation. So it is no wonder that he was elected to preside over the First Council of the Saṅgha which had been summoned on his urgent advice. It may have been on account of all these features of his personality and his life that, much later in China and Japan, Mahā Kassapa came to be regarded as the first patriarch of Ch'an or Zen Buddhism.

Like the two chief disciples, Sāriputta and Mahā Moggallāna, Mahā Kassapa too descended from the brahman caste, and again like them, he was older than the Buddha. He was born in the Magadha country, in the village Mahātittha, as the son of the brahman Kapila and his wife Sumanadevi.[3] He was called Pipphali. His father owned sixteen villages over which he ruled like a little king, so Pipphali grew up in the midst of wealth and luxury. Yet already in his young years there was in him the wish to leave the worldly life behind, and hence he did not want to marry. When his parents repeatedly urged him to take a wife, he told them that he would look after them as long as they live, but that after their deaths he wanted to become an ascetic. Yet they insisted again and again that he take a wife, so to comfort his mother he finally agreed to marry—on the condition that a girl could be found who conformed to his idea of perfection. For that purpose he shaped a golden statue of a beautiful woman, had it bedecked with fine garments and ornaments, and showed it to his parents, saying: "If you can find a woman like this for me, I shall remain in the home life." His parents approached eight brahmans, showered them with rich gifts, and asked them to take the image with them and travel around in search of a human likeness of it. The brahmans thought: "Let us first go to the Madda country, which is, as it were, a gold mine of beautiful women." There they found at Sāgala a girl whose beauty equaled that of the image. She was Bhaddā Kāpilanī, a wealthy brahman's daughter, aged sixteen, four years younger than Pipphali Kassapa. Her parents agreed to the marriage proposal, and the brahmans returned to tell of their success. Yet Bhaddā Kāpilanī also did not wish to marry, as it was her wish,

---

the mind of others, (8) remembrance of former lives, (9) the divine eye, (10) destruction of taints, i.e., Arahatship.

3. This account of Mahā Kassapa's early life is taken from the commentary to the Saṃyutta Nikāya.

too, to live a religious life as a female ascetic. Such identity between her aspiration and Pipphali Kassapa's may well point to a kammic bond and affinity between them in the past, maturing in their present life and leading to a decisive meeting between them and a still more decisive separation later on.

When Pipphali heard that what he had thought most unlikely had actually occurred, he was unhappy and sent the following letter to the girl: "Bhaddā, please marry someone else of equal status and live a happy home life with him. As for myself, I shall become an ascetic. Please do not have regrets." Bhaddā Kapilani, like-minded as she was, independently sent him a similar letter. But their parents, suspecting such an exchange would take place, had both letters intercepted on the way and replaced by letters of welcome.

So Bhaddā was taken to Magadha and the young couple were married. However, in accordance with their ascetic yearning, both agreed to maintain a life of celibacy. To give expression to their resolve, they would lay a garland of flowers between them before they went to bed, determined not to yield to sensual desire.

This young wealthy couple lived thus happily and in comfort for many years. As long as Pipphali's parents lived, they did not even have to look after the estate's farms. But when his parents died, they took charge of the large property.

One day, however, when Pipphali Kassapa was inspecting the fields, it happened that he saw, as if with new eyes, what he had seen so often before. He observed that when his people ploughed, many birds gathered and eagerly picked the worms from the furrows. This sight, so common to a farmer, now startled him. It now struck him forcefully that what brought him his wealth, the produce of his fields, was bound up with the suffering of other living beings. His livelihood was purchased with the death of so many worms and other little creatures living in the soil. Thinking about this, he asked one of his labourers: "Who will have to bear the consequences of such an action?"—"You yourself, sir," was the answer.[4]

---

4. It should be noted that the reply of the labourers does not fully accord with the Buddhist understanding of *kamma*. According to the Buddha *kamma* is constituted by volition, and where volition to take life is absent there is neither

Shaken by that insight into kammic retribution, he went home and reflected: "If I have to carry along the burden of guilt for that killing, what use is all that wealth to me? It will be better if I give it all to Bhaddā and go forth into the ascetic's life."

But at home, at about the same time, his wife had a similar experience. She too saw afresh with a deeper understanding what she had very often seen before. Sesame seeds had been spread out in the open to dry, and crows and other birds ate the insects that had been attracted by the seeds. When Bhaddā asked her servants who it was that had to account morally for the violent death of so many creatures, she was told that the kammic responsibility was hers. Then she thought: "If even by that much I commit a wrong, I won't be able to lift my head above the ocean of rebirths, even in a thousand lives. As soon as Pipphali returns, I shall hand over everything to him and leave to take up the ascetic life."

When both found themselves of one accord, they had pale-yellow cloth and clay bowls brought for them from the bazaar, and then shaved each other's head. They thus became like ascetic wanderers, and they made the aspiration: "Those who are Arahats in the world, to them we dedicate our going forth!" Slinging their alms-bowls over their shoulders, they left the estate's manor, unnoticed by the house servants. But when they reached the next village, which belonged to the estate, the labourers and their families saw them. Crying and lamenting, they fell to the feet of the two ascetics and exclaimed: "Oh, dear and noble ones! Why do you want to make us helpless orphans?"—"It is because we have seen the three worlds to be like a house afire, therefore we go forth into the homeless life." To those who were serfs, Pipphali Kassapa granted their freedom, and he and Bhaddā continued on their road, leaving the villagers behind still weeping.

When walking on, Kassapa went ahead while Bhaddā followed behind him. Considering this, Kassapa thought: "Now, this Bhaddā Kāpilanī follows me close behind, and she is a woman of great beauty. Some people could easily think, 'Though they are ascetics, they still cannot live without each other! It is unseemly what they are doing.' If they spoil their minds by such wrong

---

the *kamma* of taking life nor moral responsibility for the death of those who die through actions outside one's sphere of volitional control.

thoughts or even spread false rumours, they will cause harm to themselves." So he thought it better that they separate. When they reached a crossroads Kassapa said: "Bhaddā, you take one of these roads, and I shall go the other way." She said: "It is true, for ascetics a woman is an obstacle. People might think and speak badly about us. So please go your own way, and we shall now part." She then respectfully circumambulated him thrice, saluted him at his feet, and with folded hands she spoke: "Our close companionship and friendship that had lasted for an unfathomable past[5] comes to an end today. Please take the path to the right and I shall take the other road." Thus they parted and went their individual ways, seeking the high goal of Arahatship, final deliverance from suffering. It is said that the earth, shaken by the power of their virtue, quaked and trembled.

2. Bhaddā Kāpilanī

Let us first follow Bhaddā Kāpilanī. Her road led her to Sāvatthī where she listened to the Buddha's discourses at the Jetavana monastery. As the Order of Nuns (Bhikkhunī Saṅgha) did not yet exist at that time, she took up residence at a nunnery of non-Buddhist female ascetics, not far from the Jetavana. There she lived for five years until she could obtain ordination as a bhikkhunī. It was not long afterward that she was able to attain to the goal of the holy life, Arahatship or Sainthood. One day she uttered the following verses in praise of Mahā Kassapa and declaring her own attainment:

> Son of the Buddha and his heir is he,
> Great Kassapa—his mind serene, collected.
> Vision of previous lives is his,
> Heaven and hell he penetrates.
>
> The ceasing of rebirth he has obtained,
> And supernormal knowledge he has mastered.
> With these three knowledges possessed by him
> He is a brahman true, of threefold knowledge.

---

5. Lit.: 100,000 *kalpas*.

So has she, too, Bhaddā the Kāpilanī, gained for herself
The threefold knowledge and has vanquished death.
Having bravely vanquished Māra and his host,
It is the last formation of a body that she bears.

Seeing the world's deep misery, we both went forth
And are now both free of cankers, with well-tamed minds.
Cooled of passions, we have found deliverance;
Cooled of passions, we have found our freedom.

—Thī 63–66

As an arahat bhikkhunī, Bhaddā devoted herself chiefly to the education of the younger nuns and their instruction in monastic discipline (Vinaya). In the Analysis of Nuns' Discipline (Bhikkhunī Vibhaṅga), instances are recorded involving her pupils which led to the prescribing of certain disciplinary rules for bhikkhunis.[6] There were also two instances when Bhaddā Kāpilanī had to bear the envy of another nun who was hostile towards Mahā Kassapa, too. The nun Thullanandā was learned in the Dhamma and a good preacher, but evidently she had more intelligence than gentleness of heart. She was self-willed and not prepared to change her conduct, as evidenced by several Vinaya texts. When Bhaddā, too, became a popular preacher of Dhamma, even preferred by some of Thullanandā's own pupils, Thullanandā became jealous. In order to annoy Bhaddā, once she and her pupil nuns walked up and down in front of Bhaddā's cell, reciting loudly. She was censured by the Buddha on that account.[7] Another time, at Bhaddā's request, she had arranged temporary living quarters for Bhaddā when the latter visited Sāvatthī. But then, in another fit of jealousy, she threw her out of those quarters.[8] Bhaddā, however, being an arahat, was no longer affected by such happenings and looked at them with detachment and compassion.

The Buddha praised Bhaddā as being the foremost among the nuns who could recollect past lives (Aṅguttara, Ones). The Pali commentaries and the Jātaka stories leave us a record of some of her former lives in which she had been Kassapa's wife.

---

6. *Bhikkhunī Vibhaṅga, Saṅghādisesa* 1; *Pācittiya* 10, 12, 13.

7. *Bhikkhunī Vibhaṅga, Pācittiya* 33.

8. *Bhikkhunī Vibhaṅga, Pācittiya* 35.

3. Past Lives of Kassapa and Bhaddā Kapilani

At the time of the former Buddha Vipassi, they had been a poor brahman couple. They were so extremely poor that they had only one single upper garment, and hence only one of them at a time could go out of their hut. In the record of this story, the brahman was therefore called "he with one garment" (*ekasāṭaka*). Though it may not be easy for us to understand such extreme poverty, it will be still more difficult to understand that there have been many people for whom that utter poverty did not mean subjective, personal suffering. This was so with those two beings who later were to be Kassapa and Bhaddā. In their life as that poor brahman couple, they had lived in such perfect harmony that it was easier for them to bear their poverty. Both, one after the other, had listened to the sermons of the Buddha Vipassi. Through that Buddha's teaching, the value of giving and generosity became so deeply impressed on the mind of that brahman that he wanted to offer his only upper garment to the Order of Monks. But after he had so resolved, scruples came to his mind. As it was his and his wife's only upper garment, he thought that he should first consult his wife. How could they manage if they had no upper garment at all? But he resolutely pushed aside all such hesitation and offered the garment to the monks. Having done so, he clapped his hands and joyfully called out: "I have vanquished! I have vanquished!"

When the king, who had listened to the Buddha Vipassi's sermon behind a curtain, heard that shout of victory and learned its reason, he sent sets of garments to the brahman and later made him his court chaplain. So the couple's plight had come to an end.

As a result of his selfless giving, the brahman was reborn in a celestial world. After parting from there he became a king on earth, a great benefactor of his people who generously supported ascetics and among them also the Paccekabuddhas living at that time. Bhaddā was then his chief queen.

As to Bhaddā, she was once the mother of a brahman youth who was a pupil of the Bodhisatta (the future Buddha) and wanted to become an ascetic. Kassapa was her husband, Ānanda her son.

Bhaddā had wanted her son to know the worldly life before she would permit him to become an ascetic. But that knowledge and lesson came to the young brahman in a very thorough and drastic way. His teacher's mother fell passionately in love with him and was even ready to kill her son. This encounter with reckless passion caused in him a deep revulsion for worldly life, a thorough disgust with it. After that experience his parents gave him permission to go forth as an ascetic (J 61).

Again, another time Kassapa and Bhaddā had been the brahman parents of four sons who in the future were to be our Bodhisatta, Anuruddha, Sāriputta and Mahā Moggallāna. All four wanted to become ascetics. At first the parents refused permission, but later they came to understand the fruits and benefits of the ascetic life, and they themselves became ascetics (J 509).

In still another life, two village headmen who were friends decided that if the children that they were expecting were to be of the opposite sex, they should marry. And so it happened. But in their previous life both children had been deities of the Brahma-world. Hence they had no desire for sensual pleasures and, with their parents' permission, chose the ascetic life (J 540).

Bhaddā's only wrong act reported in the stories of her past lives was this: At a time between the appearance of Buddhas of the past, when only Paccekabuddhas lived, Bhaddā was the wife of a landowner. One day, having quarrelled with her sister-in-law, she begrudged her the merit of offering almsfood to a Paccekabuddha who was on alms-round. She took the Paccekabuddha's bowl and filled it with mud. But at once she felt remorse, took the bowl back, washed it, filled it with delicious and fragrant food and offered it to the Paccekabuddha.

In her next life she possessed wealth and great beauty, but her body exuded a loathsome odour. Her husband, who later was to be Kassapa, could not bear the noxious smell and left her. As she was beautiful, she had other suitors, but all her later marriages had the same end. She was full of despair and no longer saw any meaning in her life. Preparing to dispose of her property, she had her ornaments melted down and formed into a golden brick. Taking that golden brick with her, she went to the monastery where a stupa was being erected in honour of the Buddha Kassapa, who had just passed away. For the completion of the stupa she offered that golden brick with great devotion. After she had done that, her body became fragrant again, and her first husband, Kassapa, took her back.

Two lives before her present existence, Bhaddā was queen of Benares and used to support several Paccekabuddhas. Deeply moved by their sudden death, she renounced her worldly life as a queen and lived a meditative life in the Himalayas. By the power of her renunciation and her meditative attainments, she was reborn in a Brahma-world, and so was Kassapa. After the end of the long life-span in the Brahma-world, both were reborn in the human world, in a brahman family, and were named Pipphali Kassapa and Bhaddā Kapilani.

From these accounts we gather that in their former existences both had lived a life of purity in the Brahma-worlds and that both had repeatedly been ascetic renunciates. Hence, in their final existence, it was not difficult for them to keep to a life of celibacy, to give up all possessions, and to follow the Buddha's teaching up to its culmination in Arahatship.

4. How Kassapa Came to the Buddha

Continuing our story, we shall now return to Mahā Kassapa. Where did he go after he had come to the crossroads? Tradition says that when the two separated, the earth shook by the force of the great virtue in their act of renunciation. The Buddha perceived this trembling of the earth, and he thus knew that an outstanding disciple was on the way to him. He then set out on the road himself, walking the distance of five miles to meet his future pupil—an act of compassion which later was often praised (J 469, Introd.).

On the road between Rājagaha and Nālandā, the Master sat down under a fig tree, waiting for his future disciple. When Kassapa arrived at the spot and saw the radiance of the Buddha's countenance,[9] sensing the enlightenment that shone through it, he thought, "This must be my Master for whose sake I have gone forth!" He approached the Buddha, and paying homage, fell at his

---

9. The Commentary speaks here of the Buddha's aura and also says that the thirty-two "Marks of a Great Man" had become visible to Kassapa.

feet and exclaimed: "The Exalted One, Lord, is my teacher, and I am his disciple!"

The Master said: "Sit down, Kassapa. I shall give you your heritage." He then gave the following three exhortations:

"You should train yourself thus, Kassapa: 'A keen sense of shame and fear of wrongdoing (*hiri-ottappa*) shall be present in me towards seniors, novices, and those of middle status in the Order.

"'Whatever teaching I hear that is conducive to something wholesome, I shall listen to with an attentive ear, examining it, reflecting on it, absorbing it with all my heart.

"'Mindfulness of the body linked with gladness shall not be neglected by me!' Thus should you train yourself."

Then both Master and disciple walked towards Rājagaha. On the way, the Buddha wanted to rest and went off the road to the root of a tree. Mahā Kassapa then folded his double-robe fourfold and requested the Master to sit on it as this would bring him, Kassapa, much benefit for a long time. The Buddha sat down on Kassapa's robe and said: "Soft is your robe of patched cloth, Kassapa." Hearing this, Kassapa replied: "May the Blessed One, O Lord, accept this robe of patched cloth out of compassion for me!"—"But, Kassapa, can you wear these hempen, worn-out rag-robes of mine?" Full of joy, Kassapa said: "Certainly, Lord, I can wear the Blessed One's rough and worn-out rag-robes."

This exchange of robes can be regarded as a great distinction bestowed on Kassapa, an honour which was not shared by any other disciple. By that exchange of robes the Buddha may have intended to motivate Kassapa to observe some other "austere practices" (*dhutaṅga*) as for instance, wearing only the triple set of robes, going for alms and not omitting any houses on the alms-round. This would be a mode of conduct in conformity with wearing the Buddha's patched rag-robes. Thus the commentator says. However, the Buddha's offer may have been a quite spontaneous act in response to his being offered Kassapa's robe.

Kassapa, indeed, actually took upon himself those thirteen austere practices allowed by the Buddha for the purpose of cultivating contentedness, renunciation, and energy.[10] On a later occasion, Kassapa was said by the Buddha to be foremost among the bhikkhus

---

10. See Nyanatiloka, *Buddhist Dictionary*, q.v. *dhutaṅga*.

who observed the austere practices (Aṅguttara, Ones). Kassapa's circle of personal disciples was also devoted to these practices.

It was only seven days after his ordination and the exchange of robes that Kassapa attained the goal he was striving for, Arahatship, the mind's final liberation from defilements. Recounting this episode to Ānanda at a much later time, he declared: "For seven days, friend, I ate the almsfood of the country as one unliberated, then on the eighth day the final knowledge of Arahatship arose in me" (SN 16:11).

5. Kassapa's Relationship to the Buddha

The earlier account has already shown that there was a deep inner relationship between Kassapa and the Buddha. This relationship had its root in their past lives. According to the Jātaka stories, Kassapa was connected with the Bodhisatta in nineteen existences, frequently through a close family bond. No less than six times Kassapa had been the Bodhisatta's father (J 155, 432, 509, 513, 524, 540), twice he was his brother (J,488, 522), and often his friend or teacher. As it was thus not their first meeting, we can understand why such an immediate and strong devotion and wholehearted dedication towards the Buddha arose in Kassapa's heart at the first sight of the Master.

From Kassapa's final life, many conversations are reported between the Buddha and this great disciple. It happened on three occasions that the Master spoke to him: "Exhort the monks, Kassapa. Give them a discourse on the Dhamma, Kassapa. Either I, Kassapa, should exhort the monks, or you. Either I or you should give them a discourse on the Dhamma" (SN 16:6). These words imply a high recognition of Kassapa's ability, because not every arahat has the capacity to expound the Teaching well and effectively.

The commentary raises here the question why it was Kassapa who was placed by the Buddha on an equal footing in this respect, and not Sāriputta and Mahā Moggallāna. The Buddha did so, says the commentary, because he knew that Sāriputta and Mahā Moggallāna would not survive him, but Kassapa would. It could also be that both Sāriputta and Mahā Moggallāna were no longer alive at that time.

Though the Buddha had highly praised Kassapa's ability as an exponent of the Dhamma, there were three occasions when Kassapa hesitated to instruct the monks after being asked by the Buddha to do so. He did not refuse because he wanted to avoid the effort and distraction of teaching, but because he found that those particular young monks were unresponsive to his admonitions.

In the first of the three instances, Kassapa said that it had now become difficult to speak to some of the monks; they were not amenable to advice, were intractable, and did not accept admonitions with respect. He had also heard that two monks boasted of their skill in preaching, saying: "Come, let us see who will preach more profusely, more beautifully, and at greater length!" When the Buddha was informed about this by Kassapa, he had these monks summoned and brought them back to reason, making them give up their immature conceit (SN 16:6). Hence we can see that Kassapa's negative report turned out to be of benefit to those monks. It was not done just for criticising others.

On the second occasion, too, Kassapa did not wish to instruct monks who were not amenable to admonishment, who lacked faith in the good, who lacked shame and fear of wrongdoing, who lacked energy and understanding as to the good.

This was a statement in general about a certain section of the monks, without reference of individuals. Of these monks Kassapa said further that, in their state of decline, they are like the waning moon that daily loses in beauty (confidence), in roundness (shame), in splendour (fear of wrongdoing), in height (energy), and in width (wisdom) (SN 16:7).

Also on a third occasion the Buddha asked Kassapa to instruct the monks, and Kassapa expressed his reluctance for the same reason as before. It seems that this time, too, the Buddha did not urge Kassapa to change his mind and admonish the monks, but he himself spoke of the reasons for their conduct:

"Formerly, Kassapa, there were elders of the Order who were forest-dwellers—living on almsfood, wearing rag-robes, using only the threefold set of robes, having few wants and being contented, living secluded and aloof from society, energetic, and they praised and encouraged such a way of life. When such elders or younger bhikkhus visited a monastery, they were gladly welcomed and honoured as being dedicated to the practice of the Dhamma.

Then those who thus welcomed and honoured those noble monks would also strive to emulate them in their ways of life, and this would be of great benefit to them for a long time.

> "But nowadays, Kassapa, those who are honoured when visiting a monastery are not monks of austere and earnest life, but those who are well known and popular and are amply provided with the requisites of a monk. These are made welcome and honoured, and their hosts try to emulate them, which will bring them harm for a long time. Hence one will be right in saying that such monks are harmed and overpowered by what does harm to a monk's life."

—Paraphrased from SN 16:8

On another occasion, Kassapa asked the Buddha: "What is the reason that formerly there were fewer rules, but more monks were established in the knowledge of Arahatship, while now there are more rules, but fewer monks are established in the knowledge of Arahatship?" The Buddha replied:

> "So it happens, Kassapa, when beings deteriorate and the true Dhamma vanishes: then there are more rules and fewer Arahats. There will be, however, no vanishing of the true Dhamma until a sham Dhamma arises in the world. But when a sham Dhamma arises in the world, there will be more rules and fewer Arahats.
>
> "But, Kassapa, it is not a cataclysm of the four elements—earth, water, fire and air—that makes the Dhamma disappear. Nor is the reason for its disappearance similar to the overloading of a ship that causes it to sink. It is rather the presence of five detrimental attitudes that causes the obscuration and disappearance of the Dhamma.
>
> "These are the five: it is the lack of respect and regard for the Buddha, the Dhamma, the Saṅgha, the training, and for meditative concentration, on the part of monks and nuns, and male and female lay devotees. But so long as there is respect and regard for those five things, the Dhamma will remain free of obscuration and will not disappear."

—SN 16:13

It deserves to be noted that, according to this text, the male and female lay followers are also preservers of the Dhamma. We may conclude from this that even when the Dhamma has come to oblivion among the monks, it will still remain alive when honoured and practised by the laity.

Other discourses in the Kassapa Saṃyutta deal chiefly with Mahā Kassapa's austere way of life, which was highly praised and commended by the Buddha. But on one occasion the Buddha reminded Kassapa that he had now grown old, and that he must find his coarse, worn-out rag-robes irksome to use. Therefore, the Buddha suggested, he should now wear robes offered by householders, accept also their invitations for alms offerings, and live near him. But Kassapa replied: "For along time I have been a forest-dweller, going the alms-round, and wearing rag-robes; and such a life I have commended to others. I have had few wants, lived contented, secluded, applying strenuous energy; and that too I have commended to others."

The Buddha asked: "But for what reason do you live so?" Kassapa replied that he had two reasons: his own well-being here and now, and his compassion for later generations which, when hearing about such a life, would emulate it. Then the Buddha said: "Well spoken, Kassapa, well spoken! You have lived for the happiness of many, out of compassion for the world, for the benefit and welfare of gods and men. You may then keep to your coarse rag-robes, go out for alms, and live in the forest" (SN 16:5).

"This our Kassapa," said the Buddha, "is satisfied with whatever robes, almsfood, lodging, and medicine he obtains. For the sake of these he will not do anything that is unbefitting for a monk. If he does not obtain any of these requisites, he is not perturbed; and when he obtains them, he makes use of them without clinging or infatuation, not committing any fault, aware of (possible) dangers and knowing them as an escape (from bodily affliction). By the example of Kassapa, or by one who equals him, I will exhort you, monks. Thus admonished, you should practise in the same way" (SN 16:1).

The Buddha also mentioned that Kassapa was likewise exemplary in his relation to the laity. When going among the families on his alms-round or on invitation, he did not think wishfully that people may give amply and give things of quality, that they may give quickly and respectfully. He had no such thoughts, but remained detached like the moon that sheds its mild light from a distance.

"When Kassapa goes among families, his mind is not attached, not caught up, not fettered. He rather thinks: 'Let those who want gain acquire gain! Let those who want merit do merit!' He is pleased and glad at the gains of others, just as he is pleased and glad at his own gains. Such a monk is fit to go among families.

"When he preaches the doctrine, he will not do so for the sake of personal recognition and praise, but for letting them know the Teaching of the Exalted One, so that those who hear it may accept it and practise accordingly. He will preach because of the excellence of the Teaching and out of compassion and sympathy."

—Paraphrased from SN 16:3.4

But the strongest recognition of Mahā Kassapa's achievement, the highest praise given him by the Buddha, may be found in a sutta where it is said that Mahā Kassapa could attain at will, just like the Buddha himself, the four fine-material and the four immaterial meditative absorptions, the cessation of perception and feeling, and could also attain the six supernormal knowledges (*abhiññā*), which include the supernormal powers and culminate in the attainment of Nibbāna (SN 16:9). Here his powerful meditative achievements, equaling those of the Buddha, appear as a characteristic trait of Mahā Kassapa's mind. It was because of that deep meditative calm that he could adapt himself, unperturbed, to all external situations and live as one of few wants, materially and socially.

In his verses preserved in the "Verses of the Elders" (*Theragāthā*) Mahā Kassapa praises again and again the peace of the jhānas (meditative absorptions). He was one who went from abundance to abundance. In his lay life he had lived in the abundance of wealth and harmony. As a monk he dwelt in the abundance of *jhānic* experience, furthered by his former life in the Brahma-world. While in some of the texts he appears to be very severe, this should not lead us to believe that he was harsh by nature. When he occasionally rebuked others in stem words, he did so for pedagogical reasons in order to help them. This we shall see especially when we deal with his relationship to Ānanda.

6. Encounters with Deities

Two meetings of Mahā Kassapa with deities of lower or higher order have been recorded. They are related here because they illustrate his independence of spirit and his determination to keep to his austere way of living without accepting privileges from wherever they were offered.

There was a young female deity, called Lājā, who remembered that she had obtained her present celestial happiness because in her previous human existence as a poor woman, she had offered parched rice to the Elder Mahā Kassapa with a believing heart, uttering the aspiration: "May I be a partaker of the truth you have seen!" On her way home, while reflecting on her offering, she was bitten by a snake and died, and was immediately reborn in the Heaven of the Thirty-three gods, in the midst of great splendour.

This the deity remembered, and in her gratitude she wanted now to serve the great Elder. Descending to earth, she swept the Elder's cell and filled the water vessels. After she had done that for three days, the Elder saw her radiant figure in his cell, and after questioning her, asked her to leave as he did not wish that monks of the future, knowing of it, should disapprove of him. His entreaties were of no avail; the deity rose into the air, filled with great sadness. The Buddha, aware of what had happened, appeared to the deity and consoled her by speaking of the worth of meritorious deeds and their great reward. But he also said that it had been Kassapa's duty to practise restraint (Commentary to Dhp 118).

In the other story it is told that Mahā Kassapa, while living at the Pipphali Cave, had entered a period of seven days' uninterrupted meditation, spending the time in unbroken meditative posture. At the end of that period, after arising from that meditation, he went to Rājagaha on alms-round. At that time there arose in five hundred female deities of Sakka's celestial realm the keen desire to offer almsfood to the venerable Mahā Kassapa. With the food prepared, they approached the Elder, asking for his favour by accepting their offering. But he asked them to leave as he wanted to bestow his favour on the poor so that they could benefit from their meritorious deed. As he did not yield to their repeated entreaties, they finally left. When Sakka, king of the gods, heard about their vain effort, a great desire arose in him as well to offer almsfood to that great Elder. To avoid being refused, he turned himself into an old weaver. When Mahā Kassapa approached, he offered rice to him, and at the moment the rice was accepted it turned exceedingly fragrant. Then Mahā Kassapa knew who this old weaver truly was, and he reproached Sakka: "You have done a grievous wrong, Kosiya. By doing so, you have deprived poor people of the chance to acquire merit. Do not do such a thing again!"—"We too need merit, revered Kassapa! We too are in need of it! But have I acquired merit or not by giving alms to you through deception?"—"You have gained merit, friend. Now Sakka, while departing, gave voice to the following "Solemn Utterance" (*udāna*):

> "Oh, almsgiving! Highest almsgiving!
> Well bestowed on Kassapa!"
>
> —Commentary to Dhp 56; see Udāna, 3:7

7. Relations to Pupils and Fellow Monks

One so very dedicated to the meditative life as Mahā Kassapa was cannot be expected to have been keen on accepting and training many pupils; and, in fact, the canonical texts mention only a few pupils of his.

One of Kassapa's few recorded discourses addressed to the monks deals with the subject of overestimating one's attainments:

> "There may be a monk who declares he has attained to the highest knowledge, that of Arahatship. Then the Master, or a disciple capable of knowing the minds of others, examines and questions him. When they question him, that monk becomes embarrassed and confused. The questioner now understands that the monk has made this declaration through overrating himself out of conceit. Then, considering the reason for it, he sees that this monk has acquired much knowledge of the Teaching and proficiency in it, which made him declare his overestimation of himself to be the truth. Penetrating the mind of that monk, he sees that he is still obstructed by the

five hindrances and has stopped half-way while there is still more to do."

—AN 10:86

Apart from the few instances where Mahā Kassapa is speaking to unnamed monks or a group of monks, the texts record only his relationship to Sāriputta and Ānanda.

According to the Jātakas, in former lives Sāriputta was twice the son of Kassapa (J 509, 515) and twice the brother of Kassapa (J 326, 488); he was once also Kassapa's grandson (J 450) and his friend (J 525). In his verses, Kassapa tells that he once saw thousands of Brahma-gods descend from their heaven, pay homage to Sāriputta, and praise him (Th 1082–1086).

Two conversations between Mahā Kassapa and Sāriputta have been recorded in the Kassapa Saṃyutta. On both occasions it was at evening time, after meditation, that the venerable Sāriputta went to see the venerable Mahā Kassapa.

In the first text Sāriputta asked: "It has been said, friend Kassapa, that without ardour and without fear of wrongdoing, one is incapable of gaining enlightenment, incapable of attaining Nibbāna, incapable of attaining highest security, but that with ardour and with fear of wrongdoing, one is capable of such attainments. Now in how far is he incapable of such attainments and in how far is he capable of them?"

> "When, friend Sāriputta, a monk thinks: 'If bad and unwholesome states that have so far not arisen in me were to arise, this would bring me harm,' and if then he does not arouse ardour and fear of wrongdoing, then he is lacking ardour and fear of wrongdoing. When he thinks: 'If bad and unwholesome states that have arisen now in me are not abandoned, this would bring me harm,' or: 'If unarisen wholesome states were not to arise, this would bring me harm,' or: 'If arisen wholesome states were to vanish, this would bring me harm,' if on these occasions, too, a monk does not arouse ardour and fear of wrongdoing, then he is lacking these qualities, and lacking them, he is incapable of attaining enlightenment, incapable of attaining Nibbāna, incapable of attaining the highest security. But if a monk (on those four occasions for right effort) arouses ardour and fear of wrongdoing, he is capable of attaining

enlightenment, capable of attaining Nibbāna, capable of attaining the highest security."

—SN 16:2 condensed

On another occasion Sāriputta asked Mahā Kassapa some questions which one may not have expected: whether the Perfect One (Tathāgata) exists after death, or does not exist, or (in some sense) both exists and does not exist, or neither exists nor does not exist.

In each case Mahā Kassapa replies that this was not declared by the Exalted One. And when asked why not, he said: "Because it is of no benefit and does not belong to the fundamentals of the holy life, because it does not lead to turning away (from worldliness), nor to dispassion, cessation, (inner) peace, direct knowledge, enlightenment, and Nibbāna."

"But what, friend, did the Exalted One declare?"

"This is suffering—so, friend, has the Exalted One declared. This is the origin of suffering—the cessation of suffering—the way to the cessation of suffering—so, friend, has the Exalted One declared. And why? Because it conduces to benefit and belongs to the fundamentals of the holy life, because it leads to turning away (from worldliness), to dispassion, cessation, (inner) peace, direct knowledge, enlightenment, and Nibbāna."

—SN 16:12

We have no tradition as to why Sāriputta posed these questions, which for an arahat should have been fully clear. It is, however, not impossible that this conversation took place immediately after Kassapa's ordination and before his attainment of Arahatship, and that Sāriputta wanted to test him in that way; or, perhaps, it was for the sake of other monks who may have been present.

The Majjhima Nikāya records a sutta (No. 32, Mahāgosiṅga Sutta) in which Mahā Kassapa participated in a group discussion with several other eminent disciples led by Sāriputta. At the time these elders of the Order were residing in the Gosiṅga Forest along with the Buddha, and on a clear moonlit night they approached Sāriputta for a discussion on the Dhamma. Sāriputta declared: "Delightful is this Gosiṅga Forest, it is a clear moonlit night, the sāla-trees are in full bloom, and it seems as if celestial scents are being wafted around." Then he asked each distinguished elder in the group—Ānanda, Revata, Anuruddha, Mahā Kassapa, and Mahā Moggallāna—what kind of monk could illumine that Gosiṅga Forest. Mahā Kassapa, like the others, replied according to his own temperament. He declared that a monk who could illumine the Gosiṅga Forest would be a forest-dweller, one who went on alms-round, who wore rag-robes, who possessed only three robes, who had few wishes, was content, aloof, not gregarious, energetic, and who would speak in praise of each of these qualities. He would also possess virtue, concentration, wisdom, deliverance and the knowledge and vision of deliverance, and would speak in praise of each of these attainments.

According to tradition, Mahā Kassapa also had close connections in former lives with the venerable Ānanda. Ānanda had twice been his brother (J 488, 535), once his son (J 450), once even the murderer of his son (J 540), and in this life he was his pupil (Mahā Vagga I, 74). The Kassapa Saṃyutta likewise has two conversations between them. They concern practical questions, while those with Sāriputta referred to doctrine.

On the first occasion (related at SN 16:10) Ānanda asked Kassapa whether he would go with him to the nunnery. Kassapa, however, refused and asked Ānanda to go alone. But Ānanda seemed to be keen that Kassapa should give a Dhamma talk to the nuns, and he repeated his request twice. Kassapa finally consented to go and gave a discourse to the nuns. But the result turned out to be quite different from what Ānanda had expected. One of the nuns, Thullatissā by name, raised her voice to make a rather offensive remark: "How could the Revered Kassapa presume to speak Dhamma in the presence of the Revered Ānanda, the learned sage? This is as if a needle peddler wanted to sell a needle to the needle maker."

Obviously this nun preferred the gentle preaching of Ānanda to Kassapa's stern and sometimes critical approach, which may have touched on her own weaknesses.

When Kassapa heard the nun's remarks, he asked Ānanda: "How is it, friend Ānanda, am I the needle peddler and you the needle maker, or am I the needle maker and you the needle peddler?"

Ānanda replied: "Be indulgent, venerable sir. She is a foolish woman."

"Beware, friend Ānanda, or else the Saṅgha may further examine you. How is it, friend Ānanda, was it you to whom the Exalted One referred in the presence of the Saṅgha when saying: 'I, O monks, can attain at will the four fine-material and immaterial meditative absorptions, the cessation of perception and feeling, the six supernormal knowledges; and Ānanda, too, can so attain'?"

"Not so, venerable sir."

"Or was it that he said: 'Kassapa, too, can so attain'?"

From the above account we see that the venerable Mahā Kassapa did not think that Ānanda's conciliatory reply was adequate, or did full justice to the situation. Thullatissā's remarks showed her personal attachment to Ānanda, who has always been a favourite with women, and who had also given his strong support to the founding of the Order of Nuns (Bhikkhunī Saṅgha). This emotional relation of Thullatissā's to Ānanda could not be put aside just by Ānanda's general remark. Hence Kassapa responded in a way which, at first glance, appears rather harsh: "Beware, friend Ānanda, or else the Saṅgha may further examine you!" This was to say that Ānanda should not engage himself too much in ministering to the nuns, as on their part attachment such as that of Thullatissā's could grow from it, and cause others to entertain doubts about him. Kassapa's reply has therefore to be seen as the earnest advice of a taint-free arahat to one who had not yet reached that state. When, immediately after, Kassapa mentioned that the Buddha had declared his own meditative attainments equal with those of himself, and not Ānanda's, this may be taken as pointing to the far different spiritual status of the two; and it may have served as a spur to Ānanda to strive for those attainments. The nun Thullatissā, however, left the Order.

Another conversation between the venerable Mahā Kassapa and Ānanda arose on the following occasion (related at SN 16:11). Once the venerable Ānanda went on a walking tour in the Southern Hills, together with a large company of monks. This was at a time when thirty mostly young monks, pupils of the venerable Ānanda, had given up the robe and had returned to the lay life. After the venerable Ānanda had ended his tour, he came to Rājagaha and went to see the venerable Mahā Kassapa. When he had saluted him and had sat down, Kassapa said this:

"What are the reasons, friend Ānanda, for the sake of which the Blessed One had said that only three monks should take their alms meal among families?"

"There are three reasons, venerable sir: it is for restraining ill-behaved persons, for the well-being of good monks, and out of consideration for the lay families."

"Then, friend Ānanda, why do you go on tour with those young new monks whose senses are unrestrained, who are not moderate in eating, not given to watchfulness? It seems you behave like one trampling the corn. It seems you destroy the faith of the families. Your following is breaking up, your new starters are falling away. This youngster truly does not know his own measure!"

"Grey hairs are now on my head, venerable sir, and still we cannot escape being called 'youngster' by the venerable Mahā Kassapa."

But the venerable Mahā Kassapa repeated again the very same words he had spoken.

This could have ended this matter, as Ānanda did not deny that the reproach was justified. He objected only to the hurtful way in which Mahā Kassapa had expressed his censure. In response to the admonition, Ānanda would have tried to keep his pupils under stricter discipline. But, again, this matter was complicated by a nun, Thullanandā, who along with Thullatissā was one of the "black sheep" of the Bhikkhunī Order. She had heard that Ānanda had been called a "youngster" by the venerable Mahā Kassapa, and full of indignation, she voiced her protest saying that Kassapa had no right to criticise a wise monk like Ānanda, as Kassapa had formerly been an ascetic of another school. In that way, Thullanandā diverted the matter of monastic discipline into personal detraction. Besides, she was wrong, as our earlier account has shown. (Before meeting the Buddha, Kassapa had gone forth as an independent ascetic, not as a follower of another school.) Thullanandā soon left the Order, just as the other wayward nun, Thullatissā, had done.

When the venerable Mahā Kassapa heard Thullanandā's utterance, he said to Ānanda: "Rash and thoughtless are the words spoken by Thullanandā the nun. Since I left the home life, I have had no other teacher than the Exalted One, the Holy One, the Perfectly Enlightened One" (SN 16:11).

8. After the Buddha's Parinibbāna

What remains to be said about Mahā Kassapa's relation to Ānanda is closely connected with his leading role in the Saṅgha after the passing away of the Buddha. At the demise of the Buddha, only two of the five most prominent disciples were present, the brothers Ānanda and Anuruddha. Sāriputta and Mahā Moggallāna had preceded the Master in death and Mahā Kassapa, with a large company of monks, was just then wandering on the high-road from Pāva to Kusinārā. During that walk he happened to step aside from the road and sat down under a tree to rest. Just then a naked ascetic passed that way. The ascetic had with him a Mandārava (coral tree) flower, which is said to grow only in a celestial world. When Mahā Kassapa saw this, he knew that something unusual must have happened for the flower to be found on earth. He asked the ascetic whether he had heard any news about his teacher, the Buddha, and the ascetic affirmed that he had, saying: "The recluse Gotama passed into Nibbāna a week ago. This Mandārava flower I picked up from the place of cremation."

Among the monks who heard that message, only those who were Arahats like Mahā Kassapa could remain composed and calm; but the others who were still unliberated from the passions lamented and wept: "Too soon has the Blessed One passed into Nibbāna! Too soon has the Eye of the World vanished from our sight!"

But there was one monk, Subhaddā by name, who had ordained in his old age. He addressed the other monks and said: "Enough, friends! Do not grieve, do not lament! We are well rid of that Great Ascetic. We have been troubled by his telling us: 'This is befitting, that is not befitting.' Now we can do what we like, and we won't have to do what we do not like."

It is not recorded that at that time the venerable Mahā Kassapa gave a reply to those callous words. He may not have wished just then to strike a discordant note by censuring the monk or having him disrobed as he deserved. Hence he remained silent. But, as we shall see later, Mahā Kassapa quoted that incident when he spoke of the need for summoning a council. Now, however, he admonished his group of monks not to lament, but to remember that impermanence is the nature of all conditioned things. He then continued his journey to Kusinara, together with his monks.

Until then it had not been possible to set the funeral pyre alight as the deities present wanted to wait until the venerable Mahā Kassapa came and paid his last homage to the remains of the Master. When the venerable Mahā Kassapa arrived at the place of cremation, he walked twice around the pyre, reverently, with clasped hands, and then, with bowed head paid his homage at the feet of the Tathāgata. When his group of monks had done likewise, the pyre, it is said, burst into flames by itself.

Hardly had the bodily remains of the Tathāgata been cremated when there arose a conflict about the distribution of the relics among the lay folk assembled and those who had sent messengers later. But the venerable Mahā Kassapa remained aloof in that quarrel, as did the other monks like Anuruddha and Ānanda. It was a respected brahman, Doṇa by name, who finally divided the relics into eight portions and distributed them among the eight claimants. He himself took the vessel in which the relics had been collected.

The venerable Mahā Kassapa himself brought to King Ajātasattu of Magadha his share of the relics. Having done so, he turned his thoughts to the preservation of the Master's spiritual heritage, the Teaching (Dhamma) and the Discipline (Vinaya).

The necessity to do so was demonstrated to him by Subhadda's challenge of the monastic discipline, and his advocacy of moral laxity, which Mahā Kassapa took as a warning. If that attitude were to spread, it would lead to the decline and ruin of both the Saṅgha and the Teaching. To prevent this at the very start, Mahā Kassapa proposed holding a council by which the Dhamma and Vinaya could be reliably established and secured. With that suggestion, he turned to the monks gathered at Rājagaha. The monks agreed and at their request Mahā Kassapa selected five hundred members, all but one of whom were Arahats. Ānanda, however, at that time had not yet succeeded in reaching that final attainment, but as he excelled in remembering a large number of the Buddha's discourses, he too was admitted to complete the five hundred members of the First Council.[11] All other monks were to leave Rājagaha for the duration of the council.

---

11. Determined not to attend the meeting as a mere disciple in training

As the first item of the council's proceedings, the texts of the monastic discipline were recited by the venerable Upāli, who was a Vinaya expert. The second item was the codification of the Teaching laid down in the discourses. Here it was Ānanda who, on being questioned by the venerable Mahā Kassapa, recited all those texts which were later compiled in the Five Collections (*nikāya*) of the Sutta Piṭaka. It was an outstanding feat of memory on his part.

Finally, some special matters concerning the Saṅgha were discussed. Among them, the venerable Ānanda mentioned that the Buddha, shortly before his death, had permitted the abolishment of minor rules. When Ānanda was asked whether he had inquired from the Buddha what these minor rules were, he had to admit that he had neglected to do so.

Now various opinions about this matter were expressed in the assembly. As there was no consensus, the venerable Mahā Kassapa asked the assembly to consider that if they were to abolish rules arbitrarily, the lay followers and the public in general would reproach them for being in a hurry to relax discipline so soon after the Master's death. Hence Mahā Kassapa suggested that the rules should be preserved intact without exception. And so it was decided (Cūlavagga, XI).

After the holding of the First Council, the high regard in which the venerable Mahā Kassapa was held grew still greater, and he was seen as the de facto head of the Saṅgha. His seniority would have contributed to this, as he was then one of the oldest living disciples.[12]

Later on, the venerable Mahā Kassapa handed over the Buddha's alms-bowl to Ānanda, as a symbol of continuing the faithful preservation of the Dhamma. Thus Mahā Kassapa, who had been generally recognised in the Order as the worthiest in succession, chose on his part Ānanda as being the worthiest after him.

(*sekha*), Ānanda made a dedicated effort in meditation the night before the council convened. Just as dawn was approaching, his mind was liberated from all taints, and he attended the meeting as an arahat.

12. The commentaries say that Mahā Kassapa was 120 years old at the time of the First Council, but as this chronology would mean that he was forty years older than the Buddha and thus already an old man of at least seventy-five when he met the Master, such a statement is hardly acceptable.

There is no report in the Pali literature about the time and circumstances of his death.

9. The Verses of Mahā Kassapa

In the canonical "Verses of the Elders" (*Theragāthā*), forty verses (1051–1091) are ascribed to the venerable Mahā Kassapa. These stanzas mirror some of the great Elder's characteristic qualities and virtues: his austere habits and his contentedness; his strictness towards himself and brother monks; his independent spirit and his self-reliance; his love of solitude, shunning the crowds; his dedication to the practice of meditation and the peace of the jhānas. These verses also show what does not appear in the prose texts: his sensitivity to the beauty of nature that surrounded him.

Here only a selection of the stanzas is given, which may be read in full in the translations by C.A.F. Rhys Davids and K.R. Norman.[13]

> *An exhortation to the monks to practise contentment with regard to the four basic requisites of a monk's life:*[14]

Down from my mountain-lodge I came one day
And made my round for alms about the streets.
A leper there I saw eating his meal
And courteously I halted at his side. (1054)

He with his hand all leprous and diseased
Put in my bowl a morsel; as he threw,
A finger broke off and fell into my food. (1055)

At a wall nearby I ate my share,
Not at the time nor after felt disgust. (1056)

---

13. Both published by the Pali Text Society, London. The renderings to follow are partly those of Mrs. Rhys Davids, partly adaptations or re-translations by the author.

14. The sentences introducing sections of the verses are derived from the old commentary.

> For only he who takes as they come
> The scraps of food, cow's urine for medicine,
> Lodging beneath a tree, the patchwork robe,
> Truly is a man contented everywhere.[15] (1057)

When Mahā Kassapa was asked why, at his advanced age, he still climbed daily up and down the rock, he replied:

> While some are very wearied as they climb the rocks,
> An heir of the Buddha, mindful, self-possessed,
> By force of the spirit fortified,[16]
> Does Kassapa ascend the mountain bow. (1058)

> Returning from the daily round for alms,
> He mounts again the rock and sits
> In meditation rapt, not clinging anywhere,
> For far from him has he put fear and dread. (1059)

> Returning from his daily round for alms,
> He mounts again the rock and sits
> In meditation rapt, not clinging anywhere,
> For he among those that burn is cool and still. (1060)

> Returning from his daily round for alms,
> He mounts again the rock and sits
> In meditation rapt, not clinging anywhere,
> His task is done, from cankers he is free. (1061)

People asked again why the venerable Mahā Kassapa, at his age, wishes to live in forests and mountains. Does he not like monasteries such as the Veṇuvana Vihara and others?

> These regions are delightful to my heart
> When the Kareri creeper spreads its flower wreaths,
> When sound the trumpet-calls of elephants.
> These rocky heights delight my heart. (1062)

> These rocks with hue of dark-blue clouds
> Where streams are flowing, cool and crystal-clear,

---

15. Lit.: "a man of the four directions"; that is, he is satisfied with conditions he finds wherever he lives.

16. Lit.: "supported by his supernormal powers."

With glow-worms covered (shining bright),
These rocky heights delight my heart. (1063)

Like towering peaks of dark-blue clouds,
Like splendid edifices are these rocks,
Where the birds' sweet voices fill the air,
These rocky heights delight my heart. (1064)

With glades refreshed by (cooling) rain,
Resounding with the calls of crested birds,
The cliffs resorted to by seers,
These rocky heights delight my heart. (1065)

Here is enough for me who, resolute,
Desires to meditate (in solitude).
Here is enough for me, a monk determined,
Who seeks to dwell in the highest goal's attainment.[17] (1066)

Here is enough for me who, resolute,
Desires to live in happy ease (and free).
Here is enough for me who is on effort bent,
(Devoted to the practice) as a monk determined. (1067)

Like dark-blue blooms of flax they are,
Like autumn sky with dark-blue clouds,
With flocks of many kinds of birds,
These rocky heights delight my heart. (1068)

No crowds of lay folk have these rocks,
But visited by herds of deer.
With flocks of many kinds of birds,
These rocky heights delight my heart. (1069)

Wide gorges are there where clear water flows,
Haunted by monkeys and by deer,
With mossy carpets covered, moist,
These rocky heights delight my heart. (1700)

---

17. *Alaṃ me atthakāmassa*; lit.: "enough for me who desires the goal." But as Mahā Kassapa had already arrived at the goal of Arahatship, our free rendering is justified. Alternative rendering: "Who desires his purpose."

No music with five instruments
Can gladden me so much
As when, with mind collected well,
Right insight into Dhamma dawns. (1701)

In the following verses the venerable Mahā Kassapa voices his own "Lion Roar."

In the whole field of the Buddha's following,
Except for the mighty Master himself,
I stand the foremost in ascetic ways;
No one practises them so far as I. (1087)

The Master has been served by me,
And all the Buddha's teaching has been done.
Low have I laid the heavy load I bore,
Cause for rebirth is found in me no more. (1088)

Gotama the immeasurable does not cling
To robe, to food or place of lodging.
Like spotless lotus blossom he is free from taints,
Bent on renunciation he transcends the three worlds. (1089)

The four foundations of mindfulness are his neck;
The great Seer has faith and confidence for hands;
Above, his brow is perfect wisdom; nobly wise,
He ever wanders with all desire quenched. (1090)

Buddhist Perspectives on the Ecocrisis

With a Declaration on Environmental Ethics

Edited by
Klas Sandell

WHEEL PUBLICATION NO. 346/347/348

Copyright © Kandy; Buddhist Publication Society, (1987)

Foreword

Bhikkhu Bodhi

The current crisis arising over environmental pollution and the over-exploitation of our natural resources has gripped the attention and aroused the concern of virtually every human being alive today. The anxiety provoked by the "ecocrisis" stems from a cause lying far deeper than the immediate predicament which it creates. For the ecocrisis does not confront us simply as one more set of problems to be disposed of through further research and legislation. It comes upon us, rather, as a disturbing manifestation of the dangers inherent in unbridled technological proliferation and industrial growth and a grim portent of even graver dangers ahead if current trends continue unchecked. Thereby it causes us to reassess some of the basic premises upon which modern Western civilization is grounded and the goals towards which so much of our energy and wealth are directed.

The development of Western technology was spurred by the belief that applied science could eliminate all human wants and usher in a golden age of unlimited prosperity for all. Now, having utilised technology to subjugate nature and to serve human desire, we have doubtlessly succeeded in making life more comfortable and secure in many respects than it had been in an earlier era. However, our smog-covered cities, polluted waterways, devastated forests and chemical dumps remind us painfully that our material triumphs have been gained at a terrible price. Not only is the beauty of the natural environment being gradually destroyed, but its very capacity to sustain life is seriously threatened, and in the process of vanquishing nature, man himself has placed himself in danger of losing his own humanity.

In most industrialised nations, and in much of the Third World, national authorities have endeavoured to prevent the further spread of environmental pollution, sometimes under pressure. Despite partial success, however, the ecocrisis continues to mount, and as it does so it becomes increasingly clear that the deficiencies in our programmes are not merely quantitative but pertain to a far more fundamental level.

For the most part the approaches to environmental protection that have been sponsored and implemented in official quarters are those that are consonant with the dominant technocratic mentality. Thus they operate within the same closed frame of reference, and draw upon the same fixed premises, as the projects originally responsible for the ecocrisis. Unable to envisage any alternatives to the aims of industrial society, their proponents simply assume that our troubles stem from a lack of adequate scientific expertise and thus that they can be remedied by filling the lack through greater scientific ingenuity and more efficient technological management. However, while so much money is poured into research aimed at extending human control over the environment in order to prevent specific hazards, the basic presupposition at the root of the whole ecocrisis is allowed to stand unquestioned, namely, that the means to achieve human well-being lies in increased production and consumption.

Among a growing number of thoughtful people today it is just this presupposition that is coming to be called into question. The realisation has been dawning that if our natural environment is to be saved—indeed, if we ourselves are to be saved from destroying ourselves along with our environment—a more radical approach to the entire ecocrisis is imperative. We are now coming to recognise that the project of gaining technological mastery over nature springs from a number of assumptions specific to Western industrial society: that happiness and well-being lie in the satisfaction of our material needs and sensual desires; that the basic orientation of man to nature is one of conflict and struggle aimed at subjugation; that nature must be conquered and made subservient to the satisfaction of our desires. We can also see that these assumptions are fallacious ones which, if not challenged and replaced soon, may well have grave consequences for humanity.

At the same time that disillusionment sets in with the ends and means of industrial society, an intense search is under way for alternative world-views which can enable us to live in greater peace and harmony with nature, with our fellow beings who share this planet with us, and with ourselves. In the course of this search for alternative world-views, an increasing amount of attention has been focused on the religions and philosophies of East Asia, which advocate harmonious and peaceful co-existence between man and the natural world. Prominent among the Eastern religions in this respect is Buddhism. With its philosophic insight into the interconnectedness and thoroughgoing interdependence of all conditioned things, with its thesis that happiness is to be found through the restraint of desire in a life of contentment rather than through the proliferation of desire, with its goal of enlightenment through renunciation and contemplation and its ethic of non-injury and boundless loving kindness for all beings, Buddhism provides all the essential elements for a relationship to the natural world characterised by respect, humility, care and compassion.

In the present Wheel publication, Klas Sandell—a serious student of Buddhism and a researcher in ecology—has brought together articles from several Buddhist scholars and thinkers dealing with the relevance of Buddhism to the ecocrisis. This compilation, we hope, will help to initiate an ongoing dialogue between concerned Buddhists and those ecologists who are open to new perspectives on this crisis now threatening the very survival of the human race. It is our further hope that this work will do more than stimulate thought, that it will also exert a wholesome influence upon those charged with the protection of the environment. To the West the Buddhist world-view offers a fruitful holistic alternative to the mechanistic and reductionistic modes of thinking at the root of our crisis, while its way of life offers a means to deep satisfaction without need for a superabundance of material goods. In the East the Buddhist outlook on nature must also be newly articulated to underline its practical implications for environmental policy to those responsible for economic development. Otherwise, it is very likely that the traditional homelands of Buddhism, seduced by the wealth, power and glitter of the West, may abandon their own valuable heritage to embark upon a course that may ultimately prove self-destructive.

This compilation on Buddhism and the ecocrisis makes it abundantly clear that Buddhism, inheriting a continuous 2500 year-old tradition and a way of thinking astonishingly modern, can offer those concerned with the future of life on our planet a lofty inspiration and solid grounding for many of the attitudes central to the new ecological awareness.

Introduction—The Ecocrisis

Klas Sandell

Alarming reports about contaminated waterways, polluted air and depletion of natural resources reach us with increasing frequency. Today, it is becoming customary to talk in terms of a crisis, an "ecocrisis," in matters concerning society and its relation to the natural environment. This development, which a number of specific instances dramatically illustrate, signifies a growing concern for the survival prospects of coming generations.

In the World Conservation Strategy drawn up by the United Nations and other world organisations the following can be read:

1. Thousands of millions of tonnes of soil are lost every year as a result of deforestation and poor land management.
2. At least 3000 square kilometres of prime farmland disappear every year under buildings and roads in developed countries alone.
3. In widening swaths around their villages the rural poor strip the land of trees and shrubs for fuel so that now many communities do not have enough wood to cook food or keep warm.
4. The coastal support systems of many fisheries are being destroyed or polluted (in the United States the annual cost of the resulting losses is estimated at $86 million).[1]

Environment problems exist both in the industrialised countries and in the Third World, albeit in different forms. In industrialised countries toxic discharges in air, water and soil, estrangement from nature, etc. are the consequences of the existing system based on mass production. Here, it is important to abandon over-consumption and short-term speculations in favour of non-material values and forethought.

In the Third World, however, it is above all a question of a sensitive balance between population pressures and natural

---

1. World Conservation Strategy (International Union for Conservation of Nature and Natural Resources (IUCN), 1196 Gland, Switzerland, 1980), IV.

resources, bearing in mind such risks as erosion, unsanitary living conditions, desertification, declining ground water supplies, etc. The UN Conference in Stockholm on the Human Environment says in its declaration: "In the developing countries most of the environmental problems are caused by under-development."[2] International dependency, e.g. via international companies, is also a significant factor. World industry demands cheap raw materials and exploits the Third World via forms of production and selling that are often forbidden in the industrialised countries themselves.

However, the ecocrisis is not solely a technological problem. Better purification methods, alternative energy technologies, more stringent laws—all may prove effective as emergency measures and may suffice as short-term solutions, but in the long run they are inadequate. The Norwegian philosopher, Arne Naess, mentions a "shallow" and a "deep" ecology movement.[3] While the shallow movement involves itself in a limited struggle for better management of resources, population stability, and the prevention of pollution, the deep ecology movement tackles a whole series of questions concerning economics and values. In modern industrialised society man is becoming increasingly isolated and estranged from his natural environment, and this drastically increases the risk of short-sighted exploitation rooted in the thoughtless urge to possess. The ecocrisis, especially in industrialised countries, has come about mainly due to our own basic sense of values, as a result of our particular approach to nature. The seriousness of this situation is made all the more apparent when we consider that the prevailing attitude towards nature in industrialised society today is one of exploitation and that this attitude is swiftly gaining ground in the Third World.

Three Aspects of the Ecocrisis

The ecocrisis manifests itself in a variety of ways, and here I would particularly like to point out three important aspects: (1) The technological ecocrisis, which arises due to modern production

---

2. UN Conference in Stockholm on the Human Environment (The Swedish Ministry of Foreign Affairs, 11:25, Stockholm, 1972), p. 83.

3. Arne Naess, "The Shallow and the Deep, Long-range Ecology Movement: A Summary," Inquiry (Oslo) 16 (1973): 95–100.

methods applied within agriculture, communication, housing, etc., methods which are responsible for a rapidly expanding process of contamination and depletion of natural resources. (2) The political ecocrisis, which involves the ways in which economy, laws, commerce and dependent factors encourage a short-sighted exploitation of nature both locally and globally. (3) The value-related ecocrisis, which involves basic values concerning man's relation to nature today, values which through their growing influence present a threat to the long-term survival prospects of the human race.

Energy supply can serve to illustrate these three aspects of the ecocrisis. The technological aspect concerns, among other things, a choice between different kinds of energy technologies: on the one hand, renewable energy sources such as solar energy, wind and biodynamic fuels, and on the other, energy sources that in human perspective are non-renewable, such as oil, coal and nuclear energy. The political aspect of energy supply relates to such things as taxation, costs and laws which may be favourable or unfavourable towards different energy systems. A significant factor of the political ecocrisis is that the non-renewable energy sources are given priority from a research point of view. The value aspect of energy supply can apply to weighing material needs (which are energy-demanding) against non-material needs. Here, in addition, questions like the time aspect must be considered (how do we evaluate the living environment of future generations?) and also the geographical aspect (to what extent should we be allowed to export waste and pollution, and to what extent is the importation of resources desirable?).

It is important to remember that similar approaches to nature can manifest themselves in a variety of ways depending upon natural conditions and available technology. For example, from time immemorial it has been customary to proclaim certain areas or elements in nature sacred (e.g. trees and mountains), and it has often been claimed that if these particular areas were destroyed, then various punishments would be inflicted upon man. Modern nature-conservation movements, though they do not speak in terms of sacredness, have, via their knowledge of ecology, been able to point to innumerable instances where man through careless exploitation (e.g. of forests and mountainsides) has with devastating force inflicted great damage upon himself. Despite dissimilarities, it is apparent that parallels can be drawn between these two views of nature, even though they may find entirely different forms of expression and may recur in cultures and epochs far removed from one another.

The Aim of this Book

This book seeks to present some aspects of Buddhist philosophy as one source of inspiration for developing a more enduring and harmonious relationship between man and nature. Buddhist philosophy does not presuppose the existence of any God, but is based on individual insight, and thus ought to have a great deal to contribute in a world continually influenced by scientific thought. Buddhist religion, like all other religions, is extremely complex, embracing philosophy, moral standards, religious practices, etc., all of which have been influenced and modified by the passage of time and contact with different cultures. Thus, Buddhism today is by no means a univocal concept, but is interpreted and applied in various ways and in various circumstances. Buddhism as discussed in this book represents the principles of Theravada Buddhism as outlined in the books and articles from the Buddhist Publication Society. Nature is defined principally as the non-cultural physical and biological environment, e.g. vegetation, mountains, rivers, animals and certain aspects of the human body.

The book consists of five chapters, and each author is responsible for the content of his or her own chapter. The first chapter presents the Buddhist view of nature via references to the Pali texts and is written by Professor Lily de Silva of the Department of Buddhist Studies at the Peradeniya Campus, University of Sri Lanka. The second chapter attempts to throw light upon some aspects of a Buddhist approach to nature by linking them to current discussions centred on a more ecologically conscious "alternative" development. This perspective ties up with my work as research assistant at the Department of Water in Environment and Society, University of Linkoping, Sweden. This chapter might serve as a point of departure for others interested in this source of inspiration for a more sustainable man-nature relationship.

Professor Padmasiri de Silva is the head of the Department of Philosophy at the Peradeniya Campus, University of Sri Lanka.

He has written a chapter concerning the search for a Buddhist environmental ethics. The next, more "action-oriented" chapter by the well recognised Norwegian Buddhist ecophilosopher, Sigmund Kvaloy, gives examples of the potential of the Buddhist outlook for ecodevelopment. The book concludes with a statement on the Buddhist Perception of Nature project by the project's founder and international coordinator, American conservationist, Nancy Nash. The project also provided the declaration on environmental ethics by H. H. the Dalai Lama which opens this compilation. The Dalai Lama's message is dated 5 June 1986, in recognition of World Environment Day, and that day's 1986 theme, Peace and the Environment.

Hopefully the whole book can serve as a starting point for further discussion and action centred around these issues. Comments and viewpoints are welcome.

In conclusion, I would like to offer my sincerest thanks to the Buddhist Publication Society. Without their help this book could not have been put together.

An Ethical Approach to Environmental Protection

His Holiness the Dalai Lama

Peace and survival of life on earth as we know it are threatened by human activities which lack a commitment to humanitarian values.

Destruction of nature and natural resources result from ignorance, greed and lack of respect for the earth's living things.

This lack of respect extends even to earth's human descendants, the future generations who will inherit a vastly degraded planet if world peace does not become a reality, and destruction of the natural environment continues at the present rate.

Our ancestors viewed the earth as rich and bountiful, which it is. Many people in the past also saw nature as inexhaustibly sustainable, which we now know is the case only if we care for it.

It is not difficult to forgive destruction in the past which resulted from ignorance. Today, however, we have access to more information, and it is essential that we re-examine ethically what we have inherited, what we are responsible for, and what we will pass on to coming generations.

Clearly this is a pivotal generation. Global communication is possible, yet confrontations more often than meaningful dialogues for peace take place.

Our marvels of science and technology are matched if not outweighed by many current tragedies, including human starvation in some parts of the world, and extinction of other life forms.

Exploration of outer space takes place at the same time as the earth's own oceans, seas, and fresh water areas grow increasingly polluted, and their life forms are still largely unknown or misunderstood.

Many of the earth's habitats, animals, plants, insects, and even micro-organisms that we know as rare may not be known at all by future generations. We have the capability, and the responsibility. We must act before it is too late.

The Buddhist Attitude Towards Nature

Lily de Silva

Modern man in his search for pleasure and affluence has exploited nature without any moral restraint to such an extent that nature has been rendered almost incapable of sustaining healthy life. Invaluable gifts of nature, such as air and water, have been polluted with severely disastrous consequences. Man is now searching for ways and means of overcoming the pollution problem as his health too is alarmingly threatened. He also feels that it is irresponsible and morally wrong on his part to commit the future generations to a polluted planet. If man is to act with a sense of responsibility to the natural world, to his fellow human beings and to unborn future generations, he has to find an appropriate environmental ethic today to prevent further aggravation of the present pollution problem. Hence his search for wisdom and attitudes in a hitherto neglected area of knowledge, namely, religion.

Buddhism strictly limits itself to the delineation of a way of life designed to eradicate human suffering. The Buddha refused to answer questions which did not directly or indirectly bear on the central problem of human suffering and its ending. Furthermore, environmental pollution is a problem of the modern age, unheard of and unsuspected during the time of the Buddha. Therefore it is difficult to find any specific discourse which deals with the topic we are interested in here. Nevertheless, as Buddhism is a full-fledged philosophy of life reflecting all aspects of experience, it is possible to find enough material in the Pali Canon to delineate the Buddhist attitude towards nature. The word "nature" means everything in the world which is not organised and constructed by man. The Pali equivalents which come closest to "nature" are *loka* and *yathābhūta*. The former is usually translated as "world" while the latter literally means "things as they really are." The words *dhammatā* and *niyama* are used in the Pali Canon to mean "natural law or way."

Nature Is Dynamic

According to Buddhism changeability is one of the perennial principles of nature. Everything changes in nature and nothing remains static. This concept is expressed by the Pali term *anicca*. Everything formed is in a constant process of change (*sabbe saṅkhārā aniccā*).[4] The world is therefore defined as that which disintegrates (*lujjati ti loko*); the world is so called because it is dynamic and kinetic, it is constantly in a process of undergoing change.[5] In nature there are no static and stable "things"; there are only ever-changing, ever-moving processes. Rain is a good example to illustrate this point. Though we use a noun called "rain" which appears to denote a "thing," rain is nothing but the process of drops of water falling from the skies. Apart from this process, the activity of raining, there is no rain as such which could be expressed by a seemingly static nominal concept. The very elements of solidity (*paṭhavī*), liquidity (*āpo*), heat (*tejo*) and mobility (*vāyo*), recognised as the building material of nature, are all ever-changing phenomena. Even the most solid looking mountains and the very earth that supports everything on it are not beyond this inexorable law of change. One sutta explains how the massive king of mountains—Mount Sineru, which is rooted in the great ocean to a depth of 84,000 leagues and which rises above sea level to another great height of 84,000 leagues and which is the very classical symbol of stability and steadfastness—also gets destroyed by heat, without leaving even ashes, with the appearance of multiple suns.[6] Thus change is the very essence of nature.

Morality and Nature

The world passes through alternating cycles of evolution and dissolution, each of which endures for a long period of time. Though change is inherent in nature, Buddhism believes that natural processes are affected by the morals of man.

According to the Aggañña Sutta,[7] which relates the Buddhist legend regarding the evolution of the world, the appearance

---

4. A IV 100.
5. S IV 52.
6. A IV 100.
7. D III 80.

of greed in the primordial beings—who at that time were self-luminous, subsisting on joy and traversing in the skies—caused the gradual loss of their radiance, the ability to subsist on joy and move about in the sky. The moral degradation had effects on the external environment too. At that time the entire earth was covered over by a very flavoursome fragrant substance similar to butter. When beings started partaking of this substance with more and more greed, on the one hand their subtle bodies became coarser and coarser; on the other hand, the flavoursome substance itself started gradually diminishing. With the solidification of bodies differences of form appeared: some were beautiful while others were homely. Thereupon, conceit manifested itself in those beings, and the beautiful ones started looking down upon the others. As a result of these moral blemishes the delicious edible earth-substance completely disappeared. In its place there appeared edible mushrooms and later another kind of edible creeper. In the beings who subsisted on them successively sex differentiation became manifest and the former method of spontaneous birth was replaced by sexual reproduction.

Self-growing rice appeared on earth and through laziness to collect each meal man grew accustomed to hoarding food. As a result of this hoarding habit, the growth rate of food could not keep pace with the rate of demand. Therefore land had to be divided among families. After private ownership of land became the order of the day, those who were of a greedier disposition started robbing from others' plots of land. When they were detected they denied that they had stolen. Thus through greed, vices such as stealing and lying became manifest in society. To curb the wrong doers and punish them a king was elected by the people and thus the original simple society became much more complex and complicated. It is said that this moral degeneration of man had adverse effects on nature. The richness of the earth diminished and self-growing rice disappeared. Man had to till the land and cultivate rice for food. This rice grain was enveloped in chaff; it needed cleaning before consumption.

The point I wish to emphasise by citing this evolutionary legend is that Buddhism believes that though change is a factor inherent in nature, man's moral deterioration accelerates the process of change and brings about changes which are adverse to human well-being and happiness.

The *Cakkavattisīhanāda Sutta* of the Dīgha Nikāya predicts the future course of events when human morals undergo further degeneration.[8] Gradually man's health will deteriorate so much that life expectancy will diminish until at last the average human life-span is reduced to ten years and marriageable age to five years. At that time all delicacies such as ghee, butter, honey, etc. will have disappeared from the earth; what is considered the poorest coarse food today will become a delicacy of that day. Thus Buddhism maintains that there is a close link between man's morals and the natural resources available to him.

According to a discourse in the Aṅguttara Nikāya, when profligate lust, wanton greed and wrong values grip the heart of man and immorality becomes widespread in society, timely rain does not fall. When timely rain does not fall crops get adversely affected with various kinds of pests and plant diseases. Through lack of nourishing food the human mortality rate rises.[9]

Thus several suttas from the Pali Canon show that early Buddhism believes there to be a close relationship between human morality and the natural environment. This idea has been systematised in the theory of the five natural laws (*pañca niyāma-dhamma*) in the later commentaries.[10] According to this theory, in the cosmos there are five natural laws or forces at work, namely *utuniyāma* (lit. "season-law"), *bījaniyāma* (lit. "seed-law"), *cittaniyāma, kammaniyāma* and *dhammaniyāma*. They can be translated as physical laws, biological laws, psychological laws, moral laws and causal laws, respectively. While the first four laws operate within their respective spheres, the last-mentioned law of causality operates within each of them as well as among them.

This means that the physical environment of any given area conditions the growth and development of its biological component, i.e. flora and fauna. These in turn influence the thought pattern of the people interacting with them. Modes of thinking determine moral standards. The opposite process of interaction is also possible. The morals of man influence not only the psychological make-up of the people but the biological and physical environment

---

8. D III 71.
9. A I 160.
10. *Atthasālinī* 854.

of the area as well. Thus the five laws demonstrate that man and nature are bound together in a reciprocal causal relationship with changes in one necessarily bringing about changes in the other.

The commentary on the *Cakkavattisīhanāda Sutta* goes on to explain the pattern of mutual interaction further.[11] When mankind is demoralised through greed, famine is the natural outcome; when moral degeneration is due to ignorance, epidemic is the inevitable result; when hatred is the demoralising force, widespread violence is the ultimate outcome. If and when mankind realises that large-scale devastation has taken place as a result of his moral degeneration, a change of heart takes place among the few surviving human beings. With gradual moral regeneration conditions improve through a long period of cause and effect and mankind again starts to enjoy gradually increasing prosperity and longer life. The world, including nature and mankind, stands or falls with the type of moral force at work. If immorality grips society, man and nature deteriorate; if morality reigns, the quality of human life and nature improves. Thus greed, hatred and delusion produce pollution within and without. Generosity, compassion and wisdom produce purity within and without. This is one reason the Buddha has pronounced that the world is led by the mind, *cittena niyati loko*.[12] Thus man and nature, according to the ideas expressed in early Buddhism, are interdependent.

Human Use of Natural Resources

For survival mankind has to depend on nature for his food, clothing, shelter, medicine and other requisites.

For optimum benefits man has to understand nature so that he can utilise natural resources and live harmoniously with nature. By understanding the working of nature—for example, the seasonal rainfall pattern, methods of conserving water by irrigation, the soil types, the physical conditions required for growth of various food crops, etc.—man can learn to get better returns from his agricultural pursuits. But this learning has to be accompanied by moral restraint if he is to enjoy the benefits of natural resources for a long time. Man must learn to satisfy his needs and not feed

---

11. Dhp-a III 854.
12. S I 39.

his greed. The resources of the world are not unlimited whereas man's greed knows neither limit nor satiation. Modern man in his unbridled voracious greed for pleasure and acquisition of wealth has exploited nature to the point of near impoverishment.

Ostentatious consumerism is accepted as the order of the day. One writer says that within forty years Americans alone have consumed natural resources to the quantity of what all mankind has consumed for the last 4000 years.[13] The vast non-replenishable resources of fossil fuels which took millions of years to form have been consumed within a couple of centuries to the point of near exhaustion. This consumerism has given rise to an energy crisis on the one hand and a pollution problem on the other. Man's unrestrained exploitation of nature to gratify his insatiate greed reminds one of the traditional parable of the goose that laid the golden eggs.[14]

Buddhism tirelessly advocates the virtues of non-greed, non-hatred and non-delusion in all human pursuits. Greed breeds sorrow and unhealthy consequences. Contentment (santuṭṭhi) is a much praised virtue in Buddhism.[15] The man leading a simple life with few wants easily satisfied is upheld and appreciated as an exemplary character.[16] Miserliness[17] and wastefulness[18] are equally deplored in Buddhism as two degenerate extremes. Wealth has only instrumental value; it is to be utilised for the satisfaction of man's needs. Hoarding is a senseless anti-social habit comparable to the attitude of the dog in the manger. The vast hoarding of wealth in some countries and the methodical destruction of large quantities of agricultural produce to keep the market prices from falling, while half the world is dying of hunger and starvation, is really a sad paradox of the present affluent age.

Buddhism commends frugality as a virtue in its own right. Once Ānanda explained to King Udena the thrifty economic use of robes by the monks in the following order. When new robes

---

13. Quoted in Vance Packard, *The Waste Makers* (London 1961), p. 195.
14. Cp. J I 475 f.
15. Dhp 204.
16. A IV 2, 220, 229.
17. Dhp-a I 20 ff.
18. Dhp-a III 129 ff.

are received the old robes are used as coverlets, the old coverlets as mattress covers, the old mattress covers as rugs, the old rugs as dusters, and the old tattered dusters are kneaded with clay and used to repair cracked floors and walls.[19] Thus nothing usable is wasted. Those who waste are derided as "wood-apple eaters."[20] A man shakes the branch of a wood-apple tree and all the fruits, ripe as well as unripe, fall. The man would collect only what he wants and walk away leaving the rest to rot. Such a wasteful attitude is certainly deplored in Buddhism as not only anti-social but criminal. The excessive exploitation of nature as is done today would certainly be condemned by Buddhism in the strongest possible terms.

Buddhism advocates a gentle non-aggressive attitude towards nature. According to the *Sigālovāda Sutta* a householder should accumulate wealth as a bee collects pollen from a flower.[21] The bee harms neither the fragrance nor the beauty of the flower, but gathers pollen to turn it into sweet honey. Similarly, man is expected to make legitimate use of nature so that he can rise above nature and realise his innate spiritual potential.

Attitude towards Animal and Plant Life

The well-known Five Precepts (*pañca sīlā*) form the minimum code of ethics that every lay Buddhist is expected to adhere to. Its first precept involves abstention from injury to life. It is explained as the casting aside of all forms of weapons, being conscientious about depriving a living being of life. In its positive sense it means the cultivation of compassion and sympathy for all living things.[22] The Buddhist layman is expected to abstain from trading in meat too.[23]

The Buddhist monk has to abide by an even stricter code of ethics than the layman. He has to abstain from practices which would involve even unintentional injury to living creatures. For instance, the Buddha promulgated the rule against going on a journey during the rainy season because of possible injury to worms and insects that

---

19. Vin II 291.
20. A IV 283.
21. D III 188.
22. D I 4.
23. A III 208.

come to the surface in wet weather.[24] The same concern for non-violence prevents a monk from digging the ground.[25] Once a monk who was a potter prior to ordination built for himself a clay hut and set it on fire to give it a fine finish. The Buddha strongly objected to this as so many living creatures would have been burnt in the process. The hut was broken down on the Buddha's instructions to prevent it from creating a bad precedent for later generations.[26] The scrupulous non-violent attitude towards even the smallest living creatures prevents the monks from drinking unstrained water.[27] It is no doubt a sound hygienic habit, but what is noteworthy is the reason which prompts the practice, namely, sympathy for living creatures.

Buddhism also prescribes the practice of *metta*, "loving kindness" towards all creatures of all quarters without restriction. The *Karaṇīyametta Sutta* enjoins the cultivation of loving kindness towards all creatures, timid and steady, long and short, big and small, minute and great, visible and invisible, near and far, born and awaiting birth.[28] All quarters are to be suffused with this loving attitude. Just as one's own life is precious to oneself, so is the life of the other precious to himself. Therefore a reverential attitude must be cultivated towards all forms of life.

The *Nandivisāla Jātaka* illustrates how kindness should be shown to animals domesticated for human service.[29] Even a wild animal can be tamed with kind words. Pārileyya was a wild elephant who attended on the Buddha when he spent time in the forest away from the monks.[30] The infuriated elephant Nālāgiri was tamed by the Buddha with no other miraculous power than the power of loving kindness.[31] Man and beast can live and let live without fear of one another if only man cultivates sympathy and regards all life with compassion.

---

24. Vin I 137.
25. Vin IV 125.
26. Vin III 42.
27. Vin IV 125.
28. Sn 143–152.
29. J I 191.
30. Dhp-a I 58 ff.
31. Vin II 194 f.

The understanding of kamma and rebirth, too, prepares the Buddhist to adopt a sympathetic attitude towards animals. According to this belief it is possible for human beings to be reborn in subhuman states among animals. The *Kukkuravatika Sutta* can be cited as a canonical reference which substantiates this view.[32] The Jātakas provide ample testimony to this view from commentarial literature. It is possible that our own close relatives have been reborn as animals. Therefore it is only right that we should treat animals with kindness and sympathy. The Buddhist notion of merit also engenders a gentle non-violent attitude towards living creatures. It is said that if one throws dish-washing water into a pool where there are insects and living creatures, intending that they feed on the tiny particles of food thus washed away, one accumulates merit even by such trivial generosity.[33] According to the *Macchuddāna Jātaka* the Bodhisatta threw his leftover food into a river in order to feed the fish, and by the power of that merit he was saved from an impending disaster.[34] Thus kindness to animals, be they big or small, is a source of merit—merit needed for human beings to improve their lot in the cycle of rebirths and to approach the final goal of Nibbana.

Buddhism expresses a gentle non-violent attitude towards the vegetable kingdom as well. It is said that one should not even break the branch of a tree that has given one shelter.[35] Plants are so helpful to us in providing us with all necessities of life that we are expected not to adopt a callous attitude towards them. The more strict monastic rules prevent monks from injuring plant life.[36]

Prior to the rise of Buddhism people regarded natural phenomena such as mountains, forests, groves and trees with a sense of awe and reverence.[37] They considered them as the abode of powerful non-human beings that could assist human beings at times of need. Though Buddhism gave man a far superior Triple

---

32. M I 387 f.
33. A I 161.
34. J II 423.
35. Petavatthu II 9, 3.
36. Vin IV 34.
37. Dhp 188.

Refuge (*tisaraṇa*) in the Buddha, Dhamma and Sangha, these places continued to enjoy public patronage at a popular level, as the acceptance of terrestrial non-human beings such as devatas[38] and yakkhas[39] did not violate the belief system of Buddhism. Therefore among the Buddhists there is a reverential attitude towards specially long-standing gigantic trees. They are called *vanaspati* in Pali, meaning "lords of the forests."[40] As huge trees such as the ironwood, the sāla and the fig are also recognised as the Bodhi trees of former Buddhas, the deferential attitude towards trees is further strengthened.[41] It is well known that the *Ficus Religiosa* is held as an object of great veneration in the Buddhist world today as the tree under which the Buddha attained Enlightenment.

The construction of parks and pleasure groves for public use is considered a great meritorious deed.[42] Sakka the lord of gods is said to have reached this status as a result of social services such as the construction of parks, pleasure groves, ponds, wells and roads.[43]

The open air, natural habitats and forest trees have a special fascination for the Eastern mind as symbols of spiritual freedom. The home life is regarded as a fetter (*sambādha*) that keeps man in bondage and misery. Renunciation is like the open air (*abbhokāsa*), nature unhampered by man's activity.[44] The chief events in the life of the Buddha too took place in the open air. He was born in a park at the foot of a tree in Kapilavatthu; he attained Enlightenment in the open air at the foot of the Bodhi tree in Bodhgāya; he inaugurated his missionary activity in the open air in the sāla grove of the Mallas in Pāva. The Buddha's constant advice to his disciples also was to resort to natural habitats such as forest groves and glades. There, undisturbed by human activity, they could zealously engage themselves in meditation.[45]

---

38. S I 1–45.
39. S I 206–215.
40. S IV 302; Dhp-a I 3.
41. D II 4.
42. S I 33.
43. J I 199 f.
44. D I 63.
45. M I 118; S IV 373

Attitude towards Pollution

Environmental pollution has assumed such vast proportions today that man has been forced to recognise the presence of an ecological crisis. He can no longer turn a blind eye to the situation as he is already threatened with new pollution-related diseases. Pollution to this extent was unheard of during the time of the Buddha. But there is sufficient evidence in the Pali Canon to give us insight into the Buddhist attitude towards the pollution problem. Several Vinaya rules prohibit monks from polluting green grass and water with saliva, urine and faeces.[46] These were the common agents of pollution known during the Buddha's day and rules were promulgated against causing such pollution. Cleanliness was highly commended by the Buddhists both in the person and in the environment. They were much concerned about keeping water clean, be it in the river, pond or well. These sources of water were for public use and each individual had to use them with proper public-spirited caution so that others after him could use them with the same degree of cleanliness. Rules regarding the cleanliness of green grass were prompted by ethical and aesthetic considerations. Moreover, grass is food for most animals and it is man's duty to refrain from polluting it by his activities.

Noise is today recognised as a serious personal and environmental pollutant troubling everyone to some extent. It causes deafness, stress and irritation, breeds resentment, saps energy and inevitably lowers efficiency.[47] The Buddha's attitude to noise is very clear from the Pali Canon. He was critical of noise and did not hesitate to voice his stern disapproval whenever occasion arose.[48] Once he ordered a group of monks to leave the monastery for noisy behaviour.[49] He enjoyed solitude and silence immensely and spoke in praise of silence as it is most appropriate for mental culture. Noise is described as a thorn to one engaged in the first step of meditation,[50] but thereafter noise ceases to be a disturbance as the meditator passes beyond the possibility of being disturbed by sound.

---

46. Vin IV 205–206.
47. Robert Arvill, *Man and Environment* (Penguin Books, 1978), p. 118.
48. A III 31.
49. M I 457.
50. A V 135.

The Buddha and his disciples revelled in the silent solitary natural habitats unencumbered by human activity. Even in the choice of monasteries the presence of undisturbed silence was an important quality they looked for.[51] Silence invigorates those who are pure at heart and raises their efficiency for meditation. But silence overawes those who are impure with ignoble impulses of greed, hatred and delusion. The *Bhayabherava Sutta* beautifully illustrates how even the rustle of leaves by a falling twig in the forest sends tremors through an impure heart.[52] This may perhaps account for the present craze for constant auditory stimulation with transistors and cassettes. The moral impurity caused by greed, avarice, acquisitive instincts and aggression has rendered man so timid that he cannot bear silence that lays bare the reality of self-awareness. He therefore prefers to drown himself in loud music. Unlike classical music that tends to soothe nerves and induce relaxation, rock music excites the senses. Constant exposure to it actually renders man incapable of relaxation and sound sleep without tranquillisers.

As to the question of the Buddhist attitude to music, it is recorded that the Buddha has spoken quite appreciatively of music on one occasion.[53] When Pañcasikha the divine musician sang a song while playing the lute in front of the Buddha, the Buddha praised his musical ability saying that the instrumental music blended well with his song. Again, the remark of an Arahat that the joy of seeing the real nature of things is far more exquisite than orchestral music[54] shows the recognition that music affords a certain amount of pleasure even if it is inferior to higher kinds of pleasure. But it is stressed that the ear is a powerful sensory channel through which man gets addicted to sense pleasures. Therefore, to dissuade monks from getting addicted to melodious sounds the monastic discipline describes music as a lament.[55]

---

51. A V 15.
52. M I 16–24.
53. D II 267.
54. Th 398.
55. A I 261.

The psychological training of the monks is so advanced that they are expected to cultivate a taste not only for external silence, but for inner silence of speech, desire and thought as well. The subvocal speech, the inner chatter that goes on constantly within us in our waking life, is expected to be silenced through meditation.[56] The sage who succeeds in quelling this inner speech completely is described as a *muni*, a silent one.[57] His inner silence is maintained even when he speaks!

It is not inappropriate to pay passing notice to the Buddhist attitude to speech as well. Moderation in speech is considered a virtue, as one can avoid four unwholesome vocal activities thereby, namely, falsehood, slander, harsh speech and frivolous talk. In its positive aspect moderation in speech paves the path to self-awareness. Buddhism commends speaking at the appropriate time, speaking the truth, speaking gently, speaking what is useful, and speaking out of loving kindness; the opposite modes of speech are condemned.[58] The Buddha's general advice to the monks regarding speech is to be engaged in discussing the Dhamma or maintain noble silence.[59] The silence that reigned in vast congregations of monks during the Buddha's day was indeed a surprise even to the kings of the time.[60] Silence is serene and noble as it is conducive to the spiritual progress of those who are pure at heart.

Even Buddhist laymen were reputed to have appreciated quietude and silence. Pañcaṅgika Thapati can be cited as a conspicuous example.[61] Once Mahānāma the Sakyan complained to the Buddha that he is disturbed by the hustle of the busy city of Kapilavatthu. He explained that he experiences calm serenity when he visits the Buddha in the quiet salubrious surroundings of the monastery and his peace of mind gets disturbed when he goes to the city.[62] Though noise to the extent of being a pollutant

---

56. S IV 217, 293.
57. Sn vv. 207–221; A I 273.
58. M I 126.
59. M I 161.
60. M II 122; D I 50.
61. M II 23.
62. S V 369.

causing health hazards was not known during the Buddha's day, we have adduced enough material from the Pali Canon to illustrate the Buddha's attitude to the problem. Quietude is much appreciated as spiritually rewarding, while noise condemned as a personal and social nuisance.

Nature as Beautiful

The Buddha and his disciples regarded natural beauty as a source of great joy and aesthetic satisfaction. The saints who purged themselves of sensuous worldly pleasures responded to natural beauty with a detached sense of appreciation. The average poet looks at nature and derives inspiration mostly by the sentiments it evokes in his own heart; he becomes emotionally involved with nature. For instance, he may compare the sun's rays passing over the mountain tops to the blush on a sensitive face, he may see a tear in a dew drop, the lips of his beloved in a rose petal, etc. But the appreciation of the saint is quite different. He appreciates nature's beauty for its own sake and derives joy unsullied by sensuous associations and self-projected ideas. The simple spontaneous appreciation of nature's exquisite beauty is expressed by the Elder Mahākassapa in the following words:[63]

> Those upland glades delightful to the soul,
> Where the Kaveri spreads its wildering wreaths,
> Where sound the trumpet-calls of elephants:
> Those are the hills where my soul delights.

> Those rocky heights with hue of dark blue clouds
> Where lies embossed many a shining lake
> Of crystal-clear, cool waters, and whose slopes
> The 'herds of Indra' cover and bedeck:
> Those are the hills wherein my soul delights.

> Fair uplands rain-refreshed, and resonant,
> With crested creatures' cries antiphonal,
> Lone heights where silent Rishis oft resort:
> Those are the hills wherein my soul delights.

---

63. Th 1062–1071.

Again the poem of Kaludāyi inviting the Buddha to visit Kapilavatthu, contains a beautiful description of spring:[64]

> Now crimson glow the trees, dear Lord, and cast
> Their ancient foliage in quest of fruit,
> Like crests of flame they shine irradiant,
> And rich in hope, great Hero, is the hour.
> Verdure and blossom-time in every tree
> Wherever we look delightful to the eye,
> And every quarter breathing fragrant airs,
> While petals falling, yearning comes fruit:
> It is time,
> O Hero, that we set out hence.

The long poem of Tālaputta is a fascinating soliloquy.[65] His religious aspirations are beautifully blended with a profound knowledge of the teachings of the Buddha against the background of a sylvan resort. Many more poems could be cited for saintly appreciation of nature, but it is not necessary to burden the essay with any more quotations. Suffice it to know that the saints, too, were sensitive to the beauties and harmony of nature and that their appreciation is coloured by spontaneity, simplicity and a non-sensuous spirituality.

---

64. Th 527–529.
65. Th 1091–1145.

Conclusion

In the modern age man has become alienated from himself and nature. When science started opening new vistas of knowledge revealing the secrets of nature one by one, man gradually lost faith in theistic religions. Consequently, he developed scanty respect for moral and spiritual values as well. With the advent of the Industrial Revolution and the acquisition of wealth by mechanical exploitation of natural resources, man has become more and more materialistic in his attitudes and values. The pursuit of sense pleasures and the acquisition of possessions have become ends in themselves. Man's sense faculties dominate him to an unrelenting degree and man has become a slave to his insatiable passions. (Incidentally the sense faculties are called in Pali *indriyas* or lords, because they control man unless he is sufficiently vigilant to become their master.) Thus man has become alienated from himself as he abandoned himself to the influence of sense pleasures and acquisitive instincts.

In his greed for more and more possessions he has adopted a violent and aggressive attitude towards nature. Forgetting that he is a part and parcel of nature, he exploits it with unrestrained greed, thus alienating himself from nature as well. The net result is the deterioration of man's physical and mental health on the one hand, and the rapid depletion of non-replenishable natural resources and environmental pollution on the other. These results remind us of the Buddhist teachings in the suttas discussed above, which maintain that the moral degeneration of man leads to the decrease of his life-span and the depletion of natural resources.

Moral degeneration is a double-edged weapon, it exercises adverse effects on man's psychophysical well-being as well as on nature. Already killer diseases such as heart ailments, cancer, diabetes, AIDS, etc., are claiming victims on an unprecedented scale. In the final analysis these can all be traced to man's moral deterioration. Depletion of vast resources of fossil fuels and forests has given rise to a very severe energy crisis. It cannot be emphasised too strongly that such rapid depletion of non-renewable natural resources within less than two centuries, an infinitesimal fraction of the millions of years taken for them to form, is due to modern man's inordinate greed and acquisitiveness. A number of simple ancient societies had advanced technological skills, as is evident by their vast sophisticated irrigation schemes designed to feed the fundamental needs of several millions. Yet they survived in some countries over 2000 years without such problems as environmental pollution and depletion of natural resources. This was no doubt due to the validity of the philosophy which inspired and formed the basis of these civilizations.

In the present ecocrisis man has to look for radical solutions. "Pollution cannot be dealt with in the long term on a remedial or cosmetic basis or by tackling symptoms: all measures should deal with basic causes. These are determined largely by our values, priorities and choices."[66] Man must reappraise his value system. The materialism that has guided his lifestyle has landed him in very severe problems. Buddhism teaches that mind is the forerunner of all things, mind is supreme. If one acts with an impure mind, i.e. a mind sullied with greed, hatred and delusion, suffering is the inevitable result. If one acts with a pure mind, i.e. with the opposite qualities of contentment, compassion and wisdom, happiness will follow like a shadow.[67] Man has to understand that pollution in the environment has been caused because there has been psychological pollution within himself. If he wants a clean environment he has to adopt a lifestyle that springs from a moral and spiritual dimension.

Buddhism offers man a simple moderate lifestyle eschewing both extremes of self-deprivation and self-indulgence. Satisfaction of basic human necessities, reduction of wants to the minimum, frugality and contentment are its important characteristics. Each man has to order his life on normal principles, exercise self-control in the enjoyment of the senses, discharge his duties in his various social roles, and conduct himself with wisdom and self-awareness in all activities. It is only when each man adopts a simple moderate lifestyle that mankind as a whole will stop polluting the environment. This seems to be the only way of overcoming the present ecocrisis and the problem of alienation. With such a lifestyle, man will adopt a non-exploitative, non-aggressive, gentle attitude towards nature. He can then live in harmony with nature,

---

66. Arvill, *Man and Environment*, p. 170.
67. Dhp 1, 2.

utilising its resources for the satisfaction of his basic needs. The Buddhist admonition is to utilise nature in the same way as a bee collects pollen from the flower, neither polluting its beauty nor depleting its fragrance. Just as the bee manufactures honey out of pollen, so man should be able to find happiness and fulfilment in life without harming the natural world in which he lives.

Buddhist Philosophy as Inspiration to Ecodevelopment

Klas Sandell

"We need to reassess our attitudes towards the natural world on which our technology intrudes."

—Barry Commoner

Ecodevelopment[68]

Ecodevelopment should be seen as an integral part of the pursuit of an "alternative" or "another" development. It involves a search for alternatives to the predominant concepts of modernization and industrialization that have been the guiding influences during the postwar era. According to McNerfin an ideal development should have the following characteristics: it should be need-oriented, endogenous, self-reliant, ecologically sound, and based on structural transformations.[69] A stable, long-term relationship with nature should, therefore, be regarded as an essential basis for all efforts towards alternative development. When ecological awareness and man's relationship with nature are stressed in such development, the term "ecodevelopment" is often applied.[70]

The term "ecodevelopment" can be divided into two parts, "eco" and "development," in reference to which I would like to apply the key concepts "sustainability" and "self-reliance," respectively. Sustainability expresses the need for an approach

---

68. M T. Farvar and J. P. Milton, eds., *The Careless Technology: Ecology and International Development* (New York: The Natural History Press, 1972), p. xxix.

69. N. McNerfin, ed., *Another Development: Approaches and Strategies* (Uppsala: The Dag Hammarskjold Foundation, 1977), p. 10.

70. See B. Hettne, *Development Theory and the Third World* (Stockholm: SAREC Report, 1982); R. Riddel, *Ecodevelopment* (Gower, New Hampshire, 1981); I. Sachs, "Ecodevelopment," Ceres, Nov.-Dec. 1974, pp. 8–12.

(inclusive of technology) which does not endanger the long-term fertility of ecosystems. The concept of self-reliance indicates the wish to pursue a course of development originating in a specific natural and cultural environment. In this connection terms like "appropriate technology," "people's participation" and "diversity" are applied.[71]

Buddhist Inspiration

What, then, does all this have to do with Buddhist philosophy? Though Buddhism does not advocate specific political forms or propose specific economic programmes, it is my strong belief that in the perspective of the ecocrisis we should scrutinise, in terms of both philosophy and practice, different sources of inspiration for a sustainable development. This is why the title of this chapter deals with Buddhism as an inspiration to ecodevelopment. Padmasiri de Silva writes: "There are two possible approaches to nature within the Buddhist tradition: mastering and harnessing the natural resources for man's use, and the adoption of the contemplative attitude where we discern in nature our own images of peace and tranquillity. Both these attitudes can be brought together and contrasted with the aggressive and violent attitude towards nature."

I would like to arrange my thinking about Buddhism and ecodevelopment under the following four headings: (i) Man's mortality, which primarily concerns his approach to matter and natural laws; (ii) The significance of spiritual development, especially as a counterpoint to short-sightedness and materialism; (iii) The difference between attached and detached love, which involves the ability to appreciate and develop a non-demanding, non-attached relationship; (iv) The possibility of a harmonious relationship between man and nature, based on man's unique position in relation to other physical and biological elements.

Man's Mortality

Buddhism places a great deal of emphasis on the need to see things as they really are. It is only through the attainment of individual

---

71. Padmasiri de Silva, *Value Orientation and Nation Building* (Colombo: Lake House, 1976), p. 37.

insight into the true nature of the world that man is able to dissociate himself from the perpetual cycle of insatiable needs and his attempts to fulfil them.

Man is a part of nature and no sharp distinctions can be drawn between him and his surroundings, as everything is impermanent and subject to the same natural laws. "For according to Buddhism the factors of existence are interconnected by laws of causality. Although the factors are not fractions of a whole, yet they are interconnected and interdependent.[72] Lily de Silva writes that as "man and nature are mutually related to one another, a change in one is apt to bring about a change in the other."[73]

These views on action and reaction in man's relationship with nature seem to come very close to certain modern scientific concepts. It is above all ecology and human ecology that have observed how various elements in nature are interconnected and how human encroachment in one way or another leads to repercussions in time and space. A further parallel between Buddhism and modern science can be found in the concept of evolution, which emphasises man's role as an impermanent component in an ever-changing situation: "According to Buddhism the world we live in has come to be what it is as the result of a gradual process of evolution spread out over a vast period of time."[74]

Man's perception of the world around him and the feelings that result from this give rise to the illusion of a "self." This, in its turn, results in the need to protect that self, the pursuit of pleasures, the urge to possess, and the attempt to avoid all forms of insecurity. Considering the above statement that everything is impermanent, as a consequence a constant sense of unsatisfactoriness arises. Man's only hope of deliverance from this condition lies in his awareness and acceptance of the impermanence and inconstancy of himself and everything around him.

This awareness of the fact that everything, including man himself, is impermanent, and that man is subject to the laws

---

72. Y. Karunadasa, *The Buddhist Analysis of Matter* (Colombo: Government Press, 1967), p. 176.

73. Lily de Silva, "Psychological and Ethical Dimensions of Humanity's Relation to Nature," Dialogue (Colombo), 5 (1978):6.

74. Ibid., p. 5.

of causality, must be seen as an important basis for a proper understanding of man's role in nature. Such an awareness promotes humility and thoughtfulness.

The Significance of Spiritual Development

Buddhism emphasises the need for every human being to attain a greater understanding of the nature of the world via spiritual development, and in this way become aware of his short-sighted, insatiable needs. Moreover, in various ways the Buddha has stressed the need for close contact with nature and pointed out how advancement of mind leads to a greater appreciation of nature.

> Delightful are the forests
> Where ordinary people find no pleasure.
> There the passionless will rejoice,
> For they seek no sensual pleasures.
>
> Dhammapada v. 99

It would seem, then, obvious that a greater sense of proportion is needed between things spiritual and material, especially in our modern consumer society where a closer contact with nature may be regarded as an important foundation for the pursuit of spiritual development. A better sense of proportion and a withdrawal from exaggerated material needs should be regarded as essential ingredients to ecodevelopment. The earth will never be able to satisfy man's apparently insatiable longing for material things. Spiritual development, on the other hand, can serve both as an aim and as a means for achieving a greater sense of proportion in development.

Attached and Detached Love

In the section above I discussed the need to deal with the "urge to possess." It is not uncommon when discussing environmental degradation and nature preservation, to comment on the necessity of a deeper appreciation and love of nature. One important aspect of this is the way in which concepts such as love and appreciation acquire a new connotation when applied to "development of mind," and it is my belief that one of Buddhism's most important contributions to the concept of ecodevelopment lies here.

Buddhism points to the difference between unselfish love and the kind of love that is linked to attachment and the urge to possess. It stresses the need to learn how to appreciate someone or something without a feeling of attachment. Douglas M Burns writes: "Persons who have attained Nirvāna can fully admire beauty, but they do not cling to it. It is said that they appreciate without attachment."[75]

Naturally it is extremely difficult for most of us to come anywhere near a relationship in which we are able to appreciate somebody or something without feeling any attachment or any urge to possess or exploit. We have only to consider this in relation to people we love: how difficult it is to think of them without becoming attached and without experiencing grief when they die.

But this does not mean that the cultivation of detachment is of no great significance to developing an approach to nature that favours a stable long-term interrelation, one that encourages an unselfish appreciation and enjoyment of nature without the thought of profit or exploitation.

We can also describe the contrast between attached and detached love as the difference between greed and need. It is quite obvious that a large proportion of the production that today leads to an intensification of environmental problems and to the impoverishing of the earth comes under the category of greed, e.g. several cars per family, home computers, expendable packaging, not to mention armaments and the space race. Serious debate and a greater awareness of the difference between greed and need must be seen as a basis for the future utilisation of nature.

Harmonious Man-Nature Relationship

It is obvious that man has a capability to manipulate his environment far exceeding that of all other species. Despite what has been said above regarding natural laws and impermanence, Buddhism still holds that man's position in nature is a unique one. Padmasiri de Silva says of man that "he has the freedom to mould his natural world as well as the moral and spiritual life in accordance with the laws of causality."[76]

---

75. Douglas M Burns, *The Population Crisis and Conservation*, Bodhi Leaves B 76 (Kandy: Buddhist Publication Society, 1977), p. 15.

76. Padmasiri de Silva, op. cit., p. 37.

But how are we to avoid a situation in which man's unique position leads to an attempt to dominate nature? Here, following the above discussion on impermanence, etc., the concept of loving kindness (*metta*) comes in. This should be seen as an element in the Buddhist philosophy of non-violence, which, however, goes further than the ideas usually associated with non-violence.

Metta is the first of four contemplations termed the "Divine Abidings," which are intended to develop a peaceful relationship to other living beings. The other three are *karuṇā* (compassion), *mudita* (gladness at others' success), and *upekkha* (equanimity).

In the *Karaṇīyametta Sutta* from the Suttanipāta, the following can be read:

> May creatures all be of a blissful heart.
> Whatever breathing beings there may be,
> No matter whether they are frail or firm,
> With none excepted, be they long or big
> Or middle-sized, or be they short or small
> Or thick, as well as those seen or unseen,
> Or whether they are dwelling far or near,
> Existing or yet seeking to exist,
> May creatures all be of a blissful heart.[77]

This philosophy of non-violence should, therefore, be seen as an approach to life rooted in a feeling of tender affection towards everything around us and without the urge to get something in return.

This combination—the recognition of man's unique position in nature together with the ideal of spiritual development and humility towards nature—gives support to the achievement of a harmonious relationship between man and nature. This implies the possibility of a withdrawal from the usual ways of thinking, ranging from man's submission to nature to his domination of nature. A harmonious relationship with nature leading to cooperation with it should, therefore, be seen as a "third alternative" and not as a compromise between submission and domination. In the search for such a cooperative attitude towards nature Buddhist philosophy can be an important source of inspiration.

---

77. Ñāṇamoli Thera, *The Practice of Loving-kindness*, Wheel No. 7 (Kandy: Buddhist Publication Society, 1981), p. 19.

In Search of a Buddhist Environmental Ethics

Padmasiri de Silva

"I believe that only a religious ethic (towards nature) will serve to protect us, an ethic that regards man as the trustee of nature for the welfare of all people now and into the remote future."

Bentley Class[78]

The term "ethics" may be used in three different but related senses:

1. A general pattern or way of life;
2. A set of rules or a moral code;
3. An inquiry about ways of life, rules of conduct and basic terms used in the evaluation of human behaviour, such as good and bad, right and wrong, etc.

In more recent times, the study of ethics has by sheer necessity expanded into the arena where we deal with the encounter between traditional ethical systems and changing social conditions, where the focus is on the application of moral principles to practical situations, and some of these situations are of a very complex and even dilemmatic nature.

In this context, like most religious and ethical systems, the Buddha presents a way of life which includes a moral code for the layman as well as the monk. But both these aspects are deeply rooted in a reflective inquiry about the basis of this way of life and rules of conduct. The Buddha, where necessary, also clarifies the concepts and terms he uses for evaluating behaviour and he discusses the diverse types of reasons offered for beliefs in ethical contexts. The application of the principles of ethics to specific contexts has to be gleaned from his discourses.

---

78. Bentley Class, "The Scientist: Trustee for Humanity," *Bioscience 27* (1977): 277–278.

The clarification of the logic and usage of moral terms is a central dimension of modern ethics, referred to as "metaethics," and while this perspective has its uses, the complexity of the modern situation has generated a great interest in what may be called "applied-ethics."

Today, there is no consistent ethical perspective to deal with the issues thrust on us by new advances in biological and medical sciences like the questions of genetic engineering or those pertaining to the terminal patient who does not want to live; the case of armaments being used for self-defence and nuclear warfare; or the problem of handling sporadic forms of terrorism. As science and technology develop, traditional values are undergoing a great deal of strain in this call to adjust to new situations. Though questions pertaining to the ethics of conservation are not as sharply dilemmatic as some of the issues cited, they still belong to the technological and socioeconomic setting in the modern world and call for a new orientation in values. It is in the need for a new value orientation that a Buddhist contribution appears to be relevant. While we have explored some general Buddhist perspectives regarding the overall disturbing condition elsewhere,[79] this short analysis will explore Buddhist reflections on the ecocrisis in relation to ethical issues.

World-View Orientation and Ecological Values

What we need is not merely a discovery of certain Buddhist values but the integration of values, a certain holistic perspective which reverberates through most of our activities. Today the natural and social environment has been integrated into "one universe."

Environmentalists point out that today, more than ever, the earth has become a delicately balanced system of interdependent parts—an "ecosystem." If a person is considerate and generous in social services and community work but in his work is callous and aggressive towards the natural environment, there is a note of deep discordance. If one is callous towards the natural environment, then one is creating problems for others and for generations to come.

---

79. A forthcoming work will explore the theme "Buddhist Ethics and Ethical Dilemmas."

In the past people were not concerned with the environment; it was something given and to be used. If it was coal we needed, then the land was there to be stripped of its hidden treasure. If industrial waste had to be removed, then nature had conveniently supplied us with rivers for this very purpose. Nature existed as a system of inexhaustible and ever-renewable resources.[80] Today we possess a great deal of information about our natural environment and its relation to the quality of life as well as the duration of life. Issues like the pollution of our air, water and food, overcrowding, the depletion of natural resources, aesthetically deteriorating landscapes, etc. figure prominently in our concern with the natural environment. In the words of Barbara Ward: "Wasted, polluted, corrupted earth, filled with junked cars and old iron, is more than just sloppy and ugly. It spells indifference to human need, a wanton neglect of fundamental decencies."[81] But when far reaching issues like nuclear experiments and cancer or food poisoning emerge, we find that whether we like it or not we are deeply embedded in the natural world. It is by human intervention that man has polluted the natural environment and again it is by human intervention and a new sense of responsibility to our fellow beings and to generations to come that our natural environment can be changed. A critique of the ecosystem involves, from the Buddhist standpoint, a critique of one's sense of the self. The world-view orientation which can feed a Buddhist environmental ethics is this critique of one's sense of the self.

If nature becomes the object of our greed and avarice, and the victim of our acquisitive instinct, a gentle and non-violent man-nature orientation is not possible. Schumacher has admirably pointed out that a non-violent and gentle attitude to nature is the ecological stance of Buddhism.[82] The violent and aggressive approach to the natural world is fed by man's greed for short-term spectacular success without care for the long-term ill-effects on another generation. As Roderick Nash points out, if we have

---

80. The pioneering work on the search for an environmental ethic in the West is found in the writings of Albert Schweitzer and, more recently, the philosopher William Blackstone.

81. Barbara Ward, *The Home of Man* (London, 1976), p. 99.

82. See E. F. Schumacher, *Small is Beautiful* (London, 1973).

a proper environmental ethic, the "raping of nature" can be as morally repulsive as the raping of a woman. A healthy achievement motivation can promote economic growth, but uncontrolled greed and avarice are as detrimental as laziness and apathy.

We have pointed out elsewhere that two possible approaches to nature are found within the Buddhist tradition: one is the mastering and harnessing of the natural resources for man's use done by humanising the habitat; the other is the contemplative attitude by which we discern in nature our own image of peace and tranquillity. These attitudes can be integrated and blended to form a viable Buddhist stance on nature, one which can be contrasted with the current aggressive, dominating and violent attitude towards nature.[83]

Springing from this contemplative attitude, there is an interesting aesthetic dimension which stabilises our move towards conservation. There are many references in the Buddhist texts to instances where men of great spiritual heights appreciated scenic beauty. The Buddhist is able to look at the mirror of nature without attachment, and with a mind of equanimity he can discern the most profound truths in this mirror. He is able to see the nature of transience in the very rhythms of nature, in the falling of flowers, the decay of leaves and the change of seasons. All this is significant because it reveals an attunement with nature as well as an acute sensitivity towards nature. It is also important because we extend these attitudes to people and animals. Today there is a spell of impersonality in the way we handle people, animals and trees; we have become used to handling them in the way we handle machines and tractors. We have lost that touch of gentleness, care and concern—the non-violent and compassionate element which goes to generate creative human relations. We develop mechanistic, instrumental and impersonal attitudes to fellow humans, animals and nature.

A profound man-nature orientation also pervades the Buddhist exploration of the correct environment for the practice of meditation. The Buddhist monk is a lover of solitude and seeks out the empty places (*suññagāra*) of nature. The open, empty and

---

83. Padmasiri de Silva, *Value Orientation and Nation Building* (Colombo, 1976), p. 37.

tranquil woods provide the ideal environment for one in search of spiritual solace.

World-View Orientation And Human Needs

While the most significant aspect of the world-view orientation in the context of ecological issues is its man-nature relationship, a second aspect, equally important, is the Buddhist lifestyle. The economic needs of man have created pressing problems today because a simple way of life does not satisfy man and he longs for diverse types of goods and services. A modest concept of living, simplicity, frugality, and emphasis on essential goods, cutting down wastage and a basic ethic of restraint can supplement the Buddhist man-nature orientation. In the West, public discussion has been more concerned with the adequacy of resources than with the viability of human needs and lifestyles. Exceptions to this attitude in the West may be found in William Leiss's *The Limits to Satisfaction*[84] and Schumacher's *Small is Beautiful*.[85]

R. M Salas, a UN expert on population studies who delivered the Colombo University Special Convocation Lecture in 1979, made the following observations: "But I believe that what is more important than all these, is that the people of this country are blessed by one other resource that stands above all others—the ethic of restraint. Development in its broadest integration demands the consciousness of limits to enable people to act without degrading themselves and their environment."[86] He concludes by saying that the Buddha's attempt to overcome man's basic unruly craving provides an ethic for the next century. But we are caught up between, on the one hand, a dynamic and vibrant drive for development and, on the other, the besetting attractions of the high-intensity market setting and the lifestyles of the affluent coming from the West. We lack a clear self-critical tone in our attempts to integrate these oncoming development models. This is a common issue for Third World countries and these realities have to be consistently kept in mind when

---

84. William Leiss, *The Limits to Satisfaction* (Toronto, 1976).

85. Op. cit.

86. R. M. Salas, *Convocation Lecture* (University of Colombo, 1979).

we explore our traditional heritage to find answers for modern issues. Today, we are not only threatened by the pollution of the environment but by an insidious pollution of the mind, which has already affected the youth in the form of drug addiction. Thus in this context, today more than ever, the pollution of the environment and the pollution of the mind have to be dealt with as facets of the same problem.

Ecology and Psychology

If we accept the thesis that the pollution of nature and the pollution of the mind are facets of one problem, exploring a viable "environmental psychology" becomes a significant venture for the ecologist. Though environmental psychology, like environmental ethics, is a relatively new discipline, it helps us to get a more holistic vision of environmental problems and does so admirably in the Buddhist context.

The new environmental psychology is examining the links and the inter-relations between the psychological aspects of man and his physical environment. As the old balance and equilibrium between man and nature have broken down in the face of the new technologies, an attempt has to be made to restore this balance. Sometimes it is wrongly held that environmental psychology is a narrow discipline merely concerned with issues like the impact of a skyscraper building on its inhabitants, the effect of metal on people who are involved in the manufacture of cars, the effect of industrial smoke on workers, etc. These issues are important, but in a deeper sense environmental psychology is concerned with people searching for a more comprehensive meaning in the man-nature relationship: "In this sense, not only the environment but an ethos is preserved. For the extent to which we achieve an identity in the environment is not simply in the prudent use we make of it, but in the human values we express through our willingness to shape it to an ethical end ... Environmental man is not only critical in relation to the ecosystem but to his own sense of self."[87]

---

87. Ittelson, Proshansky, Rivlin and Winkel, eds., *An Introduction to Environmental Psychology* (New York, 1974), pp. 9–10.

In searching for a place to live in, man is not only concerned with comfort and shelter, for he does create something more than a mere physical environment. In planning the structure of the physical space, he instils it with meaning and symbols which give a sense of life and expression to his values. Thus the new environmental psychology has to be linked to this search for an environmental ethics. Erich Fromm has recently shown an interesting relation between personality types and ecology.[88] In a work entitled *To Have or To Be?*, he says that there are two modes of existence, the "having mode" and the "being mode." The "having mode" expresses man's basic acquisitiveness, his desire for power and aggressiveness, and generates greed, envy and violence; the "being mode" is an expression of man's desire to care for others, to give to others, to share and sacrifice. The latter mode encourages conservation of resources, while the former mode can lead to ecological disaster. Fromm sees in the teaching of the Buddha as well as some other religions an explication of the idea that the "having mode" leads to a callous and irresponsible attitude towards nature as well as towards other persons.

In general the Buddhist sees greed (*lobha*), hatred (*dosa*) and delusion (*moha*) as the roots of the acquisitive, destructive and confused lifestyles. Excessive greed finds expression in diffused life orientations bound to sensuality and hedonism in the form of *kāmataṇhā* (sensuous gratification); greed also manifests in limitless expansion and a possessive stance bound to *bhava-taṇhā* (craving for selfish pursuits); a destructive and violent attitude to oneself, others and the natural world finds a point of anchorage in the root hatred, manifesting sometimes as a annihilistic instinct or *vibhava-taṇhā*. The false and destructive pattern of consumption generates an unending cycle of desires and satisfactions. The psychological roots of ecological disaster and recovery are factors very much related in the Buddhist context to the search for an environmental ethic.

Ecology and Ethics

Now we should return to the original question we raised about environment and ethics in the introductory section of this essay.

---

88. Erich Fromm, *To Have or To Be?* (New York, 1976).

Ethics is concerned with the evaluation of human behaviour in terms of concepts such as good and bad, right and wrong, etc. A major dimension of the study of ethics is to focus attention on the kind of moral principles and core values which guide decision-making.

(i) The concept of the "value of life" is a concept which takes a central place in recent discussions of environmental ethics. In the evolution of ethical reflections attention was focused on the individual and family, tribes, regions, nations, and so on to include all humankind. Now this is being extended to non-human forms of life, especially animals and the natural environment. In the case of the natural environment, as vegetables are used for human consumption, the emphasis is on avoiding the callous destruction of nature and the pollution of the natural environment, rather than the destruction of life. Albert Schweitzer is one of those philosophers who have emphasised the philosophy of reverence for life including all non-human forms of life. A more recent philosophical work in this vein is the book by Peter Singer, *Animal Liberation*.[89]

(ii) The second important principle which regulates ecological ethics is the principle of reciprocity. The day-to-day maintenance of the life support system is dependent on a functional interaction of countless interdependent biotic and physiochemical factors. In the way that the value of life is a "core value" in Buddhist ethical codes, the notion of reciprocity and interdependence fits in with the Buddhist notion of a causal system. A living entity cannot isolate itself from this causal nexus and it has no essence of its own. Reciprocity also conveys the idea of mutual obligation, between nature and man and between man and man.

(iii) The third is a commitment to the future survival and development of mankind. Apart from promoting conservation, remedial action to improve the present position is a fundamental premise. The ethical concept involved here is the concept of responsibility to society and future generations, a premise which fits into the Buddhist ethical framework. People should not engage in activities detrimental to the environment and they should generate positive programmes for ecological education.

---

89. Peter Singer, *Animal Liberation* (New York, 1975).

(iv)   The fourth principle is the primacy of the value factors over the technological. The concern with the environment has to be placed in the proper context of ecological ethics as being just as much a matter of ethics as of technology, economics, law, the fear of survival, etc. Is it not possible to consider the need to preserve the environment as a biological need and cannot technology be considered as the means to redress nature's imbalance? Biology is important, technology may be useful to counteract the ill-effects of pollution, but the ethical claims have an independent appeal to human dignity and responsibility. In fact, the term "bio-ethics" is being used to convey the important notion of an ethics fed by biology—useful ecological information.

In the final analysis, as Klas Sandell says in the introduction to this work, the ecocrisis is not solely a technological problem.

Norwegian Ecophilosophy and Ecopolitics and Their Influence from Buddhism

Sigmund Kvaloy

My point of departure is Norwegian ecophilosophy and ecopolitics, with reference mainly to the work of the Ecophilosophy Group, which I have worked with since its start in 1969. I can here give only a few glimpses of what we have been doing during those years, and I will partly focus on my own contribution, since that materialised gradually, as an attempt to combine Western ideas with Buddhism and Gandhian action philosophy—which I also interpret in a Buddhist direction (that is easily done, since the Buddhist influence on Gandhi was strong).

The themes I am going to focus on are mainly two: time (or process) and what I call "radical human/environmental complexity." These two themes are interrelated. They were not only developed philosophically, but evolved as centrally related to ecopolitical activity. We have had a tendency here to combine theory and practice—in keeping with both the Buddha and Gandhi—that is, to be interested in theory only in so far as it is useful for practice. We were quite conscious in letting this South Asian attitude influence us, but it came easily, since there is also a Norwegian precedent for it—one going counter to Western-learned neutrality and detachment. It has been an attempt to weave thought and action into a single multi-coloured fabric. Furthermore, ecophilosophy in our mode presupposes no definite beginning nor any climactic conclusion, as it is supposed to reflect life more than logic. My glimpses are of an ongoing spiritual-material activity.

Several of the group members had a university background, but we learned quickly that going into ecophilosophy required of us that we spend much time talking and listening to people with no academic training. But to have fruitful exchanges in this direction it proved necessary for us, the "academically prepared" group members, to spend several years de-learning our "off-the-ground" language. As part of that, I gradually came to use a lot of visual illustrations, like cartoons telling stories, and as symbols, also under inspiration from Buddhist culture. If we are looking for a new, universal paradigm, a new basic pattern for understanding, new glasses to reveal a new "reality," something that will replace the mechanistic, analytical approach—still the vehicle in which the West travels—it is essential to speak a language so that the effort, step by step, is shared by the world community at large.

Along that way, visual elements are useful in engaging people's imagination and recollection of personally experienced situations. I will, however, hasten to say that there is one danger in using pictures—at least when your location is the academic milieu. This is that pictures tend to arrest in time the onlooker more than words do, to fix him in space, while I mentioned before that time or flow or process is one central message of ecophilosophy-process in our conception is something eminently available as the generator of a new paradigm. My thinking here may have a counterpart in very early Buddhism, as expressed through its total avoidance of any visualisation of the figure of the *Tathāgata*.[90] Later paintings and statues may be a Western influence, e.g. through Gandhāra, the north-western province in old India where Greek influence was strong.

As a starting point, I will go back sixteen years when we were more academic than we are now, and I will just state the definition of "ecophilosopher" that we made at that time. It runs as follows:

An ecophilosopher is one who occupies himself or herself with the following four kinds of pursuit, never forgetting their inter-relatedness:

(1) Studies of the global ecosocial system and local subsystems and of man and human groups as dynamic entities at various depths of complex integration with that system; the latter conceived of as a self-regulating macro-organism in interplay with matter and energy, awareness focused particularly upon relationships of process, communication and structural shifts.

---

90. "The One who, like the many previous Enlightened Ones, has come to direct us and then passed away." Several of the various translations of this old designation of the Buddha seem to me to underline the process perspective.

(2) In this study it is attempted to use all human faculties—of intellect, sensitivity, feeling, intuition and practical experience—to grasp and integrate consciously as much as possible of the total network of interdependencies and the dynamisms of the life process, so that these insights and sensibilities are, among other things, directed towards:

(3) A critical evaluation of relevant scientific, technological and economic-political views and regimes, their basic assumptions and their impact on human attitudes and activities as well as on their relation to nature and to human society; and towards:

(4) The formulation of values, norms and strategies pertinent to human activities aiming at the strengthening of the dynamic steady state or "homeorhesis"[91] of the life process as well as the continuing growth of the "organic complexity" of that process and the formulation of criticism of values, norms and procedures that tend to weaken homeorhesis and to stunt that growth.

To this definition we added a commentary from which I will just quote a part:

> Ecophilosophy is here conceived of as something more than an academic discipline in the traditional sense. It is thought of as a total engagement. It should strive to be as wide in scope as the attack upon the life-strength of the ecosystem and of human society as today. Ecophilosophy is a form of activity and a direction of thought that appears as something not freely chosen but as a necessity—a response required by the total system crisis we are experiencing in the world, challenging us to attempt a deep level revision of the basic notions of our Euro-American civilization. In such an extraordinary situation, the limitations of the academic tradition-values—

---

91. We prefer the latter term, which denotes a concept invented by the British geneticist C. H. Waddington, as being more in keeping with our process philosophy. A homeorhetic system does not swing around a fixed time trajectory. It never returns to a previous state; instead, even its "centre of balance" is on the move, changing. Homeorhesis is "inventive," but orderly. Homeostasis, in contradistinction, is the balancing of a system around a fixed time trajectory.

neutral and strictly intellectual—must, at least for the present, be broken out of ...

This was our starting point, and it was not just a definition, but a programme that we subsequently tried to follow as a gradually expanding string of groups. But of course we did not start in an historical vacuum. It has been said that the movement got off the ground earlier in Norway than elsewhere in Europe. In some respect I think that observation is correct, and one hypothesis to explain that is the very late industrialization of Norway, coupled with the fact that Norwegians were always travelling around the world like mad, eagerly gaping at what people elsewhere were doing; and that again coupled with a strange labour movement, where half its members were small farmers. Then, when industrialization finally came, it happened as an explosion, but was met with quite a bit of awareness and suspicion. It actually all occurred during my lifetime. I grew up on a mountain farm, with practices still but little removed from the Middle Ages, and at twenty-two I was an electric systems specialist on jet fighters in the Norwegian air force!

That collision between the old and the new cultures and its endless range of interdependent effects has gradually occupied more and more of my attention since the founding of the ecophilosophy group. It has structured a lot of projects. Right now, for instance, I have a Buddhist Sherpa friend—Tashi Tsangbo, from a remote Himalayan village—visiting at my farm in Norway. Together we are comparing the Sherpa tradition of semi-nomadic farming and cattle-herding and the similar tradition in Norway, and we are finding that these traditions are so close in vital human and social aspects that the difference is greater between my little Norwegian mountain community and Oslo, than between that community and Tashi's village!

This situation underlines the fact that industrialization and commercialization have not, so far, led to a homogeneous, uniform transition in my society. Instead, a high and hard barrier has been thrown up right through it as a whole, and due to ecopolitical activity, "green activism" and the like, that barrier has grown and is quite a bit more pronounced today than, say, fifteen years ago. And the comparison we are doing between Norway and the Buddhist Himalayas illustrates a further discovery: that this barrier is a global one and that it divides both the Third World and our own. Norwegian mountain farmers are part of a struggle that today engages "green Indians" all over the world in confrontation with industrio-competitive "pale-face" forces.[92] In our modern European predicament, we have actually been looking to South Asia and her "experiments with Truth" for help. That illustrates not only the industrialization of the world, but the parallel globalisation of the green movement as a common and unifying response.

So many of my people learn at school and through the mass media that "natural," pre-industrialised Norway offers a standardised environment, where children are bored, forced to engage in daily dreary work routines, given no room for play, etc., while our modern industrial society is the complex one. It has become a part of the Norwegian ecophilosophical/ecopolitical project to show that a closer look reveals the opposite

I have often used one specific pair of drawings to illustrate the transition, both of them referring to one typical Norwegian fjord landscape (figure 1).

The first, depicting a situation with industrialization still under control (in its mild 1930–1950 version), I call "Life Necessities Society" (LNS); it represents a somewhat modernised sub-class under that category, while the other one represents "Industrial Growth Society" (IGS). Among various items in the IGS picture, the new large centralised school is an important seminal object, with its attached phalanx of school buses. The portrayed institution immediately signals to you, since it is a contemporary worldwide phenomenon, that the pictured IGS-town has created a large periphery of communities that are being emptied of human activity, and finally, of people too. In this typical Norwegian case, what we observe is an effect of the transformation of the natural river system into an industriocentralized resource, serving some power-consuming world market production. It indicates the creation of a world dependency, a consequent vulnerability, and a loss of economic democracy. Jobs are specialised and standardised;

---

92. I mean here: American Indians, who have become an important inspiration to the North American and European green movement. "Paleface" was the North American Indian name for "white" European intruders.

the loss of self-reliance is directly reflected in a loss of existential meaning. Disney-landish weekend diversions do not compensate for that.

Figure 1 - Norwegian Landscape: Two Views

This kind of reflection got us started in 1969, after a couple of years of loose discussions. That summer, just after the founding of the organisation, we made the decision that all the members of the ecophilosophy group also should be members of one of the ecopolitical groups, and we took this very seriously. We read Gandhi, who says that the most important source of vital knowledge for a human being is to be had not at a seminar room, nor at some political convention, but right in the centre of social conflict, in non-violent struggle for Truth through Satyagraha. I do not want to go into a discussion about "Truth" here, but most—maybe all—of my readers should be acquainted with Gandhi and his use of the word "Truth." Particularly important to us became his (and the Bhagavad Gita's) "norm of selfless action" and its Buddhist counterparts, given in many versions throughout Buddhist literature. I would say striving to understand and to follow that norm gradually gave us a strength that we otherwise would have lacked.

We also read about and were inspired by Buddhist "non-attachment" and the "homeless life." Being fond of aimless wandering in the mountains, we were of course happy to find a 2500-years-old support, when the Buddha says: "I thought that life was oppressive in a house full of dust. Living in a house it is not easy to lead a full, pure and polished spiritual life, but the open air is better." (Majjhima Nikāya) So we thought: "Let us use our love for the open air and for wild nature, and go up into the mountains and do politics there!"

So that is part of the background for the decision both to philosophise and be politically active simultaneously and to fight for nature in nature. Actually, quite a bit of our ecophilosophy was conceptualised during direct, non-violent actions in the mountains, the forests, the fields, along the coast, in the villages, and on the streets of the cities. Throughout, we were trying to protect rivers, fertile soil, fishing grounds, open-air kindergartens, etc. against heedless onslaughts by single-minded industrialism. And, as it turned out, our most successful campaigns were those in which we were able to go beyond just protesting and to build positive, constructive actions in the classical Gandhian sense, i.e. actions by which we were able to demonstrate our alternative, the kind of society we wanted instead of the disintegrated state resulting from competitive industrial growth.

First and foremost, the Bhagavad Gita's "norm of selfless action" was our guiding star. The norm says: "Act, but do not strive for the fruit of the action!" This sounds crazy to the West, attached as it is to results that enhance individual permanency, but our step-by-step discovery was that this is the central key to everything. The norm says that the road is important, not your personal reaping of the harvest of your toil. And it is an illusion that the road has an end. At the deepest level, Buddhism teaches us that even our own toiling selves are illusory. Accepting this means a complete turn-about of lifestyle compared to the normal "means-to-an-end" practices of the West. And following the norm, we experienced something unexpected—invulnerability! Even if we lost a kindergarten to a four-lane road or a fishing ground to oil drilling, we didn't feel beaten down and we didn't stop acting. Having acted—with all our care and strength—was our success! And slowly the politicians and the broader public began seeing the light.

Through this, we have been able at least to begin to show the strength of Buddhism, that the individual's "reaping of fruit" is an expression of egotistical desire (*taṇhā*), which is not only something morally negative, but represents a misconception of reality. Reality is process, and that turns out to be the full logical consequence of the ecological perspective. A lifestyle based on this is invulnerable—because your antagonist finds nothing to hit! And the final outcome of our campaigns has actually been a substantial change of attitudes and practices towards the environment in Norway—even new laws passed recently by our Parliament. Compared to that, the loss of some individual objects is not all-important.

In this way, we were testing the East in practice in the modern West. Gandhi was a child of two worlds. That is why, with him as a bridge, we may—in a non-romantic way—gain access to Buddhism and other resources of the East, a priceless asset in an epoch when our Western resources have run dry.

A central part of our ecophilosophical activity—actually the starting point that we have kept coming back to all along—is the analysis of Industrial Growth Society. Our model has generally been a pyramidal structure (figure 2) tapered towards four governing principles:

(1) IGS is tending automatically towards an accelerating expansion of the production of industrial commodities and services (and this is its recurring measure of success) and the use of industrial methods: standardised mass-production, concentrated in a few, urbanised centres and carried out by specialists on all levels.
(2) It is based on individual competition, in every human field of endeavour.
(3) Its main resource for expansion is applied science.
(4) Its main device for registering, analysing and responding to troubles is quantification.

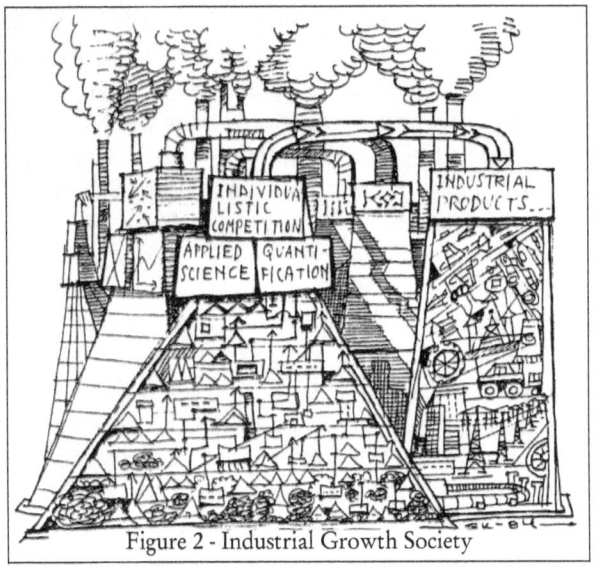
Figure 2 - Industrial Growth Society

These four principles should be seen as always interdependent, the way they have developed historically. Each one of them is in operation fortifying the others. Our Western society, is not, as yet, perfectly governed by this foursome (it could never reach that stage and survive), but it is tending towards that and it is doing it through various sorts of positive feedback. (It is mending its cracks by adding new ones deeper down.) The development in question is one that presupposes two specific conditions to be fulfilled: (1) that the earth's resources are unlimited, and (2) that human society and nature are machine-like in form. Both are untenable assumptions—I should think we are all agreed on that. So, what I am describing is a self-destructive social organism. What we today talk about as "the global socio-ecological crisis" is—that has been our contention—a direct and inevitable outcome of IGS in operation, i.e. a social system tending, characteristically, to fulfil the described model. IGS-managers—top to bottom—try to run society as if it were a machine, as if it were complicated, a structure reducible to elementary logical and mathematical entities and operations. Quality and novelty do not enter this picture and any development is in principle treated as reversible, the way it is in a machine.

In the Norwegian ecophilosophy group we reserved the word "complex" for natural and social processes, generally conceived of as contrasting with machine operations in being irreversible, qualitative and dialectical, tending to produce novelty—gradually or in unpredictable leaps, developments that are surprising even if rhythmical (an important notion when dealing with homeorhetic living processes), sometimes chaotic. So this became a pair of contrasting concepts to us: "complicated" versus "complex." It is a characteristic feature of IGS that it thrives (the organisational system, not its human members) as long as complication is spreading throughout society, replacing complexity.

The top of the IGS pyramid, seen as a centralised social organisation, may also be compared to the governing station of a machine—the single position from which you start and stop it and control all its functions. It is a basic characteristic of a machine to have just one such control centre, while a living, organic process has many, or you might say, none: the whole is governing itself. But if you are looking for governing centres to explain various functions, you will see several (never one that dominates all) and these may even be in conflict with each other. While in a machine—even in an advanced computer—if there were independent governing centres, you would have to scrap it. It would be unreliable, even self-destructive, because a machine is strictly and unidirectionally dichotomous in all its operations; it lacks completely the qualitative process-character of organic entities. The latter thrive on certain varieties of uncertainty and conflict, even need them for their continuous existence.

The all-quantifying, complicated control scheme characteristic of IGS is a spatializing system—it tends to reduce all time processes to space parameters—and I will just in passing refer to Henri Bergson here and recommend his contribution, a unique one on the European stage. As regards the Norwegian ecophilosophy group, however, we received our main ideas in this direction from Buddhism and Gandhi. Bergson has been so effectively repressed by European space-bound philosophy that his relevance was revealed to us only recently. Since that has happened, I am ready to name him as Europe's first ecophilosopher.

Buddhism, however, as it is interpreted in some of the branches of its gigantic historical-cultural tree, constitutes the most radical process philosophy the world has seen. Since it goes back two and a half millennia, that is remarkable indeed, considering the modernity of process thinking as brought about by ecology and the new physics. Whitehead should also be mentioned here (William James and James Joyce are also relevant). In view of what's happening, I predict an imminent widespread recognition of both Bergson and Whitehead, and that their contributions this time will be discussed in conjunction with Buddhism. That did not happen before, since Western philosophers were largely ignorant of the East (and even to the Buddhologists the process character of Buddhism was not clear until the works of Stcherbatsky and Rosenberg in the twenties). The time has now come.

Our analysis of IGS led us to the conclusion that it is a sociopolitical and socio-mental system that cannot survive beyond a few decades; you cannot mend its ways for the better, since it is a characteristic of the system that it thrives on or exists through an accelerated depletion of resources and an expanding simplification and standardisation of global process complexity. For that reason, after a few years, we stopped having as our aim the diversion of IGS onto a socio-ecologically sound track. Instead, we started investing our activist energy into inspiring as many people as possible to experiment with a basis for a viable society to replace the one that is now step by step cracking up at its base. I will also say this, however, that the Industrial Growth Civilisation may be utilised as mankind's most effective teacher so far. In that way we have started to look upon it not as something purely negative. It demonstrates to us, by extreme contrasts, what man is, what his potentialities are, as well as his limitations. It offers us many perspectives, mutually superimposed, because it attacks all cultures globally with one and the same standardised set of methods. At a level that perhaps is the deepest of all, it presents to us the ultimate experiment to see how far society may be pushed in spatializing time before all ends in chaos.

I will, presently, try to elucidate somewhat our notion of time. Due to my ecopolitical context, my concern here lies, of course, not so much in the infra or ultra domains—although I share with others the inspiration from the "new physics" and contemporary cosmology—as in the middle domain, in the range of human life. Let us go a little further into how one culture may be mainly time-based in the sense mentioned earlier, while another—our own—has this strong spatial bias. Let us look at a Sherpa village in Nepalese Himalaya. Westerners passing by tend to say "How primitive!" and "We cannot possibly have anything to learn here!"

Let us take a look at a traditional Sherpa house (figure 3). There is not one perfectly straight line in it, not one perfect right angle, the walls lack any semblance of standardised smoothness. No two buildings are the same, however each one expresses the safety of shared requirements. After having pondered over these structures and how they are somehow never completed, contrasting them with European architecture today, I have come to the conclusion that even the word "architecture" is inappropriate as applied to this building culture. It just leads us to judge it within a frame of concepts that is foreign to the builders themselves, and we miss their intentions, their aims. We might instead talk of their way of "living with a building," or how buildings are part of a household.

Figure 3 - The Invading Army of "Spatialists

A Western method that might help in giving us a local frame of reference is the following: Place a movie camera in front of the Sherpa building and let one single frame of the film be exposed each day and keep doing that for fifty years. Then develop the film and let it run at normal speed. What would then be revealed to us is a house that is never a fixed structure; it is a process having a flowing "amoebic" pattern, shifting functions around—we might even be tempted to drop the very word "structure." Stones are moved in the walls, the roof planking is constantly being shifted about, new parts are being added to the house, old parts removed, lichens grow on the walls, maybe a little tree on the roof, a different species of plant is coming up alongside the wall to the southwest, animals—domestic during the day, wild during the night—are flowing in and out and around, children and adults likewise (*yetis* at night!), etc. What we see is something rhythmic, something organic, a living, pulsating duration-time being created. Mind you, not something happening in time: thinking that way we would be back in a spatializing frame of ideas. Living with this "house" as the Sherpa does, we are part of time.

As for aesthetics: whether the building is beautiful or not has to be discovered through watching—or better, by being part of—the movement that was just revealed to us. You have to stop and stay and even work with the Sherpas. Here, you cannot isolate aesthetics from any other area of human concern, as little as you may isolate the Sherpa building from its many functional aspects that characterise the wholeness of Sherpa life and Himalayan nature. The house is an extension—temporary like everything else—of the human beings who built it and keep building it every day. The Buddhist process paradigm works perfectly as a reference pattern for this society, and any aid to the Sherpas today should spring out of a strengthening of that tradition. A "modernization" within that framework would strengthen their own identity, instead of undermining it, as is happening now.

So this is an illustration of two different world paradigms, as represented by two different cultures through their building traditions, and in the old Norwegian mountain farms I now see reflected the same process-character as the one I have found with the Sherpas. The "Greek" tradition with its technological successes reached the cities of Norway some time ago, but the remote rural areas only superficially. So there are unexpected allies to be found around the globe for an international "green" process movement. Of course, I am not here just talking about buildings and technology, but about a whole outlook on life. Neither am I talking about a reversal of history; a process cannot be reversed anyway.

One word I have used for this time-oriented ontology, ethics and aesthetics is "the philosophy of positive decay." In order to have continuous growth, where continuous withering is the daily reminder, unbroken human creativity is needed. In this perspective—again using the building as a symbol—you cannot just leave the design of your house to an architect, then stay in it for a brief spell leaving the repairs to others, then go off to some other place. That would be tantamount to leaving your own body.

I was a research fellow in human ecology and environmental philosophy for five years at the Oslo School of Architecture, and during that time I had fruitful exchanges with architects on these matters, and I brought four of them with me to Nepal. We started to call the contemporary Western house (in the double sense) a "paper structure," referring back to its inception on the designer's perfectly white paper sheet with its thin, ruler-drawn lines. Let's say we have a less-than-perfect architect smoking a pipe as I do, one day by mishap leaving a sooty fingerprint on the just completed drawing. All of a sudden it has lost all value, except for the trash collector. Not only the drawing, but also the finished building is treated this way! A little crack in its smooth wall, and it looks terrible. It is a kind of structure that cannot bear the "tooth of time." If the crack is not patched up in a week or two, passers-by will start thinking something is wrong with the economy of the company or the city or whatever owns the building (still using the double sense).

But the Sherpa house is made to be cracked! It is not a paper structure. Of course I am not here speaking about the virtue of having a house that cracks. I am trying to elucidate, in contemporary terms, the contrast between a Buddhist world conception and lifestyle and the West, where clinging to individuality and permanence is the very basis for society. And I am saying that the might of our modern West is built on illusion in Buddhist terms, and it must therefore be self-destructive. And the Buddhist attitude is well represented in other, non-Western cultures, in relation to which Buddhist philosophy may well serve as a tool for clarification and as a key to a united effort against Western destructiveness.

All pyramidal societies have been short-lived and all grand-scale efforts at fortified permanency have led to grand-scale devastations. Our Western society is imbued with internal psychic and social contradictions, expressive of how we are forced to live as atomised individuals, on a map, while by nature we are eddies in the stream! There never was a better illustration of the Buddhist *dukkha*—and how it propagates—than the West today!

I have a tendency to think that the West and the East have been moving away from each other, starting with those Greek philosophers who based their philosophy on permanency and perfection as the marks of reality itself. Heraclitus, with his "everything flows" (*panta rhei*), represented a potential in the opposite direction, but it came to nothing. It had no impact to speak of on later European philosophy and religion, since it offered no basis for technological and economic growth!

Mathematizing, spatializing and individualising the world were fortified through material success, and finally today we are in this position from which I think it is nearly impossible for a Westerner to bridge over into, say, the Hindu identification with Brahman, or—even more radical—the Buddhist way of dissolving everything into emptiness, *shunyata*.

Buddhism developed, in certain aspects, in the opposite direction from the West. The various branches of the gigantic religio-cultural tree of Buddhism that grew and matured through the centuries present to us a multitude of philosophical viewpoints in spirited but tolerant discussion with each other. What strikes me, looking at this tree from the West, is that throughout this differentiation, a basic unity is preserved, revealed as a unanimous negation of the spatializing and individualising tendency that characterises Western philosophy. All of it may be seen as attempts at a purification and radicalisation of process thinking. One illustration of the width of this gap between Eastern and Western thought is given by the Bodhisattva ideal as it evolved in certain branches of Mahayana, where finalising the time stream in Nirvana has almost been pushed out of view, and where even conflict and pain is something one returns to, because escaping complex time as an individual is seen as an illusion. Whether this is a deviation from the Buddha's basic intuitions is a matter of controversy, but it serves well as an example of a manner of thinking that is as far away from the Western Christian and scientific approach as it is possible to get. It represents one way of taking the ultimate logical step towards a complete eradication of permanence and clinging.

The Buddha's disintegration of the self left us with the five aggregates (*skandhas*): groups of functionally united "existence factors," namely, body, feeling, perception, mental formations, and consciousness. Between the composite individual and the Whole, modern organic systems theory today teaches us to find layer upon layer of hierarchically ordered, system-seeking organ-entities. On top of that, Hegel and Marx have given us the idea of dialectical breakthroughs. Attempting to combine these various ideas, I have ventured the thought that the human being, when born, potentially has an extra level of complexity beyond what has been conceived by Western anthropology and psychology. That extra level is one where capacity is given to grow more than one person-stream, or "personality." Let me just use this latter term without defining it, since I am short of space. I am not talking about playing different roles. If you have the opportunity during your lifetime to become immersed in or integrated with more than one distinct environment, you have the endowment to develop one personality for each, as distinctive as its corresponding environment. In each case "your" (meaning "your person-manifold's") system-seeking tendency should be in operation.

This capacity that a human being has is not allowed to flourish in a pyramidal society, such as Industrial Growth Society, because that is a structure which needs a base of small human "pyramids," organisational copies of the large one. You have once again the old mechanistic model of the universe; you need a definite governing station (the pyramid's top) from which the structure of this system is controlled, and you need ultimate, hard building blocks, or atoms, to be able to monitor and operate the complete structure efficiently, e.g. to reverse processes if they go wrong. But natural processes can never be reversed, since they are in fact not pyramidal. Breaking with this kind of rationality is a necessity that Industrial Growth Society teaches us when it reveals its oppressive character, and this is where my "middle domain" ties in with the "infra" and "ultra" domains of the new physics and cosmology, and where Buddhist concepts and modern variations on them are becoming vitally relevant. There are common conceptual forms here, inspirational takeoff points to be shared.

Well, if you have understood me correctly so far in these few pages, you are also ready to understand—if not to accept—that the individual human person process can be active in several different places simultaneously. For instance, mentioning "myself," "I" have another personality that right now is active at home on the farm because personality is not bounded by the skin of a body; in my paradigm or ontology it defines itself through activity and through intimate interaction with people, nature and landscape. Reasoning along the same line, it is not limited by death either—and here is again one point where these ideas tie in with Buddhism.

Let me round this off by just mentioning the reactions of some young people after one of our recent nature-protective campaigns—a constructive campaign in the sense mentioned, where the campaign's meaningful function completely depended upon the participants' identification with nature and humankind's future generations.[93] These youngsters came to me and said that for the first time in their life they had experienced meaningful existence. My first thought was that this is certainly a revealing comment on the normal existence that modern Western society offers young people. Further inquiry convinced me that their feeling of having lived through something deeply meaningful sprang from a positive loss of their ego's significance. Later on, it dawned on me that this campaign, the way it finally found its relaxed, resilient but insistent "middle way" form, had functioned to many as a modern Western version of Buddhist insight meditation. After

---

93. A detailed description of these campaigns and a discussion of their relationship to Buddhism's Noble Eightfold Path may be obtained through the following address: The Ring of Ecopolitical Cooperation, Saetereng, 7496 Kotsoy, Norway.

all, meditation in this sense may employ any method that leads the seeker onward to enlightenment, i.e. Nibbāna.

Here, as at several of our earlier campaigns, we were decisively influenced by what in our situation are the two most relevant well-springs of the East, Buddhism's way of liberation from the ego and the Bhagavadgīta's action gospel, easily combined! And we are today just one little member of a rapidly growing global community of practical activist groups that draw inspiration from these same sources in their struggle for a green world. My experience during the last fifteen years tells me that it is this practical struggle that will gradually give birth to the much sought-for "New Paradigm," the paradigm of resilient, creative, limitless life.

The Buddhist Perception of Nature Project

Nancy Nash

"The world grows smaller and smaller, more and more interdependent. Today more than ever before life must be characterised by a sense of Universal Responsibility, not only nation to nation and human to human, but also human to other forms of life."

—H. H. the Dalai Lama

Buddhist Perception of Nature, a project created to improve awareness, attitudes, and actions concerning the natural environment, took root with this statement by His Holiness the Dalai Lama during the course of an interview in 1979, and has been nurtured at every step with inspiration and support from the world's foremost Buddhist leader.

Our work involves researching, assembling, and putting to use as educational tools, Buddhist teachings about man's responsibilities to the natural world and all living beings. Many of the lessons from Buddhist literature and art date back more than 2,500 years, but they are as valid today as they have ever been, and capable of reaching out in many modern forms in contemporary society. Buddhism, in fact, was selected for the pilot project in new perspectives for environmental education because it is an ancient, enduring philosophy, embodying strongly themes of awareness and compassion for all life.

The faith is also influential in many parts of Asia that have unique and endangered species of animals, plants and habitats, and has been demonstrated to have a direct, beneficial effect in saving some species of wildlife and threatened habitats.

The conservation effect for the most part may be described as passive protection. Animals inhabiting the grounds of temples, for example, have automatic sanctuary for Buddhist faithful; in Thailand rules for monks living in forest monasteries are so strict that their areas are naturally well cared for. Tibet, by all accounts, was until the culture was disrupted by the Chinese takeover in 1950, a land where people and wildlife lived together in extraordinary harmony.

The environmental crisis we face today, however, needs active help, and the world's estimated 500 million Buddhists can make a major, positive impact by becoming active conservationists.

A focus on human, spiritual and cultural values in no way ignores the role of science, which itself is also part of the human cultural world. Our project recognises that science is essential, first to set priorities for the work, and to persuade educated leaders and decision-makers. Then our best scientific minds are needed to help rectify the ecological disasters we face resulting from ignorance, greed, and lack of respect for the earth.

Objective scientists are the first professionals to point out and prove that the earth's capacity to support life is clearly being reduced at the time it is needed most as rising human numbers, expectations, and consumption make increasingly heavy demands. But science outlines the state of the earth. Religion and cultural traditions are the repositories of human values, and many people today feel it is only with aroused personal and social values that we may begin to deal with our current problems in a way which will benefit life on earth now, and in the future.

The importance of excellence in scholarship cannot be overestimated in a project of this kind, and we are fortunate that from the commencement of work, research has been under the direction of highly respected institutions, and carried out by superb scholars.

The Council for Religious and Cultural Affairs and the Information Office of His Holiness the Dalai Lama have provided direction for Mahayana studies. For Theravada traditions, work has been guided by Wildlife Fund Thailand in association with experts from the Thai Ministry of Education and Thammasat University. Our chief scholars—Dr. Chatsumarn Kabilsingh in Bangkok, and Venerable Karma Gelek Yuthok in Dharamsala, India—and their colleagues assisting with research, compiling and translating, have done a remarkable job involving a vast literature and history, in a very short space of time.

Deputy Minister for Education in His Holiness the Dalai Lama's Kashag (Cabinet), Lodi Gyaltsen Gyari, is Buddhist

Perception of Nature's Tibetan Coordinator, and our Thai Coordinator is Mr. Sirajit Waramontri, Member of the Board of Trustees of Wildlife Fund Thailand. Both have given this project valuable time, energy, and creative talent to launch the work, and keep it going.

Tibetan and Thai Buddhists have undertaken the initial work for the simple reason that they were sympathetic and influential individuals willing to take on the burden of the tasks. Contacts with other Buddhist communities and countries have come about in the normal course of events and all are welcome to participate.

Because of the global concerns of conservation, this project from the beginning was envisioned as important, first among Buddhists, but also as an adaptable blueprint for research and achievement for similar projects involving other faiths and cultural traditions. Buddhist Perception of Nature aims to provide samples of the project design and educational materials to all groups, governmental and private, Buddhist and other faiths, wishing to study and use them. All of us involved with the work are therefore touched, and inspired by the interest already shown by individuals and groups from many different parts of the world, and different religions and cultural traditions, who find the project not only a viable response to the ecological problems today, but also an element in a much-needed renaissance of environmental ethics.

Inspiration from Enlightened Nuns

by
Susan Elbaum Jootla

Copyright © Kandy; Buddhist Publication Society, (1988)

Introduction

In this booklet we will be exploring poems composed by the Arahat bhikkhunīs or enlightened Buddhist nuns of old, looking at these poems as springs of inspiration for contemporary Buddhists. Most of the poems we will consider come from the *Therīgāthā*, a small section of the vast Pali Canon. The *Therīgāthā* has been published twice in English translation by the Pali Text Society, London: first in 1909 (reprinted in 1980) by C. A. F. Rhys Davids in verse under the title *Psalms of the Early Buddhists: The Sisters*; and second in 1971 by K. R. Norman in prose under the title *The Elders' Verses, II*. We have used quotations from both translations here, referring to *Psalms of the Early Buddhists* by page number and to *The Elders' Verses* by verse number. Mrs. Rhys Davids' translations have sometimes been slightly modified. Our discussion will also draw upon the verses of bhikkhunīs from the Saṃyutta Nikāya (*Kindred Sayings*), included by Mrs. Rhys Davids at the end of *Psalms of the Sisters*.

From the poems of the enlightened nuns of the Buddha's time contemporary followers of the Noble Eightfold Path can receive a great deal of instruction, help and encouragement. These verses can assist us in developing morality, concentration and wisdom, the three sections of the path. With their aid we will be able to work more effectively towards eliminating our mental defilements and towards finding lasting peace and happiness.

In some respects, the inspiration from these poems may be stronger for women than for men, since these are in fact women's voices that are speaking. And when the theme of the poem is the mother-child bond, this is bound to be the case. However, at a deeper level the sex of the speakers is irrelevant, for the ultimate truths which they enunciate explain the universal principles of reality which are equally valid for men and for women.

The verses of the nuns, if systematically examined, can help serious Buddhist meditators to understand many central aspects of the Dhamma. The background to the verses, including biographical information on the nuns who uttered them, is provided by the ancient commentary on the *Therīgāthā* by the venerable Ācariya Dhammapāla. Mrs. Rhys Davids has included some of these background stories in *Psalms of the Early Buddhists*, and in the first part of this essay we will look at these stories and consider the themes they suggest that are relevant to contemporary students of Buddhist meditation. Then we will go on to discuss a selection of the poems themselves, which deal with many specific teachings of the Buddha.

We of the twentieth century who are seeking to attain liberation will find ourselves deeply grateful to these fully awakened Buddhist nuns of old for their profound assistance in illuminating the Dhamma for us in their own distinctly personal ways.

I. The Background Stories

The ancient commentaries give us information about each nun's background and also explain the poems themselves. Two major themes of relevance to contemporary students of the Dhamma run through these stories: (1) the immeasurably long time that we have all been lost in *saṃsāra*, the round of birth and death; and (2) the working of the impersonal law of kammic cause and effect which brought these women into contact with the Buddha's teachings in what was to be their final lifetime.

The Long Duration of Saṃsāra

In the original Pali commentaries, the tales of the nuns began many, many rebirths and aeons prior to their final existence at the time of Buddha Gotama. We read how over ages and ages all these women had been living out the results of their old *kamma* and how they created powerful new *kamma* based on wisdom, which finally culminated in the attainment of Arahatship, full awakening. Each woman—or, more accurately, each succession of aggregates—had to undergo infinite aeons of suffering in its gross and subtle forms before she was prepared to gain complete insight. But finally she gave up all clinging and was freed from the need ever again to be reborn and suffer, on any plane.

Vipassanā meditators trying to develop this same understanding of the ultimate nature of conditioned existence can find inspiration if they would apply these tales to their own lives. When we realise how long we ourselves have been wandering in ignorance, constantly generating more and more unwholesome *kamma*, we will be able to remain patient when our early efforts to train the mind tend to falter or fail. Some of the bhikkhunīs who had sufficient *pāramīs*—virtues cultivated in previous lives— even to gain Arahatship, still had to put in many years of arduous and sometimes seemingly fruitless effort before they could attain the goal.

For example, Sīhā entered the Sangha as a young woman but could not learn to contain her mind's attraction to external objects for seven years. Another nun worked for twenty-five years without finding any substantial peace because of her strong attachment to sense desire. But both these bhikkhunīs, when all the appropriate conditions were finally fulfilled, found their patience and continued efforts fully rewarded. So too will we, if we diligently and strictly keep to the Noble Eightfold Path until we become Ariyas, noble ones. Once we have done this, we are assured that we will completely eliminate the causes of all suffering.

By making this effort to live in accordance with the Dhamma and to understand the true nature of existence, we begin to develop strong wholesome mental volitions, *kamma* that will have effects in future births as well as in this one. The continued efforts in this direction become easier and more natural because, as we wear away ignorance and the other defilements through insight meditation, our minds come to be more strongly conditioned by wisdom (*paññā*). Recollecting this infinite span of time behind us, and the vast mass of wholesome volitional activities accumulated therein, will help us keep our efforts at purification balanced and strong.

These rebirth stories, illustrating the continuous suffering which every sentient being has undergone during the rounds of *saṃsāra,* can also encourage us to work hard in the Dhamma. Understanding this weighty aspect of the First Noble Truth stimulates us to put forth the great effort required to overcome suffering by penetrating and uprooting its causes, which the Buddha explains are basically craving and ignorance.

Bhikkhunī Sumedhā, in her poem, repeats one of the Buddha's powerful injunctions to eliminate the source of the ceaseless stream of suffering that has rushed on in our previous lives, and will otherwise continue on in the same way throughout the infinite future. Sumedhā is pleading with her parents and fiancé to allow her to enter the Sangha rather than force her to marry:

> Journeying-on is long for fools and for those who lament again and again at that which is without beginning and end, at the death of a father, the slaughter of a brother, and their own slaughter.
>
> Remember the tears, the milk, the blood, the journeying-on as being without beginning and end; remember the heap of bones of beings who are journeying-on.

> Remember the four oceans compared with the tears, milk and blood; remember the heap of bones (of one man) for one aeon, (as) equal (in size) to Mount Vepulla.
>
> vv. 495–497

"Journeying-on" is *saṃsāra*. In the lines beginning "Remember the four oceans compared," Sumedhā is reminding her family of a discourse which they must have heard from the Buddha. Each of us, the Buddha tells us, has shed vast oceans of tears over the loss of loved ones and in fear of our own doom as the succession of aggregates has arisen and vanished throughout *samara's* weary ages. During all these lifetimes, as the verse declares, we have drunk seas and seas of mother's milk, and the blood that was shed when violent death ended our lives also amounts to an immeasurable volume. How could even one gory death be anything but terrible suffering? The Buddha perceived all this with his infinite wisdom and so described it to his followers.

The vastness of *saṃsāra* that we endured before meeting the Dhamma in this life can easily be extrapolated from the stories of these nuns. We must also sustain the patience in our endeavour to wear down ignorance and to develop the awareness of omnipresent suffering which is life in *saṃsāra*, as the First Noble Truth makes known.

Kammic Cause and Effect

The second commentarial theme that can be helpful to us in developing our own understanding of the ultimate nature of reality is the working of the law of kammic cause and effect. None of these nuns was emancipated because one day she decided, "Now I am going to cut off all craving." Nor did the grace of a guru or the power of God or the Buddha himself enlighten them. Rather, it was a very long process in the evolution of the "life continuum" that gradually permitted the conditions for liberation to develop and eventually culminate in Arahatship. Freeing the mind of ignorance, like all activities, is an impersonal cause and effect process. Natural laws of this sort are cultivated and utilised by mental volition to bring about purification. By repeatedly seeing all the phenomena of life as they are by means of concentrated

Vipassanā meditation, we gradually wear away the defilements that becloud the mind and cause rebirth with its attendant misery.

For example, Selā took robes when she was a young woman and "worked her way to insight and because of the promise in her and the maturity of her knowledge, crushing the *saṅkhāras* (conditioned phenomena), she soon won Arahatship" (p. 43). For aeons, Selā had done many good deeds, such as making offerings to and looking after previous Buddhas and their monks. As a result of these meritorious actions over many lifetimes, she was reborn in the heavenly deva planes or in comfortable situations on earth. Eventually, at the time of Buddha Gotama, each of the bhikkhunīs, including Selā, came into the Sangha in her own way. Because the time was right for their *pāramīs* to bear fruit, all the factors conducive to enlightenment could develop, their defilements could be effaced, and the goal could be achieved.

Sukha left the world under one of the earlier Buddhas, but she died without becoming an Ariya. Under subsequent Buddhas "she kept the precepts and was learned and proficient in the doctrine." Finally, "in this Buddha era she found faith in the Master at her own home, and became a lay disciple. Later, when she heard Bhikkhunī Dhammadinnā preach, she was thrilled with emotion and renounced the world under her" (pp. 40-41). All her efforts in past lives then bore their appropriate fruit as Sukha attained Arahatship and became in turn a great preacher of the Dhamma. Only a small number of nuns are renowned for their skill in teaching, and it is likely that the need to develop the extra *pāramīs* to teach the Dhamma made it necessary for Sukha to study under earlier Buddhas for so long without gaining the paths and fruits.

Similar stories tell of how other bhikkhunīs performed good works and put forth effort in previous lives, building various kinds of *pāramīs* which allowed them to completely give up all attachment to the world at the time of our Buddha. If we consider the process by which they gradually matured towards liberation, we can see how every mental volition and every deed of body and speech at some time or other bears fruit.

It is due to our own *pāramīs*, our own good *kamma* of the past, that we have the rare and great opportunity to come into contact with the teachings of a Buddha in this lifetime. It is because of wisdom already cultivated that we now have the opportunity to develop greater wisdom (*paññāpāramī*) through insight meditation. Wisdom has the power to obliterate the results of past *kamma* since it comprehends reality correctly. In addition, if we continue to generate such wholesome volitions now, more good *kamma* is built up which will continue to bear beneficial fruit and bring us closer to the goal.

However, wisdom cannot be cultivated in the absence of morality. The Buddha taught that in order to move towards liberation, it is necessary to keep a minimum of five precepts strictly at all times: abstention from killing, stealing, sexual misconduct, lying and consuming intoxicants. If the precepts are broken, the bad *kamma* thus created will bring very painful results. Without purity of body and speech, purity of mind cannot be developed as the mind will be too agitated by sense desires, regrets and aversion to settle on its meditation subject properly.

Some of the earlier rebirth stories of Arahat bhikkhunīs tell of lives in which they did not keep the precepts. Several of them suffered the results of their unwholesome deeds in animal births or in low forms of human existence. Aḍḍhakāsī, for example, had a mixed background. She had become a bhikkhunī established in morality under Kassapa Buddha, the Buddha immediately preceding Gotama. But once, due to anger, she referred to a fully liberated senior nun as a prostitute. As a result of that wrong speech, she was reborn in one of the lower realms, for to say or do anything wrong to an Ariya creates worse *kamma* than to say or do the same thing against a non-Ariya. When the fruit of that bad deed was mostly used up, as a residual effect she herself became a prostitute in her final life. By this time her previous good *kamma* was the stronger and she ordained as a nun. Keeping the bhikkhunī life pure, Aḍḍhakāsī attained the goal.

Causes and effects work themselves out and keep the life process going through *saṃsāra*. So long as the mind is attached to anything at all, we will engage in volitional actions, make new *kamma*, and will have to experience their results. Cultivating good *kamma* will save one from much suffering and prepare the mind for the most powerful wholesome *kamma* of all, that born of wisdom, which can eliminate all kammic creation.

II. The Teachings of the Poems

The actual poems composed by the nuns exhibit a wide range in tone and subject matter. They were almost all spoken after the author had realised that rebirth and all its associated suffering had been brought to an end by the perfection of insight and total elimination of defilements. So virtually all the poems contain some form of "lion's roar," an exclamation that the author has become awakened.

Trivial Incidents Spark Enlightenment

In some cases the poems describe the circumstances which brought the woman into the Sangha or which precipitated her awakening. Both of these can inspire contemporary followers of the Buddha. Sometimes the most mundane event stimulates a ripe mind to see the truth perfectly. Bhikkhunī Dhamma returned from her almsround one day exhausted from heat and exertion. She stumbled, and as she sprawled on the ground a clear perception arose in her of the utter suffering inherent in the body, bringing about total relinquishment. She describes the incident in the following lines:

> Having wandered for alms, leaning on a stick, weak, with trembling limbs I fell to the ground in that very spot, having seen peril in the body. Then my mind was completely released.
>
> v. 17

If someone could gain awakening based on such an event, surely there are an infinite number of potentially enlightening experiences available to all of us for contemplation. Systematic attention (*yoniso manasikāra*) given to any subject will show up its impermanence (*anicca*), unsatisfactoriness (*dukkha*), and essenceless nature (*anattā*) and so encourage us to stop craving. However, unless we carefully apply our minds in Vipassanā meditation under the guidance of a competent teacher, it is unlikely that we will be able to utilise our daily encounters with these basic characteristics as means towards liberation. This is because the mind's old conditioning is based on ignorance—the very *inability* to see things as they really are. Only concentrated mindfulness of phenomena in meditation can enable us to comprehend correctly our everyday experiences, because such methodical culture of insight through Vipassanā meditation loosens the old mental tendencies by giving us direct experience of the impermanence of our mind and body.

Entering the Sangha after a Child's Death

Quite a number of women entered the Sangha after their small children had died. Grief is put to good use if it is made the motivation to develop the "path leading to the cessation of suffering." Ubbirī greatly mourned the death of her infant daughter until the Buddha pointed out to her that right in the same charnel ground where she had left this baby's body, she had similarly parted with thousands of children to whom she had given birth in previous lives. Because she had acquired strong merit in the past, this brief personalised discourse was enough to turn Ubbirī from a lamenting mother into an Arahat on the spot. As she clearly saw the vastness of *saṃsāra*, she was prepared to leave it behind. Her profound gratitude to the Buddha is described in these simple lines:

> He has thrust away for me my grief for my daughter ... I am without hunger, quenched.
>
> vv. 51, 53

With the quenching of ignorance and craving, nothing remains but a pure mind, inherently peaceful. Ubbirī had a pliable, well-prepared mind, and thus she understood, through the Buddha's instructions, that the source of all her suffering had been craving. After countless millions of lifetimes spent rolling in *saṃsāra*, Ubbirī realised how her deep motherly attachment to her children had always caused her much anguish; for sons and daughters, like everything else, are subject to the law of impermanence. We cannot make our loved ones live beyond the span set by their own *kamma*. This was an insight so powerful for her that no object at all seemed worthy of interest any longer because of the potential pain permeating them all. Thus all tendency to cling was broken, never to reappear.

The life story of Paṭācārā before she came to the Dhamma, described in considerable detail in the commentary to the *Therīgāthā*, is even more dramatic. She lost her entire family, her husband, two small children, parents and brothers in various accidents within a few days. She went insane from the sorrow, but the Buddha's compassion combined with Paṭācārā's *pāramīs* from the past enabled her to regain her right mind. When she came into his presence, he taught her to understand how often before she had hopelessly exhausted herself grieving for the dead. She became a Stream-enterer (*sotāpanna*), one at the first stage of irreversible progress on the path to liberation, and she was ordained. Later, as she was one day pouring water to wash her feet and watching it trickle away—as life does sooner or later for all beings—her mind became utterly free from clinging. Paṭācārā, like Dhamma, had thoroughly developed seeds of understanding, so a very minor mundane incident at just the right moment cleared her mind of every trace of ignorance.

Many other women entered the Sangha in circumstances similar to those of Ubbirī or Paṭācārā. A woman distraught over the death of a child must have been very common in India in those days when limited medical knowledge could not counter a very high infant mortality rate. Therī Paṭācārā spoke to a group of five hundred such grief-stricken mothers, expressing what she had so powerfully learned from similar experience herself:

> The way by which men come we cannot know;
> Nor can we see the path by which they go.
> Why mourn then for him who came to you,
> Lamenting through the tears? ...
> Weep not, for such is the life of man.
> Unasked he came and unbidden he went.
> Ask yourself again whence came your child
> To live on earth this little time?
> By one way come and by another gone,
> As human to die, and pass to other births—
> So hither and so hence—why should you weep?
>
> p. 78

In this way Paṭācārā illustrates for these mothers the natural connection, the invisible, impersonal causal nexus between death and life, life and death. They too took robes and eventually became Arahats. Their joint "lion's roar" culminates in the lines:

> Today my heart is healed, my yearning stayed,
> Perfected deliverance wrought in me.
> I go for refuge to the Buddha, the Sangha, and the Dhamma.

p. 77

Because of their physiology and their conditioning by family and society, women are more prone to attachment to their offspring than are men, and so will suffer all the more from their loss. However, if women train their minds to understand how clinging causes enormous suffering, how birth and death are natural processes happening as effects of specific causes, and how infinite the history of such misery is, they can utilise their feminine sufferings in the quest for awakening. In the *Kindred Sayings* (Vol. IV, pp. 162-163), the Buddha himself pointed out the five kinds of suffering unique to women. Three are physiological—menstruation, pregnancy, and childbirth. The other two are social, and perhaps not as widely relevant today as they were in ancient Indian society: having to leave her own family to live with her husband and in-laws, and having "to wait upon a man." All five must be the results of past unwholesome deeds, yet each one can be made a basis for insight. Women can train their minds to turn to advantage these apparent disadvantages. They can then make full use of their stronger experiences of the universality and omnipresence of suffering to condition themselves to let go of everything in the conditioned realm.

For some individuals, intense suffering is needed to make the mind relinquish its misconceptions and desires. Paṭācārā is one example of this; Kisāgotamī is a second. The latter was so unwilling to face the truth of her child's death that she carried the dead baby around with her hoping to find one who could give her medicine to cure him. The Buddha guided her into a realisation of the omnipresence of death by sending her in search of some mustard seed. This is a common ingredient in Indian kitchens, but the Buddha specified that these seeds must come from a household where no one had ever died.

Kisāgotamī went looking for this "medicine" for her baby, but because of the prevalent joint family system in which three or more generations lived together under one roof, every house she went to had seen death. Gradually, as she wandered through the village, she realised that all who are born must die. Her great *pāramīs* then enabled her to understand impermanence so thoroughly that soon afterwards the Buddha confirmed her attainment of Stream-entry. She then spoke these lines:

> No village law is this, no city law,
> No law for this clan, or for that alone;
> For the whole world—and for the gods too—
> This is the law: All is impermanent.

p. 108

Kisāgotamī thus transcended the limits of a woman's personal grief to understand one of the basic characteristics of all existence.

Kisāgotamī later attained Arahatship. Some of the verses she spoke on that occasion give useful lessons to any striver on the Noble Eightfold Path:

> Resorting to noble friends, even a fool would be wise. Good men are to be resorted to; thus the wisdom of those who resort to them increases. Resorting to good men one would be released from all pains.
>
> One should know suffering, the cause of suffering and its cessation, and the Eightfold Path; (these are) the Four Noble Truths.

vv. 213–215

The company of the wise, especially the guidance of a teacher, is an invaluable help in getting oneself established on the path. But the company of people not involved in the Dhamma will tend to be distracting. Those who are not trying to practise the Buddha's teachings will usually lead us in the worldly direction to which their own minds incline. Thus, when we can, it is best to choose our friends from among meditators.

The Four Noble Truths

As Kisāgotamī urges in the final lines quoted above, meditators need to train their minds constantly to see the Four Noble Truths in all their ramifications. This is wisdom, *paññā*, the remedy for the ignorance and delusion which are at the root of all suffering as shown in the formula of dependent origination. To develop wisdom one has to ponder these four truths over and over again: (1) the Noble Truth of Suffering (*dukkha*) which includes all forms of suffering from severe agony to the pervasive unsatisfactoriness and instability inherent in individual existence in all planes of becoming; (2) the Noble Truth of the Cause of Suffering—craving (*taṇhā*), which drives the mind outwards after sense objects in a state of perpetual unrest; (3) the Noble Truth of the Cessation of Suffering—Nibbāna, which is attained when the causes of suffering, ignorance and craving, have been utterly uprooted; and (4) the Noble Truth of the Way leading to the Cessation of Suffering—the Noble Eightfold Path discovered and taught by the Buddha, consisting in the assiduous practice of morality (*sīla*), concentration (*samādhi*) and wisdom (*paññā*).

The Four Noble Truths are concisely expressed in a verse spoken by Mahā Pajāpatī, the Buddha's maternal aunt who brought him up when his own mother, Queen Mahāmāyā, died a week after his birth. It was at the insistence of Mahā Pajāpatī that the Buddha founded the Bhikkhunī Sangha. In her poem she first praises the Buddha for the unique help he has given to so many beings by training them in the way to liberation; then she briefly sums up the Four Noble Truths which she has so thoroughly experienced as ultimate truth. It would be beneficial for modern meditators to consider these lines carefully:

> Now have I understood how ill does come,
> Craving, the Cause, is dried up in me.
> Have I not walked, have I not touched the End
> Of ill—the Ariyan, the Eightfold Noble Path.
>
> p. 89

Buddhist meditators have to train themselves to know these truths as deeply as they can by seeing them in every aspect of existence. We follow the mundane level of the Noble Eightfold Path in order to reach the supramundane (*lokuttara*) path with the attainment of Stream-entry. Then the constituents of the path—morality, concentration and wisdom—are cultivated to the highest degree and the end of suffering, Nibbāna, is realised.

Reaching the Goal after a Long Struggle

When we read the stories of these great bhikkhunīs, we see that many of them attained the highest fruits either instantaneously or soon after coming into contact with the Buddha or his Dhamma. This could have happened because they had built up *pāramīs* in many previous lives, creating pure *kamma* of body, speech and mind, while simultaneously wearing out the effects of past *kamma*.

Yet not all the people whose *pāramīs* permitted them to actually hear the Buddha preach were able to become Arahats so quickly in their final lives. When we confront our rebellious minds as we try to follow his path, we can take heart from the tales of nuns who had to put forth years and years of intense persistent effort before they eliminated all their defilements.

A youthful Cittā ordained at her home town of Rājagaha and spent her whole adult life as a nun striving for enlightenment. She finally attained her goal only as a weak old woman, as she laboriously climbed up the landmark of Vulture Peak. When she had done so, she said:

> Having thrown down my outer robe, and having turned my bowl upside down, I propped myself against a rock, having torn asunder the mass of darkness (of ignorance).
>
> v. 27

If we diligently, strictly, and vigorously practise the Noble Eightfold Path, developing insight into the true nature of existence, the opacity of delusion must eventually become completely transparent, cleared by wisdom. It may require many years or many lifetimes of work, but then patience is one of the qualities we must cultivate from the time we first set foot on the path.

Another bhikkhunī who took years to reach enlightenment was Mittākālī. She took robes after hearing the Satipaṭṭhāna Sutta. In her "lion's roar" she describes the errors that cost her seven years to gain Nibbāna. Her poem can be instructive to other meditators both within and outside the Sangha:

> Having gone forth in faith from the house to the houseless state, I wandered here and there, greedy for gain and honour.

> Having missed the highest goal, I pursued the lowest goal.
> Having gone under the mastery of the defilements, I did not
> know the goal of the ascetic's state.
>
> vv. 92–93

The Buddha pointed out on many occasions that it is dangerous for monks and nuns to pursue gains or favours from the laity, as such activities nullify any attempts they may make to purify their minds. The layman gives gifts to bhikkhus and bhikkhunīs to earn merit. If the mind of the recipient is pure, free from greed and other defilements, the merit accruing to the lay disciple is far greater than if the recipient's mind is filled with craving. One of the epithets given to Arahats, whose purity is permanently perfect, is "worthy of the highest offerings." All those, ordained or not, who allow craving to overtake them and waste the precious opportunity they have to practise the Dhamma, will delay their own liberation and increase their suffering.

In the simile of the poisonous snake in the *Middle Length Sayings* (Vol I, pp. 171-72), the Buddha points out that his teaching has only one aim, freedom from suffering. An incorrect approach that seeks to misuse the Dhamma will lead to increased suffering, just as grasping a snake by the body or tail will result in one's being bitten. The same venomous snake, if grabbed with the help of a forked stick by the neck just behind its head, will safely yield up its poison for medicinal use. The Buddha declares that similarly only those who wisely examine the purpose of his teachings will be able to gain insight and actually experience their purpose—the elimination of the causes of suffering.

When Mittākālī perceived that old age and death were rapidly approaching, she finally came to realise the urgency of the task after wasting years in the pursuit of gain and honour. Since we can never be sure how much longer we will live, it is risky to put off meditation. We have come into contact with the Dhamma under conditions conducive to pursuing the Buddha's goal. Such conditions as youth and human birth will come to an end— either gradually or abruptly—so we can never be certain that the conditions to practise the Dhamma will remain ideal. Mittākālī took years to comprehend that with advancing age, rigidity of mind and bodily ailments were making the job of purification ever more difficult. But once she did realise this, she was able to achieve the goal. Studying this verse of hers may help us to avoid wasting precious time:

> I felt a sense of urgency as I was seated in my little cell; (thinking) "I have entered upon the wrong road; I have come under the mastery of craving. My life is short. Old age and sickness are destroying it. There is no time for me to be careless before this body is broken."
>
> Looking at the arising and passing away of the elements of existence as they really are, I stood up with my mind completely released. The Buddha's Teaching has been done.
>
> vv. 94–95

By observing the rise and fall at every instant of body, feelings, perceptions, mental formations, and consciousness, Mittākālī's mind was freed from misconceptions of any lasting "I" or self. After those seven long years of being trapped in the net of desires, she saw through her foolish and dangerous interest in mundane matters. She was then able to see the elements or aggregates as they actually are: utterly transient (*anicca*), hence incapable of providing any satisfaction (*dukkha*), working automatically without any lasting core (*anattā*). All her worldly involvements dropped away as she attained Arahatship and thenceforth passed beyond all sorrow and suffering.

Perhaps the most moving story of a nun who had to undergo a long struggle from the time she first ordained until she became fully enlightened is that of Puṇṇā. Under six earlier Buddhas, in the vast aeons prior to the Buddha Gotama's dispensation, Puṇṇā was a bhikkhunī "perfect in virtue, and learning the three Piṭakas (the Buddhist scriptures) she became very learned in the Norm and a teacher of it. But because of her tendency to pride (each time), she was unable to root out the defilements." Even at the time of Buddha Gotama, she had to work out some bad *kamma* and so was born as a slave. Hearing one of the Buddha's discourses, she became a Stream-enterer. After she helped her master clear his wrong view, in gratitude he freed her and she ordained. After so many lifetimes of striving, the *pāramīs* she had built up as a nun under previous Buddhas ripened. Pride or conceit, always one of the last defilements to go, finally dissolved and she attained Arahatship.

By pondering the accounts of women who attained full awakening after much application and effort, we can be encouraged to continue our own exertions no matter how slow our progress may appear at a given time. In the *Gradual Sayings* (Vol. IV, pp. 83-84), the Buddha gives an analogy of the wearing down of the carpenter's axe handle to illustrate how the mental impurities are to be gradually worn away. Even though the woodcutter cannot say, "This much of the handle was rubbed off today, this much last week," it is clear to him that slowly, over time, the handle is being destroyed. Similarly, a meditator who has a good guide and who constantly attempts to understand the Four Noble Truths and to live in accordance with the Noble Eightfold Path, will gradually eliminate his defilements, even though the steps in the process are imperceptible. Even the Buddha declined to predict the amount of time that will elapse before the final goal is reached. This is conditioned by many interacting factors, such as the good and bad *kamma* built up in the past and the amount of effort put forth now and in the future. Whether it takes us millions of more lifetimes or a week, we will be sustained in our efforts by the faith that perfection of morality, concentration and wisdom will bring utter detachment and freedom from all suffering.

Liberation means renouncing attachment to oneself and to the world. We cannot rush the process of detachment; insight into the suffering brought about by clinging will do it, slowly. While trying to eliminate mental impurities, we have to accept their existence. We would not be here at all were it not for the ignorance and other defiling tendencies that brought us into this birth. We need to learn to live equanimously with the dirt of the mind while it is slowly being cleared away. Purification, like all other mental activities, is a cause and effect process. Clarity comes slowly with the repeated application of the wisdom of impermanence. If we are patient and cheerfully bear with moments of apparent backsliding or stupidity, if we continue to work energetically with determination, not swerving off the path, the results will begin here and now. And in due time they have to ripen fully.

Contemplation on the Sangha

The Sangha, the order of monks and nuns, preserves and perpetuates the Buddha's pure teachings, and its members have dedicated their lives to practising them. Thus contemplation on the Sangha is recommended by the Buddha to help cultivate wholesome mental states. We could begin such contemplation based on the poem of a bhikkhunī named Rohiṇī.

Her father had asked her why she thought recluses and monks were great beings. He claimed, as might many people today—particularly in the West with its strong "work ethic"—that ascetics are just lazy; they are "parasites" who do nothing worthwhile and live off the labour of others. But Rohiṇī proclaimed her faith in the work and lives of pure recluses. She thereby inspired her father's confidence, and at her bidding he then took refuge in the Buddha, the Dhamma, and the Sangha. Her poem can also inspire us:

> They are dutiful, not lazy, doers of the best actions; they abandon desire and hatred ...

> They shake off the three roots of evil doing pure actions; all their evil is eliminated ...

> Their body-activity is pure; and their speech-activity is likewise; their mind-activity is pure ...

> They are spotless like mother-of-pearl, purified inside and out; full of good mental states ...

> Having great learning, expert in the doctrine, noble, living in accordance with the doctrine, they teach the goal and the doctrine ... with intent minds, (they are) possessed of mindfulness ...

> Travelling far, possessed of mindfulness, speaking in moderation, not conceited, they comprehend the end of suffering ...

> If they go from any village, they do not look back (longingly) at anything; they go without longing indeed ...

> They do not deposit their property in a store-room, nor in a pot, nor in a basket, (rather) seeking that which is cooked ...

They do not take gold, coined or uncoined, or silver; they live by means of whatever turns up ...

Those who have gone forth are of various families and from various countries; (nevertheless) they are friendly to one another; therefore ascetics are dear to me.

vv. 275–285

The Buddhist texts speak of two kinds of Sangha, both referred to in this poem, the Ariya Sangha and the Bhikkhu Sangha. In the opening lines Rohiṇī describes the Ariyas, "noble ones," and those striving to attain that state. The three lower kinds of Ariyas may be lay disciples or ordained monks and nuns. But because of their utter purity, the highest type, the fully liberated Arahats, can continue to live only within the Bhikkhu Sangha. It is Arahats who have completely rid their minds of greed, hatred and ignorance, the three roots of evil which Rohiṇī mentions. Other Ariyas are striving to abandon whatever of these three still remains in their minds. All Ariyas to some extent "comprehend the end of suffering," the Third Noble Truth, for it is this experience of Nibbāna which sets them apart as "noble."

Beginning with the next line, Rohiṇī specifically talks about the behaviour of monks and nuns. They wander on almsrounds through the streets with their eyes trained just a few steps ahead of them. "They do not look back" as they have no idle interest in the events that are going on around them. They do not handle money and are content with the minimum by way of the requisites—whatever their lay followers may offer them. Students of the Dhamma who are not in the monastic order would also do well to cultivate the monk's lack of interest in his surroundings. A good monk does not let his gaze wander about uncontrolled, especially when he is on almsround, because when going into the village every morning he encounters a plethora of sense objects that might entice him if he does not restrain his senses and maintain mindfulness. Attentively, the good bhikkhu goes silently from door to door and leaves when there is enough food in his bowl, without letting craving disturb his balance of mind. Such a monk is not interested in the details of the lives of those around him. His focus is always on the ultimate nature of things—their impermanence, painfulness and essencelessness. As lay meditators we too need to train ourselves to be like these bhikkhus, to remain equanimous and detached amidst all the clamour and distractions of life by reminding ourselves that none of these things is worth running after.

Rohiṇī also states that the noble monks are not greedy about money or other possessions. They do not save up their requisites out of fear for the future. Instead, they trust their good *kamma* to fulfil their daily needs. While, as laymen, we must work for our living, we should heed this behaviour and similarly adopt a detached attitude towards wealth. We work in order to sustain our bodies and those of the people who are dependent on us. But if we can learn to do this without intense longing for the "security" that money seems to provide, we will see how the law of *kamma* works.

The last verse states that within the Sangha, the family, class or national background of its members does not impede their cordial relations with each other. This kind of open good will is surely useful for laymen to put into practice in their daily lives too. Since it is by ordaining that individuals can completely dedicate their lives to the Dhamma, bhikkhus and bhikkhunīs offer us laymen many examples of how we should try to apply the teachings within the limitations of "the dust of household life." Rohiṇī's poem has pointed out some of these.

The Danger of Worldly Desire

A large number of poems by the nuns emphasise the danger of worldly desire. The bhikkhunī named Sumedhā shaved off her hair herself in order to force her parents to cancel her proposed marriage and permit her to enter the Sangha. But before she left home, Sumedhā convinced her whole family and its retinue of the validity of the Buddha's message. To her fiancé, King Anikaratta, she explained the futility of sense desires and the insatiability of the senses:

> Even if the rain-god rained all seven kinds
> Of gems, until earth and heaven were full,
> Still senses would crave and men die unsatiated.

p. 176

No matter how large a quantity of worldly goods we may have, if the mind has not gained insight, craving will recur. If ignorance has not been uprooted, desire will seek more and different objects, always hoping for lasting satisfaction. Durable happiness is impossible in the mundane sphere because all sense objects change and decay every moment, as does the mind itself. This perpetual state of underlying dissatisfaction—craving looking for gratification—is one of the many forms of present suffering. In addition, desire itself generates the kammic energy which propels life towards rebirth in order for it to continue its efforts at finding fulfilment. If desire is present in the mind at the moment of death, rebirth has to ensue.

After speaking the above verse, Sumedhā gave a lengthy discourse to the whole assembly in her palace on the great value of a human birth in the infinity of *saṃsāra*. Life in this world is precious because it provides a very rare opportunity for learning the way to put an end to rebirth and suffering, for putting into practice the teachings of the Buddha. Sumedhā also spoke on the dangers inherent in sensual joy and sense desire and she uttered verses about the Noble Eightfold Path as well. She enthusiastically exhorted her audience:

> When the undying (Nibbāna) exists, what do you want with sensual pleasures which are burning fevers? For all delights in sensual pleasures are on fire, aglow, seething.
>
> v. 504

When craving momentarily gains its aim, mind's enjoyment of the sense object brings it to a feverish state of excitement and activity. Sumedhā urges her family to look beyond such unsettling, binding pleasures and to heed the words of the Awakened One which show the way beyond all desire to utter peace. She exhorts them to keep in mind their long-term benefit and not get caught up in the fragile momentary happiness that comes with the occasional satisfaction of sense desire. She reminds them in words we too should recall: "Desires of sense burn those who do not let go" (p. 176). Clinging to pleasure always brings pain. Such agitated emotions, although perhaps pleasant in a gross way, are gone in a moment. They arise and cease due to conditions we cannot completely control. We always tend to want the pleasant to last in spite of the fact that its nature is to change, vanish, and give way to the unpleasant. Sumedhā's poem expounding this wisdom is the last one in the original *Therīgāthā* and it summarises what the Buddha taught about the dangers of craving.

The bhikkhunī named Subhā also dwells at length on the dangers of mundane wishes, using some terrifying metaphors to show the tremendous dangers inherent in attachment to the world. In the following poem taken from the Saṃyutta Nikāya a meditator can discover much by reflecting on Subhā's intense imagery:

> May I not meet (again) with sensual pleasures, in which no refuge is found. Sensual pleasures are enemies, murderers, like a mass of fire, pain-(ful).
>
> Greed is an obstacle, full of fear, full of annoyance, full of thorns, and it is very disagreeable. It is a great cause of stupefaction ...
>
> Sensual pleasures are maddening, deceiving, agitating the mind; a net spread out by Māra for the defilement of creatures.
>
> Sensual pleasures have endless perils, they have much pain, they are great poisons, they give little enjoyment, they cause conflict, drying up the virtuous.
>
> vv. 351f., 357f.

These lines show us the peril and suffering we must face when we allow ourselves to become entangled in mundane desires. Only personal comprehension of these dangers motivates a meditator to become truly mindful, aware of his physical and mental activities with ever-present detachment. Otherwise his "mindfulness" may be forced, suppressing reactions without helping to untie mental knots. Studying the suffering we have to encounter if we are carried away by our desires, naturally loosens their hold on the mind. We will realise along with Subhā that worldly lusts are enemies and that they herald all the misery of successive births.

One of our tasks in seeking liberation is to train our minds to see desire as it arises at the sense doors. We must also see desire as it persists and as it passes away. Having done this over and over again, we will understand that all desire or attachment is bound to result in unhappiness. In this way we will gradually train our minds to let go of all craving and aversion towards sense objects.

To try to practise this mindfulness without any specific training is likely to fail because the worldling, the average person, perceives no suffering in craving. A worldling can only see the expected happiness. He invariably thinks, "If only this would happen just right, all would be well." But as we purify our bodily and vocal activities through morality, still our minds through concentration, and take up insight meditation under a good teacher, we will come to see more and more clearly how all desire is suffering and brings still more suffering in the future. We will then also realise how often attaining a desired object turns out to be an anti-climax which leaves—not the anticipated happiness—but only emptiness. With a calm mind we can clearly perceive the tension, distress, and uneasiness caused by the continual dissatisfaction, which in turn is due to craving impelling the mind to various sense objects.

Thus the mind is always running—now towards what it foolishly regards as a "desirable" thing, now away from what it considers "undesirable." In Vipassanā meditation, the one-pointed mind is trained to experience directly the transitory nature of body and of mind itself, and also of external sense objects. With this direct knowledge or experiential insight, the "happiness" which is so avidly sought by the worldling is seen as really just another form of suffering, and the perpetual tension caused by the ignorance and craving latent in any unliberated mind becomes evident. As sensual pleasure is understood to be the seething fire described by our bhikkhunīs, the mind naturally lets go of all these different manifestations of craving. Such a mind has thoroughly learned the lesson that the nuns gleaned from their Master and passed on to us: suffering is inherent in desire.

The Danger in Attachment to One's Beauty

In ancient times as well as at present, women in all stations of life have used various means to enhance their beauty and to hide the signs of advancing age. This, however, is just a futile attempt to pretend that the body is not growing old, to keep it from showing outwardly that it is actually falling apart. But if, instead of creams and lotions, wisdom is applied to the ageing process, it can deepen our understanding of impermanence on all levels.

Ambapāli was a wealthy and beautiful courtesan during the time of the Buddha. Before she heard the Buddha preach, her main concern had been to cultivate and maintain her renowned beauty. With the Buddha's guidance, she was able to face the inevitability of ageing and the loss of her beauty and to comprehend the suffering of old age. Her verses can also stimulate our own understanding:

> My eyes were shining, very brilliant like jewels, very black and long. Overwhelmed by old age, they do not look beautiful. Not otherwise is the utterance of the speaker of truth ...
>
> Formerly my hands looked beautiful, possessing delicate signet rings, decorated with gold. Because of old age they are like onions and radishes. Not otherwise is the utterance of the speaker of the truth ...
>
> Formerly my body looked beautiful, like a well-polished sheet of gold. (Now) it is covered with very fine wrinkles. Not otherwise is the utterance of the speaker of the truth ...
>
> Such was this body. (Now) it is decrepit, the abode of many pains, an old house with its plaster fallen off. Not otherwise is the utterance of the speaker of the truth.
>
> vv. 257, 264, 266, 270

Ambapāli sees how all the body's charms give way to ugliness and pain as the ageing process takes its toll, as the Buddha teaches it must. All physical beauty, no matter how perfect it might seem at one youthful moment, is utterly impermanent. Even at its peak, the brilliance of the eyes is already, if invisibly, starting to grow dim; the firmness of limbs is withering; the smoothness of skin is wrinkling. Impermanence and decay, Ambapāli reminds us, is the nature of all bodies and of everything else in the universe as well.

Khemā, the queen of King Bimbisāra, was another woman who had been enthralled with her own beauty prior to meeting the Buddha. But Khemā had made a vow before one of the earlier Buddhas to become great in wisdom under the Buddha Gotama. During the dispensations of several of the intervening Buddhas, she had parks made which she donated to each Buddha and his Sangha.

But in her final lifetime Khemā strongly resisted going to see the Buddha Gotama. Perhaps her "Māra forces" were making a last effort to keep her in *saṃsāra*. They were, however, doomed to fail since by the force of her merits this was to be her final existence. King Bimbisāra almost had to trick her into going to the Buddha because Queen Khemā was so attached to her looks and was afraid that this would provoke the Buddha's disapproval. If we ever find ourselves resisting the Dhamma, we can use Khemā's example to remind ourselves of the temporary nature of this mental state. Then we will not take it as a major personal fault. Mind's old habits are not pure, so at times it is bound to struggle against the process of purification.

But the Buddha knew how to tame Khemā's vanity and conceit. He created the vivid image of a woman even more attractive than she was. When she came into his presence, Khemā saw this other lady fanning the Buddha. Then, before the queen's very eyes, the Buddha made the beautiful image grow older and older until she was just a decaying bag of bones. Seeing this, first Khemā realised that her own beauty was not unmatched. This broke her pride. Second and more important, she understood that she herself would likewise have to grow old and decrepit.

The Buddha next spoke a verse and Khemā became a Stream-enterer. Then in rapid succession she went through all the stages of enlightenment to attain Arahatship on the spot. Thereupon the Buddha told King Bimbisāra that she would either have to ordain or to pass away, and the king, unable to bear the thought of losing her so soon, gave her permission to ordain. So, already an Arahat, she was ordained—one of the very rare cases of a human being who had achieved Arahatship before entering the Sangha. Khemā had clearly built up truly unique *pāramīs* by giving great gifts to earlier Buddhas and by learning their teachings thoroughly.[1] Here again we see the great importance of creating in the present strong good *kamma* based on wisdom, even if we do not attain any of the paths or fruits in this lifetime. The more good deeds accompanied by wisdom that we do now, the easier will it be when the time actually comes for us to reach the goal. Meditation is, of course, the most valuable of such deeds.

In the *Therīgāthā*, Khemā's poem takes the form of a conversation with Māra, the being who controls and symbolises the forces of evil. Māra praised her beauty, and her reply shows how totally her view of herself and of life had changed now that she fully understood the true nature of things:

---

1. This story is related in the Commentary to the Dhammapada, translated as *Buddhist Legends* by E. W. Burlingame, published by the Pali Text Society. See Part 3, pp. 225f.

Through this body vile, foul seat of disease and corruption,
Loathing I feel, and oppression. Cravings of lust are uprooted.

Lusts of the body and mind cut like daggers and javelins.
Speak not to me of delighting in any sensuous pleasure!
All such vanities cannot delight me any more.

p. 83

Then she identifies Māra with those who believe that mere ritual observances will lead to mental purification. Khemā states that such people, who worship fire or the constellations, etc., are ignorant of reality and cannot eliminate their defiling tendencies through such practices. This is why the belief that rites and rituals can bring about liberation has to be eliminated to attain even the stage of Stream-entry.

Khemā concludes her verses with an exclamation of deep gratitude to the Buddha, the supreme among men. Her last line is a resounding "lion's roar":

(I am) utterly free from all sorrow,
A doer of the Buddha's teachings.

pp. 3-4

Khemā had "done," i.e., put into practice, the message of all the Buddhas, and this had taken her beyond the realms of suffering.

Further Conversations with Māra

Some of the other discourse-type verses in the *Therīgāthā* also take the form of a discussion with Māra. Typically, Māra asks the Arahat nun why she is not interested in the "good things of life." Māra urged Selā, for example, to enjoy sensual pleasures while youth allowed her to do so. The Therī's reply on the dangers of such delights offers similes as powerful as those used by Bhikkhunī Sumedhā:

Sensual pleasures are like swords and stakes; the elements of existence are a chopping block for them; what you call "delight in sensual pleasures" is now "non-delight" for me.

v. 58

Surely many of us have also heard our own internal Māra urge us to "go have a good time and never mind the long-term kammic consequences." But if we can remind ourselves often enough and early enough of the painful after-effects of such "joys"—especially of those that involve breaking moral precepts—we may see through the pleasures of the senses and so gradually lose our attachment to them.

In one of the discourses from the Saṃyutta Nikāya, Cala tells Māra that, unlike most beings, she finds no delight in birth in spite of the so-called sensual pleasures that life makes possible. With clear simplicity she shows that ultimately all that birth produces is suffering:

> Once born we die. Once born we see life's ills—
> The bonds, the torments, and the life cut off.
>
> p. 186

We too should cultivate this understanding in order to develop detachment from the poison-soaked sensual pleasures offered by mundane life.

The Doctrine of Anattā

One of the unique aspects of the Buddha's teaching is its doctrine of *anattā*, the impersonal, essenceless, egoless or soul-less nature of all phenomena. This universal characteristic is difficult to comprehend as it is contrary to our most deeply held assumption that "I" exist, that "I" act and "I" feel.

Sakula, in the following lines of her poem in the *Therīgāthā*, briefly expresses her understanding of the impersonal quality of all compounded things:

> Seeing the constituent elements as other, arisen causally, liable to dissolution, I eliminated all taints. I have become cool, quenched.
>
> v. 101

Sakula has attained Nibbāna because she saw with total clarity that everything normally taken to be "myself" is, in fact, devoid of any such self. She knew that all these phenomena arise and dissolve every moment strictly dependent on causes. This comprehension has rooted out all tendency to cling to the *saṅkhāras* or "constituent elements" and so all the defiling mental tendencies have ceased.

When Māra asks Sister Selā, "Who made this body, where did it come from and where will it go?", she gives him in reply (in one of the poems added from the Saṃyutta Nikāya) a discourse on egolessness:

> Neither self-made the puppet is, nor yet
> By another is this evil fashioned.
> By reason of a cause it came to be;
> By rupture of a cause it dies away.
> Like a given seed sown in the field,
> Which, when it gets the taste of earth,
> And moisture too—by these two does grow,
> So the five aggregates, the elements,
> And the six spheres of sense—all of these—
> By reason of a cause they came to be;
> By rupture of the cause they die away.

pp. 189–190

After the seed analogy, the last four lines discuss the "self" as it actually is—a compound of conditioned, changing phenomena. The five aggregates make up *nāma* (mentality) and *rūpa* (materiality), each of which is in turn made up of groups of ephemeral factors. *Nāma*, the mental side of existence, consists of the four immaterial aggregates—feeling (*vedanā*), perception (*saññā*), mental formations (*saṅkhāra*), and consciousness (*viññāṇa*)—which arise together at every moment of experience. *Rūpa*, which may be external matter or the matter of one's own body, consists of the four essential material qualities—solidity, cohesion, temperature, and vibration—along with the derivative types of matter coexisting with them in the very minute material groupings called *kalāpas*, arising and passing away millions of times per second.

Each aggregate arises due to certain causes and when these causes end, the aggregate also ceases. Causes, or conditions, are connected with effects in the law of dependent arising (*paṭiccasamuppāda*), which is at the centre of the Buddha's own awakening. The refrain from Selā's poem (lines 3-4 and 10-11) is, in fact, a reformulation of the most general exposition of that law often stated thus in the suttas:

When there is this, that comes to be;
With the arising of this, that arises.
When this is absent, that does not come to be;
With the cessation of this, that ceases.

The specific link in the cycle of dependent arising most relevant to Selā's verse is: "With consciousness as condition, mentality-materiality arises." That is, at the moment of conception, *nāma-rūpa* (in this case excluding consciousness) arises due to rebirth-linking consciousness. Later on, during the course of an existence, *nāma*, the mental aggregates, comes into being due to ignorance, past *kamma*, objects at the sense doors, and many other conditions. *Rūpa*, the matter which makes up the body, arises during life because of food, climate, present state of mind, and past *kamma*.

Selā also refers to the elements, *dhātu*, a word which the Buddha uses for several groups of phenomena. Let us look here at the eighteen elements. The five sense faculties (eye, ear, nose, tongue, body), their objects (sights, sounds, smells, tastes, touches), and the five types of consciousness dependent on their coming together make up fifteen of the elements. Mind as a faculty, mental objects (ideas), and the mind-consciousness that arises when those two come together are the sixth in each set, completing the eighteen.

The Buddha analysed the totality of conditioned phenomena into ultimate constituents in a number of ways for the benefit of listeners of varying proclivities. To some, the eighteen elements are clear, to others, the five aggregates. Either way, what we need to understand as Selā did is that none of these things is "me" or "mine" or "my self." All these phenomena—the aggregates, the elements, the spheres—arise because of certain conditions, and when those conditions end, naturally they also have to end. When the relevant causes have expended their force, all these aspects of what we erroneously take to be "me" and "mine" cease. So we see with Selā that nowhere is there any real, independent, or lasting "I" with the power to create and sustain itself. There is only the concept "I am" which is conditioned by ignorance, i.e., our inability to see mind-and-body as it really is. The idea "I" is itself essenceless, it arises due to causes; and it is also inherently impermanent, bound to completely disappear when the ignorance and other supporting conditions behind it are uprooted. This is the attainment of Arahatship.

The removal of ignorance takes place step by step in Vipassanā meditation. Every aspect of the mind-body complex comes to be clearly known at its ultimate level as conditioned, essenceless, transitory, oppressive. One comes to fully understand that only when the appropriate conditions come about will a so-called "being" be born. Only then will a five-aggregate life-continuum commence a new life with its bases, elements and sense organs. If we explore Bhikkhunī Selā's seed analogy, we will see in relation to ourselves how a strict succession of causes and effects, kammic and other, governs all of life. We will discover that there is no underlying or ongoing "I" doing or experiencing anything, and will begin to loosen our attachment to this non-existent "self." Then we start to eliminate the dreadful suffering that comes attendant on this delusion.

Suffering follows from the mistaken belief in an "I," technically called *sakkāyadiṭṭhi*, wrong view of a lasting self. On the basis of this idea the mind generates all its thoughts of craving: "I must have this," "I don't like that," "This is mine." It is basically due to this misconception of a controlling self that we have been wandering and suffering throughout aeons in *saṃsāra*. If we are to eliminate all the *dukkha* of existence, as Therī Selā did, we must develop insight through Vipassanā meditation to the point at which understanding of the ultimate truth about mind and body dissolves the mistaken belief in an "I." We can use this bhikkhunī's words to stimulate our own personal meditative experience of the essenceless nature of the five aggregates.

Men and Women in the Dhamma

The difference between the male and female in connection with the Dhamma is a minor theme running through the *Therīgāthā*. It takes two forms: poems whose subject matter is the irrelevance of one's gender for gaining insight, and instances in which a nun specifically inspires or instructs a man with a discourse. The stories of Sumedhā and Rohiṇī already discussed fit into the latter type.

An example of the first type is Somā's challenge to Māra's query about women's ability to attain Arahatship. Somā showed Māra that the capacity to gain the requisite insight for liberation need not be hindered by "woman's nature." Somā's encounter with Māra in the *Therīgāthā* proper is explained in her verses from the Saṃyutta Nikāya, where she rhetorically asks him:

> What should the woman's nature do to them
> Whose hearts are firmly set, who ever move
> With growing knowledge onward in the Path?

pp. 45; 182-183

If one is really developing morality, concentration and wisdom, it does not matter whether one was born male or female. The insight to "truly comprehend the Norm" is completely irrespective of superficial distinctions of sex, race, caste, etc. Somā adds that if one even thinks, "Am I a woman in these matters, or am I a man, or what not am I then?" one is under Māra's sway. To be much concerned with such subjects is to remain on the level of conventional truth, clinging to the non-existent self. Repeatedly worrying about which sex is better or about the "inequities" women suffer generates unwholesome *kamma*. Thoughts like this are rooted in attachment to "I" and "mine" and are associated with ill will or desire.

Moreover, spending time on such matters distracts us from the urgent task of self-purification. Meditators who wish to escape Māra's net need to cast off such thoughts as soon as they are noticed. We should not indulge in or expand upon them. Somā and all the other nuns follow the Buddha's advice closely when they urge us to stick exclusively to the work that will allow us to liberate ourselves from all suffering. All side issues will lose their importance and so pass away with further growth of wisdom. When we know fully that all beings are just impersonal, unstable mind-body processes, generating *kamma* and feeling its results, our minds will remain with the ultimate truths and have no interest in any conventional concerns.

The story of the bhikkhunī known as "Vaddha's Mother" is one in which a nun specifically guides a man in the Dhamma. This woman joined the Sangha when her son Vaddha was small; thus he had been brought up by relatives. Later, he too ordained and one day went to visit his mother in the bhikkhunīs' quarters. On that occasion, she exhorted and inspired him to seek and attain the highest goal:

Vaddha, may you not have craving for the world at any time.
Child, do not be again and again a sharer in pain.

Happily, indeed, Vaddha, dwell the sages, free from lust,
with doubts cut off, become cool, having attained self-taming,
(being) without taints.

O Vaddha, devote yourself to the way practised by seers
for the attainment of insight, for the putting an end to pain.

vv. 204–205

From these lines Vaddha deduced that his mother had reached the goal, a fact she confirmed. She again urged him to develop "the path leading to the cessation of suffering" himself. Vaddha, being deeply inspired by his mother's words, also attained the goal and then spoke the following lines praising her:

Truly my mother, because of being sympathetic, applied an excellent goad to me, (namely) verses connected with the highest goal.

Having heard her utterance, the instruction of my mother, I reached a state of religious excitement in the doctrine, for the attainment of rest-from-exertion.

vv. 210–211

Here we find a woman's example of perfect sainthood, combined with her timely Dhamma instruction, inspiring a man whose *pāramīs* were ripe to put forth the utmost effort and attain complete liberation.

The Five Aggregates and Nibbāna

The Cūlavedalla Sutta (*Middle Length Sayings,* Vol. I) is another sutta in which a bhikkhunī instructs a man. This important text takes the form of a discourse on some fine points of the Dhamma given by the Therī Dhammadinnā in reply to questions put to her by her former husband, the lay disciple Visākha. They had been married for some time when he attained the third stage of holiness, that of the Non-returner (*anāgāmī*), by eradicating all traces of ill will and sense desire. Dhammadinnā then learned from him that women too could purify their minds and she obtained his permission to take robes as a nun. By the time of this discussion, she must have already attained Arahatship, the fourth and final stage of holiness.

Visākha first asks Dhammadinnā what the Buddha actually refers to when, using conventional language, he says "own self."[2] As a Non-returner, Visākha knew the answer to this basic question, but he put it by way of introduction to his progressive series of queries. Dhammadinnā's reply is something for us to ponder. She says that the "five aggregates of grasping" (*pañcupadānakkhandhā*) comprise "own self." She defines the aggregates or groups of grasping as:

the group of grasping after material shape,
the group of grasping after feeling,
the group of grasping after perception,
the group of grasping after habitual tendencies,
the group of grasping after consciousness.

The aggregates are viewed and clung to as myself or mine: this is *sakkāyadiṭṭhi*, the view that there is a lasting self. Actually, there is no lasting controller or core corresponding to the concept "me" or "I." It is merely the grasping after these five groups, which are all that actually makes up "myself," that perpetuates our illusion that there is something substantial. If we can see this, we will be attacking *sakkāyadiṭṭhi* and will come to know that in reality there is no essence, just these five aggregates, all of whose components are continually changing.

The next question Visākha asks Dhammadinnā concerns the reasons for the arising of the aggregates. Quoting the Buddha, she replies that the cause for the aggregates is "craving (that is) connected with again-becoming, accompanied by delight and attachment, finding delight in this and that, namely, the craving for sense pleasures, the craving for becoming, the craving for annihilation."

All craving contributes to the arising of the aggregates over and over again. Being attracted to the things of this world or of

---

2. In Pali, *sakkāya*. I. B. Horner's translation of this term here as "own body" may be misleading. Although the word *kāya* does literally mean "body," it is often used to refer to a collection or assemblage of things, such as a "body of people." Here it signifies the assemblage of psycho-physical phenomena that the worldling identifies as his self.

the heavenly planes ("craving for sense pleasures") will lead to rebirth there with renewed suffering, gross or subtle. Wanting to keep on going ("craving for becoming") strengthens clinging and ignorance to force us to continue in *saṃsāra*. The belief that there is no form of life after death (rooted in "craving for annihilation") undermines the doctrine of *kamma* and its result, the understanding of which is essential to moral living.

After a long series of questions and answers which cover the Four Noble Truths, the attainment of cessation, feeling, etc., Visākha asks a final question: "And what, lady, is the counterpart (i.e. equal) of Nibbāna?" Here Dhammadinnā has to stop him:

> This question goes too far, friend Visākha, it is beyond the compass of an answer. Friend Visākha, the Brahmafaring is for immergence in Nibbāna, for going beyond to Nibbāna, for culminating in Nibbāna.

Nothing can possibly be compared with Nibbāna, as everything else, be it mental or physical, arises and ceases due to conditions. Nibbāna alone is unconditioned and unchanging. Going beyond the realm of transitory, unsatisfactory phenomena to the utter peace of Nibbāna is the aim of the teaching of the Buddha and so of serious Buddhists. It is useful to keep this goal in mind even during the early stages of meditation, when it may seem remote and vague. The aspiration to attain Nibbāna is cumulative. If it is frequently considered, repeated and combined with the practice of Vipassanā, this aspiration will become a supporting condition for the attainment itself. Frequent recollection of the goal will also keep us from being sidetracked by the pleasurable experiences one may encounter on the path.

After this question and answer session, Dhammadinnā suggests that Visākha should ask the Buddha about all this so that he is certain and learns the answers well. Visākha takes up the idea and later repeats to the Buddha his entire conversation with the Therī. The Lord replies in her praise:

> Clever, Visākha, is the nun Dhammadinnā, of great wisdom ... If you had asked me, Visākha, about this matter, I too would have answered exactly as the nun Dhammadinnā answered.

Kamma and its Fruit

Finally, let us look at a poem in which a bhikkhunī describes in detail a few of her previous lives and shows her questioner how she comprehended the law of kammic cause and effect working out behind her present-life experiences.

Isidāsī had built up many good *pāramīs* long ago during the times of former Buddhas. But some seven lifetimes back, when she was a young man, she had committed adultery. After passing away from that existence Isidāsī had to suffer the results of this immoral action:

> Therefrom deceasing, long I ripened in Avīci hell
> And then found rebirth in the body of an ape.
> Scarce seven days I lived before the great
> Dog-ape, the monkey's chief, castrated me.
> Such was the fruit of my lasciviousness.
>
> Therefrom deceasing in the woods of Sindh,
> Born the offspring of a one-eyed goat
> And lame, twelve years a gelding, gnawn by worms.
> Unfit, I carried children on my back.
> Such was the fruit of my lasciviousness.

p. 157

The next time she was born a calf and was again castrated, and as a bullock pulled a plough and a cart. Then, as the worst of that evil *kamma*'s results had already ripened, Isidāsī returned to the human realm. But it was still an uncertain kind of birth as she was the hermaphroditic child of a slave. That life too did not last long. Next, she was the daughter of a man oppressed by debts. One of her father's creditors took her in lieu of payment. She became the wife of that merchant's son, but she "brought discord and enmity within that house."

In her final lifetime, no matter how hard she tried, no home she was sent to as a bride would keep her more than a brief while. Several times her virtuous father had her married to appropriate suitors. She tried to be the perfect wife, but each time she was thrown out. This inability to remain with a husband created an opportunity for her to break through the cycle of results. After her third marriage disintegrated, she decided to enter the Sangha.

All her mental defilements were eliminated by meditation, insight into the Four Noble Truths matured, and Isidāsī became an Arahat.

She also developed the ability to see her past lives and thus saw how this whole causal chain of unwholesome deeds committed long ago brought their results in her successive existences:

> Fruit of my *kamma* was it thus that they
> In this last life have slighted me even though
> I waited on them as their humble slave.

The last line of her poem puts the past, rebirth and all its sufferings, completely behind with a "lion's roar":

> "Enough! Of all that now have I made an end."

p. 163

In Isidāsī's tale we have several instructive illustrations of the inexorable workings of the law of *kamma*. The suffering she had to undergo because of sexual misconduct lasted through seven difficult lives. But the seeds of wisdom had also been sown and when the force of the bad *kamma* was used up, the powerful *pāramīs* she had created earlier bore their fruit. Hence Isidāsī was able to become a bhikkhunī, purify her mind perfectly, and so eliminate all possible causes of future suffering. The beginning, the middle, and the ending of every life are always due to causes and conditions.

* * *

We have now come full circle with these stories of the Therīs and have returned to the theme of impersonal causes and effects working themselves out, without any lasting being committing deeds or experiencing results. The infinite sequence of lifetimes steeped in ignorance and suffering is repeated over and over until accumulated *pāramīs* and present wisdom, aided by other factors, become sufficiently strong to enable one to see through the craving which has perpetually propelled the succession of aggregates. Through this process these bhikkhunīs clearly perceived that their attachments and aversions were the source of all their suffering. Because of this insight, they were able to dissolve the knots of old delusion-based conditioning.

With their completed understanding of suffering, the First Noble Truth, and the abandoning of craving, the Second Noble Truth, their practice of the Noble Eightfold Path, the Fourth Noble Truth, was perfected. They attained the cessation of suffering, the Third Noble Truth, in that very lifetime, and were never reborn again.

The poems of these enlightened nuns, telling how they came to meet the Buddha, how they had built up wisdom and other meritorious *kamma* over many previous lives, how they understood the Buddha's teachings, and how they attained Arahatship, offer us inspiration and guidance. They can help us present-day Buddhists to practise Vipassanā meditation and to gain insight into suffering and its causes. Then we too will be able to give up all craving by developing wisdom. We can use the messages of the Therīs to assist us in putting an end to our own suffering.

Grateful for their assistance, may we all follow in the footsteps of these great nuns, true daughters of the Buddha. May our minds be perfect in wisdom, perfectly pure, and utterly free from all possibility of future suffering.

The Jhānas

In Theravada Buddhist Meditation

by
Henepola Gunaratana Mahāthera

Copyright © Kandy; Buddhist Publication Society, (1988, 2007)

Introduction

The Doctrinal Context of Jhāna

The Buddha says that just as in the great ocean there is but one taste, the taste of salt, so in his doctrine and discipline there is but one taste, the taste of freedom. The taste of freedom that pervades the Buddha's teaching is the taste of spiritual freedom, which from the Buddhist perspective means freedom from suffering. In the process leading to deliverance from suffering, meditation is the means of generating the inner awakening required for liberation. The methods of meditation taught in the Theravada Buddhist tradition are based on the Buddha's own experience, forged by him in the course of his own quest for enlightenment. They are designed to re-create in the disciple who practises them the same essential enlightenment that the Buddha himself attained when he sat beneath the Bodhi tree, the awakening to the Four Noble Truths.

The various subjects and methods of meditation expounded in the Theravada Buddhist scriptures—the Pali Canon and its commentaries—divide into two interrelated systems. One is called the development of serenity (*samathabhāvanā*), the other the development of insight (*vipassanabhāvanā*). The former also goes under the name of development of concentration (*samādhibhāvanā*), the latter the development of wisdom (*paññābhāvanā*). The practice of serenity meditation aims at developing a calm, concentrated, unified mind as a means of experiencing inner peace and as a basis for wisdom. The practice of insight meditation aims at gaining a direct understanding of the real nature of phenomena. Of the two, the development of insight is regarded by Buddhism as the essential key to liberation, the direct antidote to the ignorance underlying bondage and suffering. Whereas serenity meditation is recognised as common to both Buddhist and non-Buddhist contemplative disciplines, insight meditation is held to be the unique discovery of the Buddha and an unparalleled feature of his path. However, because the growth of insight presupposes a certain degree of concentration, and serenity meditation helps to achieve this, the development of serenity also claims an incontestable place in the Buddhist meditative process. Together the two types of meditation work to make the mind a fit instrument for enlightenment. With his mind unified by means of the development of serenity, made sharp and bright by the development of insight, the meditator can proceed unobstructed to reach the end of suffering, Nibbāna.

Pivotal to both systems of meditation, though belonging inherently to the side of serenity, is a set of meditative attainments called the *jhānas*. Though translators have offered various renderings of this word, ranging from the feeble "musing" to the misleading "trance" and the ambiguous "meditation," we prefer to leave the word untranslated and to let its meaning emerge from its contextual usages. From these it is clear that the *jhānas* are states of deep mental unification which result from the centering of the mind upon a single object with such power of attention that a total immersion in the object takes place. The early suttas speak of four *jhānas*, named simply after their numerical position in the series: the first *jhāna*, the second *jhāna*, the third *jhāna* and the fourth *jhāna*. In the suttas the four repeatedly appear each described by a standard formula which we will examine later in detail.

The importance of the *jhānas* in the Buddhist path can readily be gauged from the frequency with which they are mentioned throughout the suttas. The *jhānas* figure prominently both in the Buddha's own experience and in his exhortation to disciples. In his childhood, while attending an annual ploughing festival, the future Buddha spontaneously entered the first *jhāna*. It was the memory of this childhood incident, many years later after his futile pursuit of austerities, that revealed to him the way to enlightenment during his period of deepest despondency (M I 246–47). After taking his seat beneath the Bodhi tree, the Buddha entered the four *jhānas* immediately before directing his mind to the threefold knowledge that issued in his enlightenment (M I 247–49). Throughout his active career the four *jhānas* remained "his heavenly dwelling" (D III 220) to which he resorted in order to live happily here and now. His understanding of the corruption, purification and emergence in the *jhānas* and other meditative attainments is one of the Tathāgata's ten powers which enable him to turn the matchless wheel of the Dhamma (M I 70). Just before his passing away the Buddha entered the *jhānas* in direct and reverse order, and the passing away itself took place directly from the fourth *jhāna* (D II 156).

The Buddha is constantly seen in the suttas encouraging his disciples to develop *jhāna*. The four *jhānas* are invariably included in the complete course of training laid down for disciples.[1] They figure in the training as the discipline of higher consciousness (*adhicittasikkhā*), right concentration (*sammāsamādhi*) of the Noble Eightfold Path, and the faculty and power of concentration (*samādhindriya, samādhibala*). Though a vehicle of dry insight can be found, indications are that this path is not an easy one, lacking the aid of the powerful serenity available to the practitioner of *jhāna*. The way of the *jhāna* attainer seems by comparison smoother and more pleasurable (AN II 150–52). The Buddha even refers to the four *jhānas* figuratively as a kind of Nibbāna: he calls them immediately visible Nibbāna, factorial Nibbāna, Nibbāna here and now (AN IV 453–54).

To attain the *jhānas*, the meditator must begin by eliminating the unwholesome mental states obstructing inner collectedness, generally grouped together as the *five hindrances* (*pañcanīvaraṇā*): sensual desire, ill will, sloth and torpor, restlessness and worry and doubt.[2] The mind's absorption on its object is brought about by five opposing mental states—applied thought, sustained thought, rapture, happiness and one pointedness[3]—called the *jhāna factors* (*jhānaṅgāni*) because they lift the mind to the level of the first *jhāna* and remain there as its defining components.

After reaching the first *jhāna* the ardent meditator can go on to reach the higher *jhānas*, which is done by eliminating the coarser factors in each *jhāna*. Beyond the four *jhānas* lies another fourfold set of higher meditative states which deepen still further the element of serenity. These attainments (*āruppa*), are the base of boundless space, the base of boundless consciousness, the base of nothingness, and the base of neither-perception-nor-non-perception.[4] In the Pali

---

1. See for example, the Samaññaphala Sutta (DN 2), the Cullahatthipadopama Sutta (MN 27), etc.
2. *Kāmacchanda, byāpāda, thīnamiddha, uddhaccakukkucca, vicikicchā.*
3. *Vitakka, vicāra, pīti, sukha, ekaggatā.*
4. *Ākāsānañcāyatana, viññāṇañcāyatana, ākiñcaññāyatana, nevasaññā-nāsaññāyatana.*

commentaries these come to be called the *four immaterial jhānas* (*arūpajhāna*), the four preceding states being renamed for the sake of clarity, the *four fine-material jhānas* (*rūpajhāna*). Often the two sets are joined together under the collective title of the eight *jhānas* or the eight attainments (*aṭṭha-samāpattiyo*).

The four *jhānas* and the four immaterial attainments appear initially as mundane states of deep serenity pertaining to the preliminary stage of the Buddhist path, and on this level they help provide the base of concentration needed for wisdom to arise. But the four *jhānas* again reappear in a later stage in the development of the path, in direct association with liberating wisdom, and they are then designated the *supramundane* (*lokuttara*) *jhānas*. These supramundane *jhānas* are the levels of concentration pertaining to the four degrees of enlightenment experience called the supramundane paths (*magga*) and the stages of liberation resulting from them, the four fruits (*phala*).

Finally, even after full liberation is achieved, the mundane *jhānas* can still remain as attainments available to the fully liberated person, part of his untrammelled contemplative experience.

Etymology of Jhāna

The great Buddhist commentator Buddhaghosa traces the Pali word "*jhāna*" (Skt. *dhyāna*) to two verbal forms. One, the etymologically correct derivation, is the verb *jhāyati*, meaning to think or meditate; the other is a more playful derivation, intended to illuminate its function rather than its verbal source, from the verb *jhāpeti* meaning to burn up. He explains: "It burns up opposing states, thus it is *jhāna*" (Vin-a I 116), the purport being that *jhāna* "burns up" or destroys the mental defilements preventing the developing the development of serenity and insight.

In the same passage Buddhaghosa says that *jhāna* has the characteristic mark of contemplation (*upanijjhāna*). Contemplation, he states, is twofold: the contemplation of the object and the contemplation of the characteristics of phenomena. The former is exercised by the eight attainments of serenity together with their access, since these contemplate the object used as the basis for developing concentration; for this reason these attainments are given the name "*jhāna*" in the mainstream of Pali meditative exposition. However, Buddhaghosa also allows that the term "*jhāna*" can be extended loosely to insight (*vipassanā*), the paths and the fruits on the ground that these perform the work of contemplating the characteristics of things: the three marks of impermanence, suffering and non-self in the case of insight, Nibbāna in the case of the paths and fruits.

In brief the twofold meaning of *jhāna* as "contemplation" and "burning up" can be brought into connection with the meditative process as follows. By fixing his mind on the object the meditator reduces and eliminates the lower mental qualities such as the five hindrances and promotes the growth of the higher qualities such as the *jhāna* factors, which lead the mind to complete absorption in the object. Then by contemplating the characteristics of phenomena with insight, the meditator eventually reaches the supramundane *jhāna* of the four paths, and with this *jhāna* he burns up the defilements and attains the liberating experience of the fruits.

Jhāna and Samādhi

In the vocabulary of Buddhist meditation the word "*jhāna*" is closely connected with another word, "*samādhi*" generally rendered by "concentration." *Samādhi* derives from the prefixed verbal root sam + ā + √dhā, meaning to collect or to bring together, thus suggesting the concentration or unification of the mind. The word "*samādhi*" is almost interchangeable with the word "*samatha*," serenity, though the latter comes from a different root, √sam, meaning to become calm.

In the suttas *samādhi* is defined as mental one-pointedness, (*cittassekaggatā*, M I 301) and this definition is followed through rigorously in the Abhidhamma. The Abhidhamma treats one-pointedness as a distinct mental factor present in every state of consciousness, exercising the function of unifying the mind on its object. From this strict psychological standpoint *samādhi* can be present in unwholesome states of consciousness as well as in wholesome and neutral states. In its unwholesome forms it is called "wrong concentration" (*micchāsamādhi*), In its wholesome forms "right concentration" (*sammāsamādhi*).

In expositions on the practice of meditation, however, *samādhi* is limited to one-pointedness of mind (Vism 84–85; PP 84–85), and even here we can understand from the context that the word means only the wholesome one-pointedness involved in the deliberate transmutation of the mind to a heightened level of calm. Thus Buddhaghosa explains *samādhi* etymologically as "the centering of consciousness and consciousness concomitants evenly and rightly on a single object ... the state in virtue of which consciousness and its concomitants remain evenly and rightly on a single object, undistracted and unscattered" (Vism 84–85; PP 85).

However, despite the commentator's bid for consistency, the word *samādhi* is used in the Pali literature on meditation with varying degrees of specificity of meaning. In the narrowest sense, as defined by Buddhaghosa, it denotes the particular mental factor responsible for the concentrating of the mind, namely, one-pointedness. In a wider sense it can signify the states of unified consciousness that result from the strengthening of concentration, i.e., the meditative attainments of serenity and the stages leading up to them. And in a still wider sense the word *samādhi* can be applied to the method of practice used to produce and cultivate these refined states of concentration, here being equivalent to the development of serenity.

It is in the second sense that *samādhi* and *jhāna* come closest in meaning. The Buddha explains right concentration as the four *jhānas* (D II 313), and in doing so allows concentration to encompass the meditative attainments signified by the *jhānas*. However, even though *jhāna* and *samādhi* can overlap in denotation, certain differences in their suggested and contextual meanings prevent unqualified identification of the two terms. First behind the Buddha's use of the *jhāna* formula to explain right concentration lies a more technical understanding of the terms. According to this understanding *samādhi* can be narrowed down in range to signify only one mental factor, the most prominent in the *jhāna*, namely, one-pointedness, while the word "*jhāna*" itself must be seen as encompassing the state of consciousness in its entirety, or at least the whole group of mental factors individuating that meditative state as a *jhāna*.

In the second place, when *samādhi* is considered in its broader meaning it involves a wider range of reference than *jhāna*. The Pali exegetical tradition recognises three levels of *samādhi*: preliminary concentration (*parikammasamādhi*), which is produced as a result of the meditator's initial efforts to focus his mind on his meditation subject; access concentration (*upacārasamādhi*), marked by the suppression of the five hindrances, the manifestation of the *jhāna* factors, and the appearance of a luminous mental replica of the meditation object called the counterpart sign (*paṭibhāganimitta*); and absorption concentration (*appanāsamādhi*), the complete immersion of the mind in its object effected by the full maturation of the *jhāna* factors.[5] Absorption concentration comprises the eight attainments, the four immaterial attainments, and to this extent *jhāna* and *samādhi* coincide. However, *samādhi* still has a broader scope than *jhāna*, since it includes not only the *jhānas* themselves but also the two preparatory degrees of concentration leading up to them. Further, *samādhi* also covers a still different type of concentration called momentary concentration (*khaṇikasamādhi*), the mobile mental stabilisation produced in the course of insight contemplation of the passing flow of phenomena.

The Preparation for Jhāna

The *jhānas* do not arise out of a void but in dependence on the right conditions. They come to growth only when provided with the nutriments conductive to their development. Therefore, prior to beginning meditation, the aspirant to the *jhānas* must prepare a groundwork for his practice by fulfilling certain preliminary requirements. He first must endeavour to purify his moral virtue, sever the outer impediments to practise, and place himself under a qualified teacher who will assign him a suitable meditation subject and explain to him the methods of developing it. After learning these, the disciple must then seek out a congenial dwelling and diligently strive for success. In this chapter we will examine in order each of the preparatory steps that have to be fulfilled before commencing to develop *jhāna*.

The Moral Foundation for Jhāna

A disciple aspiring to the *jhānas* first has to lay a solid foundation of moral discipline. Moral purity is indispensable to meditative progress for several deeply psychological reasons. It is needed first,

---

5. See Narada & Bodhi, *A Comprehensive Manual of Abhidhamma* (Kandy: Buddhist Publication Society, 1980), pp. 389, 395–96.

in order to safeguard against the danger of remorse, the nagging sense of guilt that arises when the basic principles of morality are ignored or deliberately violated. Scrupulous conformity to virtuous rules of conduct protects the meditator from this danger disruptive to inner calm, and brings joy and happiness when the meditator reflects upon the purity of his conduct (see AN V 1–7).

A second reason a moral foundation is needed for meditation follows from an understanding of the purpose of concentration. Concentration, in the Buddhist discipline, aims at providing a base for wisdom by cleansing the mind of the dispersive influence of the defilements. But in order for the concentration exercises to effectively combat the defilements, the coarser expressions of the latter through bodily and verbal action first have to be checked. Moral transgressions being invariably motivated by defilements—by greed, hatred and delusion—when a person acts in violation of the precepts of morality he excites and reinforces the very same mental factors his practice of meditation is intended to eliminate. This involves him in a crossfire of incompatible aims which renders his attempts at mental purification ineffective. The only way he can avoid frustration in his endeavour to purify the mind of its subtler defilements is to prevent the unwholesome inner impulses from breathing out in the coarser form of unwholesome bodily and verbal deeds. Only when he establishes control over the outer expression of the defilements can he turn to deal with them inwardly as mental obsessions that appear in the process of meditation.

The practice of moral discipline consists negatively in abstinence from immoral actions of body and speech and positively in the observance of ethical principles promoting peace within oneself and harmony in one's relations with others. The basic code of moral discipline taught by the Buddha for the guidance of his lay followers is the five precepts: abstinence from taking life, from stealing, from sexual misconduct, from false speech, and from intoxicating drugs and drinks. These principles are bindings as minimal ethical obligations for all practitioners of the Buddhist path, and within their bounds considerable progress in meditation can be made. However, those aspiring to reach the higher levels of *jhānas* and to pursue the path further to the stages of liberation, are encouraged to take up the more complete moral discipline pertaining to the life of renunciation. Early Buddhism is unambiguous in its emphasis on the limitations of household life for following the path in its fullness and perfection. Time and again the texts say that the household life is confining, a "path for the dust of passion," while the life of homelessness is like open space. Thus a disciple who is fully intent upon making rapid progress towards Nibbāna will when outer conditions allow for it, "shave off his hair and beard, put on the yellow robe, and go forth from the home life into homelessness" (M I 179).

The moral training for the bhikkhus or monks has been arranged into a system called the fourfold purification of morality (*catupārisuddhisīla*).[6] The first component of this scheme, its backbone, consists in the *morality of restraint according to the Pātimokkha*, the code of 227 training precepts promulgated by the Buddha to regulate the conduct of the Sangha or monastic order. Each of these rules is in some way intended to facilitate control over the defilements and to induce a mode of living marked by harmlessness, contentment and simplicity. The second aspect of the monk's moral discipline is *restraint of the senses*, by which the monk maintains close watchfulness over his mind as he engages in sense contacts so that he does not give rise to desire for pleasurable objects and aversion towards repulsive ones. Third, the monk is to live by a *purified livelihood*, obtaining his basic requisites such as robes food, lodgings and medicines in ways consistent with his vocation. The fourth factor of the moral training is *proper use of the requisites*, which means that the monk should reflect upon the purposes for which he makes use of his requisites and should employ them only for maintaining his health and comfort, not for luxury and enjoyment.

After establishing a foundation of purified morality, the aspirant to meditation is advised to cut off any outer impediments (*palibodha*) that may hinder his efforts to lead a contemplative life. These impediments are numbered as ten: a dwelling, which becomes an impediment for those who allow their minds to become preoccupied with its upkeep or with its appurtenances; a family of relatives or supporters with whom the aspirant may

---

6. A full description of the fourfold purification of morality will be found in the *Visuddhimagga*, Chapter 1.

become emotionally involved in ways that hinder his progress; gains, which may bind the monk by obligation to those who offer them; a class of students who must be instructed; building work, which demands time and attention; travel; kin, meaning parents, teachers, pupils or close friends; illness; the study of scriptures; and supernormal powers, which are an impediment to insight (Vism 90–97; PP 91–98).

The Good Friend and the Subject of Meditation

The path of practice leading to the *jhānas* is an arduous course involving precise techniques, and skillfulness is needed in dealing with the pitfalls that lie along the way. The knowledge of how to attain the *jhānas* has been transmitted through a lineage of teachers going back to the time of the Buddha himself. A prospective meditator is advised to avail himself of the living heritage of accumulated knowledge and experience by placing himself under the care of a qualified teacher, described as a "good friend" (*kalyāṇamitta*), one who gives guidance and wise advice rooted in his own practice and experience. On the basis of either the power of penetrating others minds, or by personal observation, or by questioning, the teacher will size up the temperament of his new pupil and then select a meditation subject for him appropriate to his temperament.

The various meditation subjects that the Buddha prescribed for the development of serenity have been collected in the commentaries into a set called the forty *kammaṭṭhāna*. This word means literally a place of work, and is applied to the subject of meditation as the place where the meditator undertakes the work of meditation. The forty meditation subjects are distributed into seven categories, enumerated in the *Visuddhimagga* as follows: ten *kasiṇas*, ten kinds of foulness, ten recollections, four divine abidings, four immaterial states, one perception, and one defining.[7]

A *kasiṇa* is a device representing a particular quality used as a support for concentration. The ten *kasiṇas* are those of earth, water, fire and air; four colour *kasiṇas*—blue, yellow, red and white; the light *kasiṇa* and the limited space *kasiṇa*. The *kasiṇa* can be either a naturally occurring form of the element or colour

---

7. The following discussion is based on Vism 110–115; PP 112–118.

chosen, or an artificially produced device such as a disc that the meditator can use at his convenience in his meditation quarters.

The ten kinds of foulness are ten stages in the decomposition of a corpse: the bloated, the livid, the festering, the cut-up, the gnawed, the scattered, the hacked and scattered, the bleeding, the worm-infested, and a skeleton. The primary purpose of these meditations is to reduce sensual lust by gaining a clear perception of the repulsiveness of the body.

The ten recollections are the recollections of the Buddha, the Dhamma, the Sangha, morality, generosity and the deities, mindfulness of death, mindfulness of the body, mindfulness of breathing, and the recollection of peace. The first three are devotional contemplations on the sublime qualities of the "Three Jewels," on the primary objects of Buddhist virtues, and on the deities inhabiting the heavenly worlds, intended principally for those still intent on a higher rebirth. Mindfulness of death is reflection on the inevitably of death, a constant spur to spiritual exertion. Mindfulness of the body involves the mental dissection of the body into thirty-two parts, undertaken with a view to perceiving its unattractiveness. Mindfulness of breathing is awareness of the in-and-out movement of the breath, perhaps the most fundamental of all Buddhist meditation subjects. And the recollection of peace is reflection on the qualities of Nibbāna.

The four divine abidings (*brahmavihārā*) are the development of boundless loving kindness, compassion, sympathetic joy and equanimity. These meditations are also called the "immeasurables" (*appamaññā*) because they are to be developed towards all sentient beings without qualification or exclusiveness.

The four immaterial states are the base of boundless space, the base of boundless consciousness, the base of nothingness, and the base of neither-perception-nor-non-perception. These are the objects leading to the corresponding meditative attainments, the immaterial *jhānas*.

The one perception is the perception of the repulsiveness of food. The one defining is the defining of the four elements, that is, the analysis of the physical body into the elemental modes of solidity, fluidity, heat and oscillation.

The forty meditation subjects are treated in the commentarial texts from two important angles—one their ability to induce different levels of concentration, the other their suitability for differing temperaments. Not all meditation subjects are equally effective in inducing the deeper levels of concentration. They are first distinguished on the basis of their capacity for inducing only access concentration or for inducing full absorption; those capable of inducing absorption are then distinguished further according to their ability to induce the different levels of *jhāna*.

Of the forty subjects, ten are capable of leading only to access concentration: eight recollections—i.e., all except mindfulness of the body and mindfulness of breathing—plus the perception of repulsiveness in nutriment and the defining of the four elements. These, because they are occupied with a diversity of qualities and involve an active application of discursive thought, cannot lead beyond access. The other thirty subjects can all lead to absorption.

The ten *kasiṇas* and mindfulness of breathing, owing to their simplicity and freedom from thought construction, can lead to all four *jhānas*. The ten kinds of foulness and mindfulness of the body lead only to the first *jhāna*, being limited because the mind can only hold onto them with the aid of applied thought (*vitakka*) which is absent in the second and higher *jhānas*. The first three divine abidings can induce the lower three *jhānas* but not the fourth, since they arise in association with pleasant feeling, while the divine abiding of equanimity occurs only at the level of the fourth *jhāna*, where neutral feeling gains ascendency. The four immaterial states conduce to the respective immaterial *jhānas* corresponding to their names.

The forty subjects are also differentiated according to their appropriateness for different character types. Six main character types are recognised—the greedy, the hating, the deluded, the faithful, the intelligent and the speculative—this oversimplified typology being taken only as a pragmatic guideline which in practice admits various shades and combinations. The ten kinds of foulness and mindfulness of the body, clearly intended to attenuate sensual desire, are suitable for those of greedy temperament. Eight subjects—the four divine abidings and four colour *kasiṇas*—are appropriate for the hating temperament. Mindfulness of breathing is suitable for those of the deluded and the speculative temperament. The first six recollections are appropriate for the faithful temperament. Four subjects—

mindfulness of death, the recollection of peace, the defining of the four elements, and the perception of the repulsiveness in nutriment—are especially effective for those of intelligent temperament. The remaining six *kasiṇas* and the immaterial states are suitable for all kinds of temperaments. But the *kasiṇas* should be limited in size for one of speculative temperament and large in size for one of deluded temperament.

Immediately after giving this breakdown Buddhaghosa adds a proviso to prevent misunderstanding. He states that this division by way of temperament is made on the basis of direct opposition and complete suitability, but actually there is no wholesome form of meditation that does not suppress the defilements and strengthen the virtuous mental factors. Thus an individual meditator may be advised to meditate on foulness to abandon lust, on loving kindness to abandon hatred, on breathing to cut off discursive thought, and on impermanence to eliminate the conceit "I am" (AN IV 358).

Choosing a Suitable Dwelling

The teacher assigns a meditation subject to his pupil appropriate to his character and explains the methods of developing it. He can teach it gradually to a pupil who is going to remain in close proximity to him, or in detail to one who will go to practise it elsewhere. If the disciple is not going to stay with his teacher he must be careful to select a suitable place for meditation. The texts mention eighteen kinds of monasteries unfavourable to the development of *jhāna*: a large monastery, a new one, a dilapidated one, one near a road, one with a pond, leaves, flowers or fruits, one sought after by many people, one in cities, among timber or fields, where people quarrel, in a port, in border lands, on a frontier, a haunted place, and one without access to a spiritual teacher (Vism 118-121; PP 122-125).

The factors which make a dwelling favourable to meditation are mentioned by the Buddha himself. If should not be too far from or too near a village that can be relied on as an alms resort, and should have a clear path: it should be quiet and secluded; it should be free from rough weather and from harmful insects and animals; one should be able to obtain one's physical requisites while dwelling there; and the dwelling should provide ready access to learned elders and spiritual friends who can be consulted when problems arise in meditation (AN V 15). The types of dwelling places commended by the Buddha most frequently in the suttas as conductive to the *jhānas* are a secluded dwelling in the forest, at the foot of a tree, on a mountain, in a cleft, in a cave, in a cemetery, on a wooded flatland, in the open air, or on a heap of straw (M I 181). Having found a suitable dwelling and settled there, the disciple should maintain scrupulous observance of the rules of discipline, He should be content with his simple requisites, exercise control over his sense faculties, be mindful and discerning in all activities, and practise meditation diligently as he was instructed. It is at this point that he meets the first great challenge of his contemplative life, the battle with the five hindrances.

The First Jhāna and its Factors

The attainment of any *jhāna* comes about through a twofold process of development. On one side the states obstructive to it, called its factors of abandonment, have to be eliminated, on the other the states composing it, called its factors of possession, have to be acquired. In the case of the first *jhāna* the factors of abandonment are the five hindrances and the factors of possession the five basic *jhāna* factors. Both are alluded to in the standard formula for the first *jhāna*, the opening phrase referring to the abandonment of the hindrances and the subsequent portion enumerating the *jhāna* factors:

> Quite secluded from sense pleasures, secluded from unwholesome states of mind, he enters and dwells in the first *jhāna*, which is accompanied by applied thought and sustained thought with rapture and happiness born of seclusion. (M I 1818; Vibh 245)

In this chapter we will first discuss the five hindrances and their abandonment, then we will investigate the *jhāna* factors both individually and by way of their combined contribution to the attainment of the first *jhāna*. We will close the chapter with some remarks on the ways of perfecting the first *jhāna*, a necessary preparation for the further development of concentration.

The Abandoning of the Hindrances

The five hindrances (*pañcanīvaraṇa*) are sensual desire, ill will, sloth and torpor, restlessness and worry, and doubt. This group, the principal classification the Buddha uses for the obstacles to meditation, receives its name because its five members hinder and envelop the mind, preventing meditative development in the two spheres of serenity and insight. Hence the Buddha calls them "obstructions, hindrances, corruptions of the mind which weaken wisdom"(S V 94).

The hindrance of sensual desire (*kāmacchanda*) is explained as desire for the "five strands of sense pleasure," that is, for pleasant forms, sounds, smells, tastes and tangibles. It ranges from subtle liking to powerful lust. The hindrance of ill will (*byāpāda*) signifies aversion directed towards disagreeable persons or things. It can vary in range from mild annoyance to overpowering hatred. Thus the first two hindrances correspond to the first two root defilements, greed and hate. The third root defilement, delusion, is not enumerated separately among the hindrances but can be found underlying the remaining three.

Sloth and torpor is a compound hindrance made up of two components: sloth (*thīna*), which is dullness, inertia or mental stiffness; and torpor (*middha*), which is indolence or drowsiness. Restlessness and worry is another double hindrance, restlessness (*uddhacca*) being explained as excitement, agitation or disquietude, worry (*kukkucca*) as the sense of guilt aroused by moral transgressions. Finally, the hindrance of doubt (*vicikicchā*) is explained as uncertainty with regard to the Buddha, the Dhamma, the Sangha and the training.

The Buddha offers two sets of similes to illustrate the detrimental effect of the hindrances. The first compares the five hindrances to five types of calamity: sensual desire is like a debt, ill will like a disease, sloth and torpor like imprisonment, restless and worry like slavery, and doubt like being lost on a desert road. Release from the hindrances is to be seen as freedom from debt, good health, release from prison, emancipation from slavery, and arriving at a place of safety (D I 71-73). The second set of similes compares the hindrances to five kinds of impurities affecting a bowl of water, preventing a keen-sighted man from seeing his own reflection as it really is. Sensual desire is like a bowl of water mixed with brightly coloured paints, ill will like a bowl of boiling water, sloth and torpor like water covered by mossy plants, restlessness and worry like water blown into ripples by the wind, and doubt like muddy water. Just as the keen-eyed man would not be able to see his reflection in these five kinds of water, so one whose mind is obsessed by the five hindrances does not know and see as it is his own good, the good of others or the good of both (S V 121–24). Although there are numerous defilements opposed to the first *jhāna* the five hindrances alone are called its factors of abandoning. One reason according to the *Visuddhimagga*, is that the hindrances are specifically obstructive to *jhāna*, each hindrance impeding in its own way the mind's capacity for concentration.

The mind affected through lust by greed for varied objective fields does not become concentrated on an object consisting in unity, or being overwhelmed by lust, it does not enter on the way to abandoning the sense-desire element. When pestered by ill will towards an object, it does not occur uninterruptedly. When overcome by stiffness and torpor, it is unwieldy. When seized by agitation and worry, it is unquiet and buzzes about. When stricken by uncertainty, it fails to mount the way to accomplish the attainment of *jhāna*. So it is these only that are called factors of abandonment because they are specifically obstructive to *jhāna* (Vism 146: pp 152).

A second reason for confining the first *jhāna*'s factors of abandoning to the five hindrances is to permit a direct alignment to be made between the hindrances and the jhānic factors. Buddhaghosa states that the abandonment of the five hindrances alone is mentioned in connection with *jhāna* because the hindrances are the direct enemies of the five *jhāna* factors, which the latter must eliminate and abolish. To support his point the commentator cites a passage demonstrating a one-to-one correspondence between the *jhāna* factors and the hindrances: one-pointedness is opposed to sensual desire, rapture to ill will, applied thought to sloth and torpor, happiness to restlessness and worry, and sustained thought to doubt (Vism 141; PP 147).[8] Thus

---

8. Buddhaghosa ascribes the passage he cites in support of the correspondence to the "Peṭaka," but it cannot be traced anywhere in the present Tipiṭaka, nor

each *jhāna* factor is seen as having the specific task of eliminating a particular obstruction to the *jhāna* and to correlate these obstructions with the five *jhāna* factors they are collected into a scheme of five hindrances.

The standard passage describing the attainment of the first *jhāna* says that the *jhāna* is entered upon by one who is "secluded from sense pleasures, secluded from unwholesome states of mind." The *Visuddhimagga* explains that there are three kinds of seclusion relevant to the present context—namely, bodily seclusion (*kāyaviveka*), mental seclusion (*cittaviveka*), and seclusion by suppression (*vikkhambhanaviveka*) (Vism 140; PP 145). These three terms allude to two distinct sets of exegetical categories. The first two belong to a threefold arrangement made up of bodily seclusion, mental seclusion, and "seclusion from the substance" (*upadhiviveka*). The first means physical withdrawal from active social engagement into a condition of solitude for the purpose of devoting time and energy to spiritual development. The second, which generally presupposes the first, means the seclusion of the mind from its entanglement in defilements; it is in effect equivalent to concentration of at least the access level. The third, "seclusion from the substance," is Nibbāna, liberation from the elements of phenomenal existence. The achievement of the first *jhāna* does not depend on the third, which is its outcome rather than prerequisite, but it does require physical solitude and the separation of the mind from defilements, hence bodily and mental seclusion. The third type of seclusion pertinent to the context, seclusion by suppression, belongs to a different scheme generally discussed under the heading of "abandonment" (*pahāna*) rather than "seclusion." The type of abandonment required for the attainment of *jhāna* is abandonment by suppression, which means the removal of the hindrances by force of concentration similar to the pressing down of weeds in a pond by means of a porous pot.[9]

---

in the exegetical work named *Peṭakopadesa*.

9. The other two types of abandoning are by substitution of opposites (*tadaṅgapahāna*), which means the replacement of unwholesome states by wholesome ones specifically opposed to them, and abandoning by eradication (*samucchedapahāna*), the final destruction of defilements by the supramundane paths. See Vism 693–96; PP 812–16.

The work of overcoming the five hindrances is accomplished through the gradual training (*anupubbasikkhā*) which the Buddha has laid down so often in the suttas, such as the Sāmaññaphala Sutta and the Cullahatthipadopama Sutta. The gradual training is a step-by-step process designed to lead the practitioner gradually to liberation. The training begins with moral discipline, the undertaking and observance of specific rules of conduct which enable the disciple to control the coarser modes of bodily and verbal misconduct through which the hindrances find an outlet. With moral discipline as a basis, the disciple practises the restraint of the senses. He does not seize upon the general appearances of the beguiling features of things, but guards and masters his sense faculties so that sensual attractive and repugnant objects no longer become grounds for desire and aversion. Then, endowed with the self-restraint, he develops mindfulness and discernment (*sati-sampajañña*) in all his activities and postures, examining everything he does with clear awareness as to its purpose and suitability. He also cultivates contentment with a minimum of robes, food, shelter and other requisites.

Once he has fulfilled these preliminaries the disciple is prepared to go into solitude to develop the *jhānas*, and it is here that he directly confronts the five hindrances. The elimination of the hindrances requires that the meditator honestly appraises his own mind. When sensuality, ill will and the other hindrances are present, he must recognise that they are present and he must investigate the conditions that lead to their arising: the latter he must scrupulously avoid. The meditator must also understand the appropriate antidotes for each of the five hindrances. The Buddha says that all the hindrances arise through unwise consideration (*ayoniso manasikāra*) and that they can be eliminated by wise consideration (*yoniso manasikāra*). Each hindrance, however, has its own specific antidote. Thus wise consideration of the repulsive feature of things is the antidote to sensual desire; wise consideration of loving kindness counteracts ill will; wise consideration of the elements of effort, exertion and striving opposes sloth and torpor; wise consideration of tranquillity of mind removes restlessness and worry; and wise consideration of the real qualities of things eliminates doubt (S V 105–106).

Having given up covetousness (i.e., sensual desire) with regard to the world, he dwells with a heart free of covetousness; he cleanses his mind from covetousness. Having given up the blemish of ill will, he dwells without ill will; friendly and compassionate towards all living beings, he cleanses his mind from the blemishes of ill will. Having given up sloth and torpor, he dwells free from sloth and torpor, in the perception of light; mindful and clearly comprehending, he cleanses his mind from sloth and torpor. Having given up restlessness and worry, he dwells without restlessness; his mind being calmed within, he cleanses it from restlessness and worry. Having given up doubt, he dwells as one who has passed beyond doubt; being free from uncertainty about wholesome things, he cleanses his mind from doubt ...

And when he sees himself free of these five hindrances, joy arises; in him who is joyful, rapture arises; in him whose mind is enraptured, the body is stilled; the body being stilled, he feels happiness; and a happy mind finds concentration. Then, quite secluded from sense pleasures, secluded from unwholesome states of mind, he enters and dwells in the first *jhāna*, which is accompanied by applied thought and sustained thought, with rapture and happiness born of seclusion (D I 73-74).[10]

The Factors of the First Jhāna

The first *jhāna* possesses five component factors: applied thought, sustained thought, rapture, happiness and one-pointedness of mind. Four of these are explicitly mentioned in the formula for the *jhāna*; the fifth, one-pointedness, is mentioned elsewhere in the suttas but is already suggested by the notion of *jhāna* itself. These five states receive their name, first because they lead the mind from the level of ordinary consciousness to the jhānic level, and second because they constitute the first *jhāna* and give it its distinct definition.

The *jhāna* factors are first aroused by the meditator's initial efforts to concentrate upon one of the prescribed objects for

---

10. Adapted from Nyanaponika Thera, *The Five Mental Hindrances and Their* Conquest (Wheel No. 26). This booklet contains a full compilation of texts on the hindrances.

developing *jhāna*. As he fixes his mind on the preliminary object, such as a *kasiṇa* disc, a point is eventually reached where he can perceive the object as clearly with his eyes closed as with them open. This visualised object is called the learning sign (*uggahanimitta*). As he concentrates on the learning sign, his efforts call into play the embryonic *jhāna* factors, which grow in force, duration and prominence as a result of the meditative exertion. These factors, being incompatible with the hindrances, attenuate them, exclude them, and hold them at bay. With continued practice the learning sign gives rise to a purified luminous replica of itself called the counterpart sign (*paṭibhāganimitta*), the manifestation of which marks the complete suppression of the hindrances and the attainment of access concentration (*upacārasamādhi*). All three events—the suppression of the hindrances, the arising of the counterpart sign, and the attainment of access concentration—take place at precisely the same moment, without interval (Vism 126; PP 131). And though previously the process of mental cultivation may have required the elimination of different hindrances at different times, when access is achieved they all subside together:

Simultaneously with his acquiring the counterpart sign his lust is abandoned by suppression owing to his giving no attention externally to sense desires (as object). And owing to his abandoning of approval, ill will is abandoned too, as pus is with the abandoning of blood. Likewise stiffness and torpor is abandoned through exertion of energy, agitation and worry is abandoned through devotion to peaceful things that cause no remorse; and uncertainty about the Master who teaches the way, about the way, and about the fruit of the way, is abandoned through the actual experience of the distinction attained. So the five hindrances are abandoned (Vism 189; PP 196).

Though the mental factors determinative of the first *jhāna* are present in access concentration, they do not as yet possess sufficient strength to constitute the *jhāna*, but are strong enough only to exclude the hindrances. With continued practice, however, the nascent *jhāna* factors grow in strength until they are capable of issuing in *jhāna*. Because of the instrumental role these factors play both in the attainment and constitution of the first *jhāna* they are deserving of closer individual scrutiny.

Applied Thought (*vitakka*)

The word *vitakka* frequently appears in the texts in conjunction with the word *vicāra*. The pair signify two interconnected but distinct aspects of the thought process, and to bring out the difference between them (as well as their common character), we translate the one as applied thought and the other as sustained thought.

In both the suttas and the Abhidhamma applied thought is defined as the application of the mind to its object (*cetaso abhiniropana*), a function which the *Atthasālinī* illustrates thus: "Just as someone ascends the king's palace in dependence on a relative of friend dear to the king, so the mind ascends the object in dependence on applied thought" (Dhs-a 157). This function of applying the mind to the object is common to the wide variety of modes in which the mental factor of applied thought occurs, ranging from sense discrimination to imagination, reasoning and deliberation and to the practice of concentration culminating in the first *jhāna*. Applied thought can be unwholesome as in thoughts of sensual pleasure, ill will and cruelty, or wholesome as in thoughts of renunciation, benevolence and compassion (M I 116).

In *jhāna* applied thought is invariably wholesome and its function of directing the mind upon its object stands forth with special clarity. To convey this the *Visuddhimagga* explains that in *jhāna* the function of applied thought is "to strike at and thresh— for the meditator is said, in virtue of it, to have the object struck at by applied thought, threshed by applied thought" (Vism 142; PP148). The *Milindapañhā* makes the same point by defining applied thought as absorption (*appanā*): "Just as a carpenter drives a well-fashioned piece of wood into a joint, so applied thought has the characteristic of absorption" (Mil 62).

The object of *jhāna* into which *vitakka* drives the mind and its concomitant states is the counterpart sign, which emerges from the learning sign as the hindrances are suppressed and the mind enters access concentration. The *Visuddhimagga* explains the difference between the two signs thus:

In the learning sign any fault in the *kasiṇa* is apparent. But the counterpart sign appears as if breaking out from the learning sign, and a hundred times, a thousand times more purified, like a looking-glass disc drawn from its case, like a mother-of-pearl dish well washed, like the moon's disc coming out from behind a cloud, like cranes against a thunder cloud. But it has neither colour nor shape; for if it had, it would be cognizable by the eye, gross, susceptible of comprehension (by insight) and stamped with the three characteristics. But it is not like that. For it is born only of perception in one who has obtained concentration, being a mere mode of appearance (Vism 125–26; PP 130).

The counterpart sign is the object of both access concentration and *jhāna*, which differ neither in their object nor in the removal of the hindrances but in the strength of their respective *jhāna* factors. In the former the factors are still weak, not yet fully developed, while in the *jhāna* they are strong enough to make the mind fully absorbed in the object. In this process applied thought is the factor primarily responsible for directing the mind towards the counterpart sign and thrusting it in with the force of full absorption.

Sustained Thought (*vicāra*)

Vicāra seems to represent a more developed phase of the thought process than *vitakka*. The commentaries explain that it has the characteristic of "continued pressure" on the object (Vim. 142; PP 148). Applied thought is described as the first impact of the mind on the object, the gross inceptive phase of thought; sustained thought is described as the act of anchoring the mind on the object, the subtle phase of continued mental pressure. Buddhaghosa illustrates the difference between the two with a series of similes. Applied thought is like striking a bell, sustained thought like the ringing; applied thought is like a bee's flying towards a flower, sustained thought like its buzzing around the flower; applied thought is like a compass pin that stays fixed to the centre of a circle, sustained thought like the pin that revolves around (Vism 142–43; PP 148–49).

These similes make it clear that applied thought and sustained thought, functionally associated, perform different tasks. Applied thought brings the mind to the object, sustained thought fixes and anchors it there. Applied thought focuses the mind on the object, sustained thought examines and inspects what is focused on. Applied thought brings a deepening of concentration by again and again leading the mind back to the same object, sustained thought sustains the concentration achieved by keeping the mind anchored on that object.

Rapture (*pīti*)

The third factor present in the first *jhāna* is *pīti*, usually translated as joy or rapture.[11] In the suttas *pīti* is sometimes said to arise from another quality called *pāmojja*, translated as joy or gladness, which springs up with the abandonment of the five hindrances. When the disciple sees the five hindrances abandoned in himself "gladness arises within him; thus gladdened, rapture arises in him; and when he is rapturous his body becomes tranquil" (D I 73). Tranquillity in turn leads to happiness, on the basis of which the mind becomes concentrated. Thus rapture precedes the actual arising of the first *jhāna*, but persists through the remaining stages up to the third *jhāna*.

The *Vibhaṅga* defines *pīti* as "gladness, joy, joyfulness, mirth, merriment, exultation, exhilaration, and satisfaction of mind" (Vibh 257). The commentaries ascribe to it the characteristic of endearing, the function of refreshing the body and mind or pervading with rapture, and the manifestation as elation (Vism 143; PP 149). Shwe Zan Aung explains that *"pīti* abstracted means interest of varying degrees of intensity, in an object felt as desirable or as calculated to bring happiness."[12]

When defined in terms of agency, *pīti* is that which creates interest in the object; when defined in terms of its nature it is the interest in the object. Because it creates a positive interest in the object, the *jhāna* factor of rapture is able to counter and suppress the hindrance of ill will, a state of aversion implying a negative evaluation of the object.

---

11. Ven. Ñyāṇamoli, in his translation of the *Visuddhimagga*, renders piti by "happiness," but this rendering can be misleading since most translators use "happiness" as a rendering for *sukha*, the pleasurable feeling present in the jhana. We will render piti by "rapture," thus maintaining the connection of the term with ecstatic meditative experience.

12. Shwe Zan Aung, *Compendium of Philosophy* (London: Pali Text Society, 1960), p. 243.

Rapture is graded into five categories: minor rapture, momentary rapture, showering rapture, uplifting rapture and pervading rapture.[13] Minor rapture is generally the first to appear in the progressive development of meditation; it is capable of causing the hairs of the body to rise. Momentary rapture, which is like lightning, comes next but cannot be sustained for long. Showering rapture runs through the body in waves, producing a thrill but without leaving a lasting impact. Uplifting rapture, which can cause levitation, is more sustained but still tends to disturb concentration. The form of rapture most conductive to the attainment of *jhāna* is all-pervading rapture, which is said to suffuse the whole body so that it becomes like a full bladder or like a mountain cavern inundated with a mighty flood of water. The *Visuddhimagga* states that what is intended by the *jhāna* factor of rapture is this all-pervading rapture "which is the root of absorption and comes by growth into association with absorption" (Vism 144; PP 151).

Happiness (*sukha*)

As a factor of the first *jhāna*, *sukha* signifies pleasant feeling. The word is explicitly defined in the sense by the *Vibhaṅga* in its analysis of the first *jhāna*: "Therein, what is happiness? Mental pleasure and happiness born of mind-contact, the felt pleasure and happiness born of mind-contact, pleasurable and happy feeling born of mind contact—this is called 'happiness'" (Vibh 257). The *Visuddhimagga* explains that happiness in the first *jhāna* has the characteristic of gratifying, the function of intensifying associated states, and as manifestation, the rendering of aid to its associated states (Vism 145; PP 151).

Rapture and happiness link together in a very close relationship, but though the two are difficult to distinguish, they are not identical. Happiness is a feeling (*vedanā*); rapture a mental formation (*saṅkhāra*). Happiness always accompanies rapture, so that when rapture is present happiness must always be present; but rapture does not always accompany happiness, for in the

---

13. *Khuddakapīti, khaṇikapīti, okkantikapīti, ubbegapīti* and *pharaṇapīti*. Vism 143–44; PP 149–51; Dhs-a 158.

third *jhāna*, as we will see, there is happiness but no rapture. The *Atthasālinī*, which explains rapture as "delight in the attaining of the desired object" and happiness as "the enjoyment of the taste of what is required," illustrates the difference by means of a simile:

Rapture is like a weary traveller in the desert in summer, who hears of, or sees water of a shady wood. Ease (happiness) is like his enjoying the water of entering the forest shade. For a man who, travelling along the path through a great desert and overcome by the heat, is thirsty and desirous of drink, if he saw a man on the way, would ask 'Where is water?' The other would say, 'Beyond the wood is a dense forest with a natural lake. Go there, and you will get some.' He, hearing these words, would be glad and delighted and as he went would see lotus leaves, etc., fallen on the ground and become more glad and delighted. Going onwards, he would see men with wet clothes and hair, hear the sounds of wild fowl and pea-fowl, etc., see the dense forest of green like a net of jewels growing by the edge of the natural lake, he would see the water lily, the lotus, the white lily, etc., growing in the lake, he would see the clear transparent water, he would be all the more glad and delighted, would descend into the natural lake, bathe and drink at pleasure and, his oppression being allayed, he would eat the fibres and stalks of the lilies, adorn himself with the blue lotus, carry on his shoulders the roots of the *mandalaka*, ascend from the lake, put on his clothes, dry the bathing cloth in the sun, and in the cool shade where the breeze blew ever so gently lay himself down and say: 'O bliss! O bliss!' Thus should this illustration be applied. The time of gladness and delight from when he heard of the natural lake and the dense forest till he saw the water is like rapture having the manner of gladness and delight at the object in view. The time when, after his bath and dried he laid himself down in the cool shade, saying, 'O bliss! O bliss!' etc., is the sense of ease (happiness) grown strong, established in that mode of enjoying the taste of the object.[14]

Since rapture and happiness co-exist in the first *jhāna*, this simile should not be taken to imply that they are mutually exclusive. Its purport is to suggest that rapture gains prominence before happiness, for which it helps provide a causal foundation.

---

14. Dhs-a 160-61. Translation by Maung Tin, *The Expositor* (*Atthasalini*) (London: Pali Text Society, 1921), I 155-56.

In the description of the first *jhāna*, rapture and happiness are said to be "born of seclusion" and to suffuse the whole body of the meditator in such a way that there is no part of his body which remains unaffected by them:

> Monks, secluded from sense pleasure ... a monk enters and dwells in the first *jhāna*. He steeps, drenches, fills and suffuses his body with the rapture and happiness born of seclusion, so that there is no part of his entire body that is not suffused with this rapture and happiness. Just as a skilled bath-attendant or his apprentice might strew bathing powder in a copper basin, sprinkle it again and again with water, and knead it together so that the mass of bathing soap would be pervaded, suffused, and saturated with moisture inside and out yet would not ooze moisture, so a monk steeps, drenches, fills and suffuses his body with the rapture and happiness born of seclusion, so that, there is no part of his entire body that is not suffused with this rapture and happiness born of seclusion (D I 74).

One-pointedness (*ekaggatā*)

Unlike the previous four *jhāna* factors, one-pointedness is not specifically mentioned in the standard formula for the first *jhāna*, but it is included among the *jhāna* factors by the Mahāvedalla Sutta (M I 294) as well as in the Abhidhamma and the commentaries. One-pointedness is a universal mental concomitant, the factor by virtue of which the mind is centred upon its object. It brings the mind to a single point, the point occupied by the object.

One-pointedness is used in the text as a synonym for concentration (*samādhi*) which has the characteristic of non-distraction, the function of eliminating distractions, non-wavering as its manifestation, and happiness as its proximate cause (Vism 85; PP 85). As a *jhāna* factor one-pointedness is always directed to a wholesome object and wards off unwholesome influences, in particular the hindrance of sensual desire. As the hindrances are absent in *jhāna* one-pointedness acquires special strength, based on the previous sustained effort of concentration.

Besides the five *jhāna* factors, the first *jhāna* contains a great number of other mental factors functioning in unison as coordinate members of a single state of consciousness. Already the Anupada Sutta lists such additional components of the first *jhāna* as contact, feeling, perception, volition, consciousness, desire, decision, energy, mindfulness, equanimity and attention (M III 25). In the Abhidhamma literature this is extended still further up to thirty-three indispensable components. Nevertheless, only five states are called the factors of the first *jhāna*, for only these have the functions of inhibiting the five hindrances and fixing the mind in absorption. For the *jhāna* to arise all these five factors must be present simultaneously, exercising their special operations:

But applied thought directs the mind onto the object; sustained thought keeps it anchored there. Happiness (rapture) produced by the success of the effort refreshes the mind whose effort has succeeded through not being distracted by those hindrances; and bliss (happiness) intensifies it for the same reason. Then unification aided by this directing onto, this anchoring, this refreshing and this intensifying, evenly and rightly centres the mind with its remaining associated states on the object consisting in unity. Consequently possession of five factors should be understood as the arising of these five, namely, applied thought, sustained thought, happiness [rapture], bliss (happiness), and unification of mind. For it is when these are arisen that *jhāna* is said to be arisen, which is why they are called the five factors of possession (Vism 146; PP 152).

Each *jhāna* factor serves as support for the one which succeeds it. Applied thought must direct the mind to its object in order for sustained thought to anchor it there. Only when the mind is anchored can the interest develop which will culminate in rapture. As rapture develops it brings happiness to maturity, and this spiritual happiness, by providing an alternative to the fickle pleasures of the senses, aids the growth of one-pointedness. In this way, as Nāgasena explains, all the other wholesome states lead to concentration, which stands at their head like the apex on the roof of a house (Mil 38–39).

Perfecting the First Jhāna

The difference between access and absorption concentration, as we have said, does not lie in the absence of the hindrances, which is common to both, but in the relative strength of the *jhāna* factors. In access the factors are weak so that concentration is fragile, comparable to a child who walks a few steps and then falls down. But in absorption the *jhāna* factors are strong and well developed so that the mind can remain continuously in concentration just as a healthy man can remain standing on his feet for a whole day and night (Vism 126; PP 131).

Because full absorption offers the benefit of strengthened concentration, a meditator who gains access is encouraged to strive for the attainment of *jhāna*. To develop his practice several important measures are recommended.[15] The meditator should live in a suitable dwelling, rely upon a suitable alms resort, avoid profitless talk, associate only with spiritually-minded companions, make use only of suitable food, live in a congenial climate, and maintain his practice in a suitable posture. He should also cultivate the ten kinds of skill in absorption. He should clean his lodging and his physical body so that they conduce to clear meditation, balance his spiritual faculties by seeing that faith is balanced with wisdom and energy with concentration, and he must be skilful in producing and developing the sign of concentration (1–3). He should exert the mind when it is slack, restrain it when it is agitated, encourage it when it is restless or dejected, and look at the mind with equanimity when all is proceeding well (4–7). The meditator should avoid distracting persons, should approach people experienced in concentration, and should be firm in his resolution to attain *jhāna* (8–10).

After attaining the first *jhāna* a few times the meditator is not advised to set out immediately striving for the second *jhāna*. This would be a foolish and profitless spiritual ambition. Before he is prepared to make the second *jhāna* the goal of his endeavour he must first bring the first *jhāna* to perfection. If he is too eager to reach the second *jhāna* before he has perfected the first, he is likely to fail to gain the second and find himself unable to regain the first. The Buddha compares such a meditator to a foolish cow who, while still unfamiliar with her own pasture, sets out for new pastures and gets lost in the mountains: she fails to find food or drink and is unable to find her way home (AN IV 418–19).

The perfecting of the first *jhāna* involves two steps: the extension of the sign and the achievement of the five masteries. The

---

15. The following is based on Vism 126–35; PP 132–40.

extension of the sign means extending the size of the counterpart sign, the object of the *jhāna*. Beginning with a small area, the size of one or two fingers, the meditator gradually learns to broaden the sign until the mental image can be made to cover the world-sphere or even beyond (Vism 152–53; PP 158–59).

Following this the meditator should try to acquire five kinds of mastery over the *jhāna*: mastery in adverting, in attaining, in resolving, in emerging and in reviewing.[16] Mastery in adverting is the ability to advert to the *jhāna* factors one by one after emerging from the *jhāna*, wherever he wants, whenever he wants, and for as long as he wants. Mastery in attaining is the ability to enter upon *jhāna* quickly, mastery in resolving the ability to remain in the *jhāna* for exactly the pre-determined length of time, mastery in emerging the ability to emerge from *jhāna* quickly without difficulty, and mastery in reviewing the ability to review the *jhāna* and its factors with retrospective knowledge immediately after adverting to them. When the meditator has achieved this fivefold mastery, then he is ready to strive for the second *jhāna*.

The Higher Jhānas

In this chapter we will survey the higher states of *jhāna*. First we will discuss the remaining three *jhānas* of the fine-material sphere, using the descriptive formulas of the suttas as our starting point and the later literature as our source for the methods of practice that lead to these attainments. Following this we will consider the four meditative states that pertain to the immaterial sphere, which come to be called the immaterial *jhānas*. Our examination will bring out the dynamic character of the process by which the *jhānas* are successively achieved. The attainment of the higher *jhānas* of the fine-material sphere, we will see, involves the successive elimination of the grosser factors and the bringing to prominence of the subtler ones, the attainment of the formless *jhānas* the replacement of grosser objects with successively more refined objects. From our study it will become clear that the *jhānas* link together in a graded

---

16. *Āvajjanavasī, samāpajjanavasī, adhiṭṭhānavasī, vutthānavasī, paccavek-khanavasī*. For a discussion see Vism 154–55; PP 160–61. The canonical source for the five masteries is the *Paṭisambhidamagga*, I 100.

sequence of development in which the lower serves as basis for the higher and the higher intensifies and purifies states already present in the lower. We will end the chapter with a brief look at the connection between the *jhānas* and the Buddhist teaching of rebirth.

The Higher Fine-material Jhānas

The formula for the attainment of the *second jhāna* runs as follows:

> With the subsiding of applied thought and sustained thought he enters and dwells in the second *jhāna*, which has internal confidence and unification of mind, is without applied thought and sustained thought, and is filled with rapture and happiness born of concentration. (M I 181; Vibh 245)

The second *jhāna*, like the first, is attained by eliminating the factors to be abandoned and by developing the factors of possession. In this case however, the factors to be abandoned are the two initial factors of the first *jhāna* itself, applied thought and sustained thought; the factors of possession are the three remaining *jhāna* factors, rapture, happiness and one-pointedness. Hence the formula begins "with the subsiding of applied thought and sustained thought," and then mentions the *jhāna*'s positive endowments.

After achieving the five kinds of mastery over the first *jhāna*, a meditator who wishes to reach the second *jhāna* should enter the first *jhāna* and contemplate its defects. These are twofold: one, which might be called the defect of proximate corruption, is the nearness of the five hindrances, against which the first *jhāna* provides only a relatively mild safeguard; the other defect, inherent to the first *jhāna*, is its inclusion of applied and sustained thought, which now appear as gross, even as impediments needing to be eliminated to attain the more peaceful and subtle second *jhāna*.

By reflecting upon the second *jhāna* as more tranquil and sublime than the first, the meditator ends his attachment to the first *jhāna* and engages in renewed striving with the aim of reaching the higher stage. He directs his mind to his meditation subject—which must be one capable of inducing the higher *jhānas* such as a *kasiṇa* or the breath—and resolves to overcome applied and sustained thought. When his practice comes to maturity the two kinds of thought subside and the second *jhāna* arises. In the second *jhāna* only three of the original five *jhāna* factors remain—rapture, happiness, and one-pointedness. Moreover, with the elimination of the two grosser factors these have acquired a subtler and more peaceful tone.[17]

Besides the main *jhāna* factors, the canonical formula includes several other states in its description of the second *jhāna*. "Internal confidence" (*ajjhattaṃ sampasādanaṃ*) conveys the twofold meaning of faith and tranquillity. In the first *jhāna* the meditator's faith lacked full clarity and serenity due to "the disturbance created by applied and sustained thought, like water ruffled by ripples and wavelets" (Vism 157; PP 163). But when applied and sustained thought subside, the mind becomes very peaceful and the meditator's faith acquires fuller confidence.

The formula also mentions unification of mind (*cetaso ekodibhāvaṃ*), which is identified with one-pointedness or concentration. Though present in the first *jhāna*, concentration only gains special mention in connection with the second *jhāna* since it is here that it acquires eminence. In the first *jhāna* concentration was still imperfect, being subject to the disturbing influence of applied and sustained thought. For the same reason this *jhāna*, along with its constituent rapture and happiness, is said to be born of concentration (*samādhija*): "It is only this concentration that is quite worthy to be called 'concentration' because of its complete confidence and extreme immobility due to absence of disturbance by applied and sustained thought" (Vism 158; PP 164).

To attain the *third jhāna* the meditator must use the same method he used to ascend from the first *jhāna* to the second. He must master the second *jhāna* in the five ways, enter and emerge

---

17. Based on the distinction between applied and sustained thought, the Abhidhamma presents a fivefold division of the jhanas obtained by recognizing the sequential rather than simultaneous elimination of the two kinds of thought. On this account a meditator of duller faculties eliminates applied thought first and attains a second jhana with four factors including sustained thought, and a third jhana identical with the second jhana of the fourfold scheme. In contrast a meditator of sharp faculties comprehends quickly the defects of both applied and sustained thought and so eliminates them both at once.

from it, and reflect upon its defects. In this case the defect of proximate corruption is the nearness of applied and sustained thought, which threaten to disrupt the serenity of the second *jhāna*; its inherent defect is the presence of rapture, which now appears as a gross factor that should be discarded. Aware of the imperfections in the second *jhāna*, the meditator cultivates indifference towards it and aspires instead for the peace and sublimity of the third *jhāna*, towards the attainment of which he now directs his efforts. When his practice matures he enters the third *jhāna*, which has the two *jhāna* factors that remain when the rapture disappears, happiness and one-pointedness, and which the suttas describe as follows:

> "With the fading away of rapture, he dwells in equanimity, mindful and discerning; and he experiences in his own person that happiness of which the noble ones say: 'Happily lives he who is equanimous and mindful'—thus he enters and dwells in the third *jhāna*." (M I 182; Vibh 245)

The formula indicates that the third *jhāna* contains, besides its two defining factors, three additional components not included among the *jhāna* factors: equanimity, mindfulness and discernment. Equanimity is mentioned twice. The Pali word for equanimity, *upekkhā*, occurs in the texts with a wide range of meanings, the most important being neutral feeling—that is, feeling which is neither painful nor pleasant—and the mental quality of inner balance or equipoise called "specific neutrality" (*tatramajjhattatā*—see Vism 161; PP 167). The equanimity referred to in the formula is a mode of specific neutrality which belongs to the aggregate of mental formations (*saṅkhārakkhandha*) and thus should not be confused with equanimity as neutral feeling. Though the two are often associated, each can exist independently of the other, and in the third *jhāna* equanimity as specific neutrality co-exists with happiness or pleasant feeling.

The meditator in third *jhāna* is also said to be mindful and discerning, which points to another pair of frequently conjoined mental functions. Mindfulness (*sati*), in this context, means the remembrance of the meditation object, the constant bearing of the object in mind without allowing it to float away. Discernment (*sampajañña*) is an aspect of wisdom or understanding which scrutinises the object and grasps its nature free from delusion.

Though these two factors were already present even in the first two *jhānas*, they are first mentioned only in connection with the third since it is here that their efficacy becomes manifest. The two are needed particularly to avoid a return to rapture. Just as a suckling calf, removed from its mother and left unguarded, again approaches the mother, so the happiness of *jhāna* tends to veer towards rapture, its natural partner, if unguarded by mindfulness and discernment (Dhs A.219). To prevent this and the consequent loss of the third *jhāna* is the task of mindfulness and discernment.

The attainment of the *fourth jhāna* commences with the aforesaid procedure. In this case the meditator sees that the third *jhāna* is threatened by the proximity of rapture, which is ever ready to swell up again due to its natural affinity with happiness; he also sees that it is inherently defective due to the presence of happiness, a gross factor which provides fuel for clinging. He then contemplates the state where equanimous feeling and one-pointedness subsist together—the fourth *jhāna*—as far more peaceful and secure than anything he has so far experienced, and therefore as far more desirable. Taking as his object the same counterpart sign he took for the earlier *jhāna*, he strengthens his efforts in concentration for the purpose of abandoning the gross factor of happiness and entering the higher *jhāna*. When his practice matures the mind enters absorption into the fourth *jhāna*:

> With the abandoning of pleasure and pain, and with the previous disappearance of joy and grief, he enters and dwells in the fourth *jhāna*, which has neither-pain-nor-pleasure and has purity of mindfulness due to equanimity. (M I 182; Vibh 245)

The first part of this formula specifies the conditions for the attainment of this *jhāna*—also called the neither-painful-nor-pleasant liberation of mind (M I 296)—to be the abandoning of four kinds of feeling incompatible with it, the first two signifying bodily feelings, the latter two the corresponding mental feelings. The formula also introduces several new terms and phrases which have not been encountered previously. First, it mentions a new feeling, neither-pain-nor-pleasure (*adukkhamasukha*), which remains after the other four feelings have subsided. This kind of feeling, also called equanimous or neutral feeling, replaces happiness as the concomitant feeling of the *jhāna* and also figures as one of the *jhāna* factors. Thus this attainment has two *jhāna* factors: neutral feeling and one-pointedness of mind. Previously the ascent from one *jhāna* to the next was marked by the progressive elimination of the coarser *jhāna* factors, but none were added to replace those which were excluded. But now, in the move from the third to the fourth *jhāna*, a substitution occurs, neutral feeling moving in to take the place of happiness.

In addition we also find a new phrase composed of familiar terms, "purity of mindfulness due to equanimity" (*upekkhāsatipārisuddhi*). The *Vibhaṅga* explains: "This mindfulness is cleared, purified, clarified by equanimity" (Vibh 261), and Buddhaghosa adds: "for the mindfulness in this *jhāna* is quite purified, and its purification is effected by equanimity, not by anything else" (Vism 167; PP 174). The equanimity which purifies the mindfulness is not neutral feeling, as might be supposed, but specific neutrality, the sublime impartiality free from attachment and aversion, which also pertains to this *jhāna*. Though both specific neutrality and mindfulness were present in the lower three *jhānas*, none among these is said to have "purity of mindfulness due to equanimity." The reason is that in the lower *jhānas* the equanimity present was not purified itself, being overshadowed by opposing states and lacking association with equanimous feeling. It is like a crescent moon which exists by day but cannot be seen because of the sunlight and the bright sky. But in the fourth *jhāna*, where equanimity gains the support of equanimous feeling, it shines forth like the crescent moon at night and purifies mindfulness and the other associated states (Vism 169; PP 175).

The Immaterial Jhānas

Beyond the four *jhānas* lie four higher attainments in the scale of concentration, referred to in the suttas as the "peaceful immaterial liberations transcending material form" (*santā vimokkhā atikamma rūpe āruppā*, M I 33). In the commentaries they are also called the immaterial *jhānas*, and while this expression is not found in the suttas it seems appropriate in so far as these states correspond to jhānic levels of consciousness and continue the same process of mental unification initiated by the original four *jhānas*, now sometimes called the fine-material *jhānas*. The immaterial *jhānas* are designated, not by numerical names like their predecessors, but by the names of their objective spheres: the base of boundless space, the base of boundless consciousness, the base of nothingness, and the base of neither-perception-nor-non-perception.[18] They receive the designation "immaterial" or "formless" (*arūpa*) because they are achieved by surmounting all perceptions of material form, including the subtle form of the counterpart sign which served as the object of the previous *jhānas*, and because they are the subjective correlates of the immaterial planes of existence.

Like the fine-material *jhānas* they follow a fixed sequence and must be attained in the order in which they are presented. That is, the meditator who wishes to achieve the immaterial *jhānas* must begin with the base of boundless space and then proceed step by step up to the base of neither-perception-nor-non-perception. However, an important difference separates the modes of progress in the two cases. In the case of the fine-material *jhānas*, the ascent from one *jhāna* to another involves a surmounting of *jhāna* factors. To rise from the first *jhāna* to the second the meditator must eliminate applied thought and sustained thought, to rise from the second to the third he must overcome rapture, and to rise from the third to the fourth he must replace pleasant with neutral feeling. Thus progress involves a reduction and refinement of the *jhāna* factors, from the initial five to the culmination in one-pointedness and neutral feeling.

Once the fourth *jhāna* is reached the *jhāna* factors remain constant, and in higher ascent to the immaterial attainments there is no further elimination of *jhāna* factors. For this reason the formless *jhānas*, when classified from the perspective of their factorial constitution as is done in the Abhidhamma, are considered modes of the fourth *jhāna*. They are all two-factored *jhānas*, constituted by one-pointedness and equanimous feeling.

Rather than being determined by a surmounting of factors, the order of the immaterial *jhānas* is determined by a surmounting of objects. Whereas for the lower *jhānas* the object can remain constant but the factors must be changed, for the immaterial *jhānas* the factors remain constant while the objects change. The

---

18. *Ākāsānañcāyatana, viññāṇañcāyatana, ākiñcaññāyatana, nevasaññā-nāsaññāyatana.*

base of boundless space eliminates the *kasiṇa* object of the fourth *jhāna*, the base of boundless consciousness surmounts the object of the base of boundless space, the base of nothingness surmounts the object of base of boundless consciousness, and the base of neither-perception-nor-non-perception surmounts the object of the base of nothingness.

Because the objects become progressively more subtle at each level, the *jhāna* factors of equanimous feeling and one-pointedness, while remaining constant in nature throughout, become correspondingly more refined in quality. Buddhaghosa illustrates this with a simile of four pieces of cloth of the same measurements, spun by the same person, yet made of thick, thin, thinner and very thin thread respectively (Vism 339; PP 369). Also, whereas the four lower *jhānas* can each take a variety of objects—the ten *kasiṇas*, the in-and-out breath, etc.—and do not stand in any integral relation to these objects, the four immaterial *jhānas* each take a single object inseparably related to the attainment itself. The first is attained solely with the base of boundless space as object, the second with the base of boundless consciousness, and so forth.

The motivation which initially leads a meditator to seek the immaterial attainments is a clear recognition of the dangers inherent in material existence: it is in virtue of matter that injuries and death by weapons and knives occur, that one is afflicted with diseases, subject of hunger and thirst, while none of this takes place on the immaterial planes of existence (M I 410). Wishing to escape these dangers by taking rebirth in the immaterial planes, the meditator must first attain the four fine-material *jhānas* and master the fourth *jhāna* with any *kasiṇa* as object except the omitted space *kasiṇa*. By this much the meditator has risen above gross matter, but he still has not transcended the subtle material form comprised by the luminous counterpart sign which is the object of his *jhāna*. To reach the formless attainments the meditator, after emerging from the fourth *jhāna*, must consider that even that *jhāna*, as refined as it is, still has an object consisting in material form and thus is distantly connected with gross matter; moreover, it is close to happiness, a factor of the third *jhāna*, and is far coarser than the immaterial states. The meditator sees the base of boundless space, the first immaterial *jhāna*, as more peaceful and sublime than the fourth fine-material *jhāna* and as more safely removed from materiality.

Following these preparatory reflections, the meditator enters the fourth *jhāna* based on a *kasiṇa* object and extends the counterpart sign of the *kasiṇa* "to the limit of the world-sphere, or as far as he likes." Then, after emerging from the fourth *jhāna*, he must remove the *kasiṇa* by attending exclusively to the space it has been made to cover without attending to the *kasiṇa* itself. Taking as his object the space left after the removal of the *kasiṇa*, the meditator adverts to it as "boundless space" or simply as "space, space," striking at it with applied and sustained thought. As he cultivates this practice over and over, eventually the consciousness pertaining to the base of boundless space arises with boundless space as its object (Vism 327–28; PP 355–56).

A meditator who has gained mastery over the base of boundless space, wishing to attain as well the second immaterial *jhāna*, must reflect upon the two defects of the first attainment which are its proximity to the fine-material *jhānas* and its grossness compared to the base of boundless consciousness. Having in this way developed indifferent to the lower attainment, he must next enter and emerge from the base of boundless space and then fix his attention upon the consciousness that occurred there pervading the boundless space. Since the space taken as the object by the first formless *jhāna* was boundless, the consciousness of that space also involves an aspect of boundlessness, and it is to this boundless consciousness that the aspirant for the next attainment adverts. He is not to attend to it merely as boundless, but as "boundless consciousness" or simply as "consciousness." He continues to cultivate this sign again and again until the consciousness belonging to the base of boundless consciousness arises in absorption taking as its object the boundless consciousness pertaining to the first immaterial state (Vism 331–32; PP 360–61).

To attain the next formless state, the base of nothingness, the meditator who has mastered the base of boundless consciousness must contemplate its defects in the same twofold manner and advert to the superior peacefulness of the base of nothingness. Without giving any more attention to the base of boundless consciousness, he should "give attention to the present non-existence, voidness, secluded aspect of that same past consciousness belonging to the base consisting of boundless space" (Vism 333; PP 362). In other words, the meditator is to focus upon the present absence or non-existence of the consciousness belonging to the base of boundless space, adverting to it over and over thus: "There is not, there is not" or "void, void". When his efforts fructify there arises in absorption a consciousness belonging to the base of nothingness, with the non-existence of the consciousness of boundless space as its object. Whereas the second immaterial state relates to the consciousness of boundless space positively, by focusing upon the content of that consciousness and appropriating its boundlessness, the third immaterial state relates to it negatively, by excluding that consciousness from awareness and making the absence or present non-existence of that consciousness its object.

The fourth and final immaterial *jhāna*, the base of neither-perception-nor-non-perception, is reached through the same preliminary procedure. The meditator can also reflect upon the unsatisfactoriness of perception, thinking: "Perception is a disease, perception is a boil, perception is a dart… this is peaceful, this is sublime, that is to say, neither-perception-nor-non-perception" (M II 231). In this way he ends his attachment to the base of nothingness and strengthens his resolve to attain the next higher stage. He then adverts to the four mental aggregates that constitute the attainment of the base of nothingness—its feeling, perception, mental formations and consciousness—contemplating them as "peaceful, peaceful," reviewing that base and striking at it with applied and sustained thought. As he does so the hindrances are suppressed, the mind passes through access and enters the base of neither-perception-nor-non-perception.

This *jhāna* receives its name because, on the one hand, it lacks gross perception with its function of clearly discerning objects, and thus cannot be said to have perception; on the other, it retains a very subtle perception, and thus cannot be said to be without perception. Because all the mental functions are here reduced to the finest and most subtle level, this *jhāna* is also named the attainment with residual formations. At this level the mind has reached the highest possible development in the direction of pure serenity. It has attained the most intense degree of concentration, becoming so refined that consciousness can no longer be described in terms of existence or non-existence. Yet even this attainment, from the Buddhist point of view, is still a mundane state which must finally give way to insight that alone leads to true liberation.

The Jhānas and Rebirth

Buddhism teaches that all sentient beings in whom ignorance and craving still linger are subject to rebirth following death. Their mode of rebirth is determined by their *kamma*, their volitional action, wholesome *kamma* issuing in a good rebirth and unwholesome *kamma* in a bad rebirth. As a kind of wholesome *kamma* the attainment of *jhāna* can play a key role in the rebirth process, being considered a weighty good *kamma* which takes precedence over other lesser kammas in determining the future rebirth of the person who attains it.

Buddhist cosmology groups the numerous planes of existence into which rebirth takes place into three broad spheres each of which comprises a number of subsidiary planes. The sense-sphere (*kāmadhātu*) is the field of rebirth for evil deeds and for meritorious deeds falling short of the *jhānas*; the fine-material sphere (*rūpadhātu*), the field of rebirth for the fine-material *jhānas*; and the immaterial sphere (*arūpadhātu*), the field of rebirth for the immaterial *jhānas*.

An unwholesome *kamma*, should it become determinative of rebirth, will lead to a new existence in one of the four planes of misery belonging to the sense-sphere: the hells, the animal kingdom, the sphere of afflicted spirits, or the host of titans. A wholesome *kamma* of a subjhānic type produces rebirth in one of the seven happy planes in the sense-sphere, the human world or the six heavenly worlds.

Above the sense-sphere realms are the fine-material realms, into which rebirth is gained only through the attainment of the fine-material *jhānas*. The sixteen realms in this sphere are hierarchically ordered in correlation with the four *jhānas*. Those who have practised the first *jhāna* to a minor degree are reborn in the Realm of the Retinue of Brahma, to a moderate degree in the Realm of the Ministers of Brahma, and to a superior degree in the Realm of the Great Brahma.[19] Similarly, practising the second *jhāna* to a minor degree brings rebirth in the Realm of Minor Lustre, to a moderate degree in the Realm of Infinite Lustre, and to

---

19. *Brahmapārisajja, brahmapurohita, mahābrahmā.*

a superior degree the Realm of Radiant Lustre.[20] Again, practising the third *jhāna* to a minor degree brings rebirth in the Realm of Minor Aura, to a moderate degree in the Realm of Infinite Aura, and to a superior degree in the Realm of Steady Aura.[21]

Corresponding to the fourth *jhāna* there are seven realms: the Realm of Great Reward, the Realm of Non-percipient Beings, and the five Pure Abodes.[22] With this *jhāna* the rebirth pattern deviates from the former one. It seems that all beings who practise the fourth *jhāna* of the mundane level without reaching any supramundane attainment are reborn in the realm of Great Reward. There is no differentiation by way of inferior, moderate or superior grades of development. The Realm of Non-percipient Beings is reached by those who, after attaining the fourth *jhāna*, then use the power of their meditation to take rebirth with only material bodies; they do not acquire consciousness again until they pass away from this realm. The five Pure Abodes are open only to non-returners (*anāgāmis*), noble disciples at the penultimate stage of liberation who have eradicated the fetters binding them to the sense-sphere and thence automatically take rebirth in higher realms, where they attain arahatship and reach final deliverance.

Beyond the fine-material sphere lie the immaterial realms, which are four in number—the base of boundless space, the base of boundless consciousness, the base of nothingness, and the base of neither-perception-nor-non-perception. As should be evident, these are realms of rebirth for those who, without having broken the fetters that bind them to *saṃsāra*, achieve and master one or another of the four immaterial *jhānas*. Those meditators who have mastery over a formless attainment at the time of death take rebirth in the appropriate plane, where they abide until the kammic force of the *jhāna* is exhausted. Then they pass away, to take rebirth in some other realm as determined by their accumulated *kamma*.[23]

---

20. *Paritābha, appamāṇābha, abhassara.*
21. *Parittasubha, appamāṇasubha, subhakiṇhā.*
22. *Vehapphala, asaññasattā, suddhāvāsa.*
23. A good summary of Buddhist cosmology and of the connection between *kamma* and planes of rebirth can be found in Narada, *A Manual of Abhidhamma*, pp. 233–55.

Jhānas and the Supramundane

The Way of Wisdom

The goal of the Buddhist path, complete and permanent liberation from suffering, is to be achieved by practising the full threefold discipline of morality (*sīla*), concentration (*samādhi*), and wisdom (*paññā*). The mundane *jhānas*, comprising the four fine-material *jhānas* and the four immaterial *jhānas*, pertain to the stage of concentration, which they fulfil to an eminent degree. However, taken by themselves, these states do not ensure complete deliverance, for they are incapable of cutting off the roots of suffering. The Buddha teaches that the cause of suffering, the driving power behind the cycle of rebirths, is the defilements with their three unwholesome roots—greed, hatred and delusion. Concentration of the absorption level, no matter to what heights it is pursued, only suppresses the defilements, but cannot destroy their latent seeds. Thence bare mundane *jhāna*, even when sustained, cannot by itself terminate the cycle of rebirths. To the contrary, it may even perpetuate the round. For if any fine-material or immaterial *jhāna* is held to with clinging, it will bring about a rebirth in that particular plane of existence corresponding to its own kammic potency, which can then be followed by rebirth in some lower realm.

What is required to achieve complete deliverance from the cycle of rebirths is the eradication of the defilements. Since the most basic defilement is ignorance (*avijjā*), the key to liberation lies in developing its direct opposite, namely wisdom (*paññā*).

Since wisdom presupposes a certain proficiency in concentration it is inevitable that *jhāna* comes to claim a place in its development. This place, however, is not fixed and invariable, but as we will see allows for differences depending on the individual meditator's disposition.

Fundamental to the discussion in this chapter is a distinction between two terms crucial to Theravada philosophical exposition, "mundane" (*lokiya*) and "supramundane" (*lokuttara*). The term "mundane" applies to all phenomena comprised in the world (*loka*)— to subtle states of consciousness as well as matter, to virtue as well as evil, to meditative attainments as well as sensual engrossments. The term "supramundane," in contrast, applies exclusively to that which transcends the world, that is the nine supramundane states: Nibbāna, the four noble paths (*magga*) leading to Nibbāna, and their corresponding fruits (*phala*) which experience the bliss of Nibbāna.

Wisdom has the specific characteristic of penetrating the true nature of phenomena. It penetrates the particular and general features of things through direct cognition rather than discursive thought. Its function is "to abolish the darkness of delusion which conceals the individual essences of states" and its manifestation is "non-delusion." Since the Buddha says that one whose mind is concentrated knows and sees things as they are, the proximate cause of wisdom is concentration (Vism 438; PP 481).

The wisdom instrumental in attaining liberation is divided into two principal types: insight knowledge (*vipassanāñāṇa*) and the knowledge pertaining to the supramundane paths (*maggañāṇa*). The first is the direct penetration of the three characteristics of conditioned phenomena—impermanence, suffering and non-self.[24] It takes as its objective sphere the five aggregates (*pañcakkhandha*)—material form, feeling perception, mental formations and consciousness. Because insight knowledge takes the world of conditioned formations as its object, it is regarded as a mundane form of wisdom. Insight knowledge does not itself directly eradicate the defilements, but serves to prepare the way for the second type of wisdom, the wisdom of the supramundane paths, which emerges when insight has been brought to its climax. The wisdom of the path, occurring in four distinct stages (to be discussed below), simultaneously realises Nibbāna, fathoms the Four Noble Truths, and cuts off the defilements. This wisdom is called "supramundane" because it rises up from the world of the five aggregates to realise the state transcendent to the world, Nibbāna.

The Buddhist disciple, striving for deliverance, begins the development of wisdom by first securely establishing its roots—purified moral discipline and concentration. He then learns and masters the basic material upon which wisdom is to work—the aggregates, elements, sense bases, dependent arising, the Four Noble Truths, etc. He commences the actual practice of wisdom

---

24. *Anicca, dukkha, anattā.*

by cultivating insight into the impermanence, suffering and non-self aspect of the five aggregates. When this insight reaches its apex it issues in supramundane wisdom, the right view factor of the Noble Eightfold Path, which turns from conditioned formations to the unconditioned Nibbāna and thereby eradicates the defilements.

The Two Vehicles

The Theravada tradition recognises two alternative approaches to the development of wisdom, between which practitioners are free to choose according to their aptitude and propensity. These two approaches are the vehicle of serenity (*samathayāna*) and the vehicle of insight (*vipassanāyāna*). The meditators who follow them are called, respectively, the *samathayānika*, "one who makes serenity his vehicle," and the *vipassanāyānika*, "one who makes insight his vehicle." Since both vehicles, despite their names, are approaches to developing insight, to prevent misunderstanding the latter type of meditator is sometimes called a *suddhavipassanāyānika*, "one who makes bare insight his vehicle," or a *sukkhavipassaka*, "a dry-insight worker." Though all three terms appear initially in the commentaries rather than in the suttas, the recognition of the two vehicles seems implicit in a number of canonical passages.

The *samathayānika* is a meditator who first attains access concentration or one of the eight mundane *jhānas*, then emerges and uses his attainment as a basis for cultivating insight until he arrives at the supramundane path. In contrast, the *vipassanāyānika* does not attain mundane *jhāna* prior to practising insight contemplation, or if he does, does not use it as an instrument for cultivating insight. Instead, without entering and emerging from *jhāna*, he proceeds directly to insight contemplation on mental and material phenomena and by means of this bare insight he reaches the noble path. For both kinds of meditator the experience of the path in any of its four stages always occurs at a level of jhānic intensity and thus necessarily includes supramundane *jhāna* under the heading of right concentration (*samma samādhi*), the eighth factor of the Noble Eightfold Path.

The classical source for the distinction between the two vehicles of serenity and insight is the *Visuddhimagga* where it is explained that when a meditator begins the development of wisdom "if firstly, his vehicle is serenity, (he) should emerge from any fine-material or immaterial *jhāna* except the base consisting of neither-perception-nor-non-perception, and he should discern, according to characteristic, function, etc. the *jhāna* factors consisting of applied thought, etc. and the states associated with them" (Vism 557; PP 679–80). Other commentarial passages allow access concentration to suffice for the vehicle of serenity, but the last immaterial *jhāna* is excluded because its factors are too subtle to be discerned. The meditator whose vehicle is pure insight, on the other hand, is advised to start directly by discerning material and mental phenomena, beginning with the four elements, without utilising a *jhāna* for this purpose (Vism 558; PP 680). Thus the *samathayānika* first attains access concentration or mundane *jhāna* and then develops insight knowledge, by means of which he reaches the supramundane path containing wisdom under the heading of right view, and supramundane *jhāna* under the heading of right concentration. The *vipassanāyānika*, in contrast, skips over mundane *jhāna* and goes directly into insight contemplation. When he reaches the end of the progression of insight knowledge he arrives at the supramundane path which, as in the previous case, brings together wisdom with supramundane *jhāna*. This *jhāna* counts as his accomplishment of serenity.

For a meditator following the vehicle of serenity the attainment of *jhāna* fulfils two functions: first, it produces a basis of mental purity and inner collectedness needed for undertaking the work of insight contemplation; and second, it serves as an object to be examined with insight in order to discern the three characteristics of impermanence, suffering and non-self. *Jhāna* accomplishes the first function by providing a powerful instrument for overcoming the five hindrances. As we have seen, for wisdom to arise the mind must first be concentrated well, and to be concentrated well it must be freed from the hindrances, a task accomplished pre-eminently by the attainment of *jhāna*. Though access concentration will keep the hindrances at bay, *jhāna* will ensure that they are removed to a much safer distance.

In their capacity for producing concentration the *jhānas* are called the basis (*pada*) for insight, and that particular *jhāna* a meditator enters and emerges from before commencing his practice of insight is designated his *pādakajjhāna*, the basic or foundational *jhāna*. Insight cannot be practised while absorbed in *jhāna*, since insight meditation requires investigation and observation, which are impossible when the mind is immersed in one-pointed absorption. But after emerging from the *jhāna* the mind is cleared of the hindrances, and the stillness and clarity that then result conduce to precise, penetrating insight.

The *jhānas* also enter into the *samathayānika's* practice in second capacity, that is, as objects for scrutinization by insight. The practice of insight consists essentially in the examination of mental and physical phenomena to discover their marks of impermanence, suffering and non-self. The *jhānas* a meditator attains provide him with a readily available and strikingly clear object in which to seek out the three characteristics. After emerging from a *jhāna* the meditator will proceed to examine the jhānic consciousness and to discern the way it exemplifies the three universal marks. This process is called *sammasanañāṇa*, "comprehension knowledge," and the *jhāna* subject to such treatment is termed *sammasitajjhāna*, "the comprehended *jhāna*" (Vism 607–11; PP 706–10). Though the basic *jhāna* and the comprehended *jhāna* will often be the same, the two do not necessarily coincide. A meditator cannot practise comprehension on a *jhāna* higher than he is capable of attaining, but one who uses a higher *jhāna* as his *pādakajjhāna* can still practise insight comprehension on a lower *jhāna* which he has previously attained and mastered. The admitted difference between the *pādakajjhāna* and the *sammasitajjhāna* leads to discrepant theories about the supramundane concentration of the noble path, as we will see.

Whereas the sequence of training undertaken by the *samathayānika* meditator is unproblematic, the *vipassanāyānika* approach presents the difficulty of accounting for the concentration he uses to provide a basis for insight. Concentration is needed in order to see and know things as they are, but without access concentration or *jhāna*, what concentration can he use? The solution to this problem is found in a type of concentration distinct from the access and absorption concentrations pertaining to the vehicle of serenity, called "momentary concentration" (*khaṇika samādhi*). Despite its name, momentary concentration does not signify a single moment of concentration amidst a current of distracted thoughts, but a dynamic concentration which flows from object to object in the ever-changing flux of phenomena, retaining a constant degree of intensity and collectedness sufficient to purify the mind of the hindrances. Momentary concentration arises in the *samathayānika* simultaneously with his post-jhānic attainment of insight, but for the *vipassanāyānika* it develops naturally and spontaneously in the course of his insight practice without his having to fix the mind upon a single exclusive object. Thus the follower of the vehicle of insight does not omit concentration altogether from his training, but develops it in a different manner from the practitioner of serenity. Without gaining *jhāna* he goes directly into contemplation on the five aggregates and by observing them constantly from moment to moment acquires momentary concentration as an accompaniment of his investigations. This momentary concentration fulfils the same function as the basic *jhāna* of the serenity vehicle, providing the foundation of mental clarity needed for insight to emerge.

Supramundane Jhāna

The climax in the development of insight is the attainment of the supramundane paths and fruits. Each path is a momentary peak experience directly apprehending Nibbāna and permanently cutting off certain defilements. These defilements are generally grouped into a set of ten "fetters" (*saṃyojana*) which keep beings chained to the round of rebirths. The first path, called the path of stream-entry (*sotāpatti*) because it marks the entry into the stream of the Dhamma, eradicates the first three fetters—the false view of self, doubt, and clinging to rites and rituals. The disciple who has reached stream-entry has limited his future births to a maximum of seven in the happy realms of the human and heavenly worlds, after which he will attain final deliverance. But an ardent disciple may progress to still higher stages in the same life in which he reaches stream-entry, by making an aspiration for the next higher path and again undertaking the development of insight with the aim of reaching that path.

The next supramundane path is that of the once-returner (*sakadāgāmi*). This path does not eradicate any fetters completely, but it greatly attenuates sensual desire and ill will. The once-returner is so called because he is bound to make an end of suffering after returning to this world only one more time. The third path, that of the non-returner (*anāgāmī*) utterly destroys the sensual desire and ill will weakened by the preceding path. The non-returner is assured that he will never again take rebirth in the sense-sphere; if he does not penetrate higher he will be reborn spontaneously in the Pure Abodes and there reach final Nibbāna. The highest path, the path of arahatship, eradicates the remaining five fetters— desire for existence in the fine-material and immaterial spheres, conceit, restlessness and ignorance. The *arahat* has completed the development of the entire path taught by the Buddha; he has reached the end of rebirths and can sound his "lion's roar": "Destroyed is birth, the holy life has been lived, what was to be done has been done, there is nothing further beyond this."

Each path is followed immediately by the supramundane experience of fruition, which results from the path, comes in the same four graded stages, and shares the path's world-transcending character. But whereas the path performs the active function of cutting off defilements, fruition simply enjoys the bliss and peace that result when the path has completed its task. Also, where the path is limited to a single moment of consciousness, the fruition that follows immediately on the path endures for two or three moments. And while each of the four paths occurs only once and can never be repeated, fruition remains accessible to the noble disciple at the appropriate level. He can resort to it as a special meditative state called fruition attainment (*phalasamāpatti*) for the purpose of experiencing nibbānic bliss here and now (Vism 699–702; PP 819–24).

The supramundane paths and fruits always arise as states of jhānic consciousness. They occur as states of *jhāna* because they contain within themselves the *jhāna* factors elevated to an intensity corresponding to that of the *jhāna* factors in the mundane *jhānas*. Since they possess the *jhāna* factors these states are able to fix upon their object with the force of full absorption. Thence, taking the absorptive force of the *jhāna* factors as the criterion, the paths and fruits may be reckoned as belonging to either the first, second, third or fourth *jhāna* of the fourfold scheme, or to the first, second, third, fourth or fifth *jhāna* of the fivefold scheme.

The basis for the recognition of a supramundane type of *jhāna* goes back to the suttas, especially to the section of "The Great Discourse on the Foundations of Mindfulness" where the Buddha defines right concentration of the Noble Eightfold Path by the standard formula for the four *jhānas* (D II 313). However, it is in the Abhidhamma that the connection between the *jhānas*, paths and fruits comes to be worked out with great intricacy of detail. The *Dhammasaṅgaṇī*, in its section on states of consciousness, expounds each of the path and fruition states of consciousness as occasions, first, of one or another of the four *jhānas* in the fourfold scheme, and then again as occasions of one or another of the five *jhānas* in the fivefold scheme (Dhs 74–86). Standard Abhidhammic exposition, as formalised in the synoptical manuals of Abhidhamma, employs the fivefold scheme and brings each of the paths and fruits into connection with each of the five *jhānas*. In this way the eight types of supramundane consciousness— the path and fruition consciousness of stream-entry, the once-returner, the non-returner and arahatship—proliferate to forty types of supramundane consciousness, since any path or fruit can occur at the level of any of the five *jhānas*. It should be noted, however, that there are no paths and fruits conjoined with the immaterial attainments, the reason being that supramundane *jhāna* is presented solely from the standpoint of its factorial constitution, which for the immaterial attainment and the fifth *jhāna* is identical—equanimity and one-pointedness.

The fullest treatment of the supramundane *jhānas* in the authoritative Pali literature can be found in the *Dhammasaṅgaṇī* read in conjunction with its commentary, the *Atthasālinī*. The *Dhammasaṅgaṇī* opens its analysis of the first wholesome supramundane consciousness with the words:

> On the occasion when one develops supramundane *jhāna* which is emancipating, leading to the demolition (of existence), for the abandonment of views, for reaching the first plane, secluded from sense pleasures... one enters and dwells in the first *jhāna*. (Dhs 72)

The *Atthasālinī* explains the word *lokuttara*, which we have been translating "supramundane," as meaning "it crosses over the world, it transcends the world, it stands having surmounted and overcome the world." It glosses the phrase "one develops *jhāna*" thus: "One develops, produces, cultivates absorption *jhāna* lasting for a single thought-moment." This gloss shows us two things about the consciousness of the path: that it occurs as a *jhāna* at the level of full absorption and that this absorption of the path lasts for only a single thought-moment. The word "emancipating" (*niyyānika*) is explained to mean that this *jhāna* "goes out" from the world, from the round of existence, the phrase "leading to demolition" (*apacayagāmī*) that it demolishes and dismantles the process of rebirth (Dhs-a 259).

This last phrase points to a striking difference between mundane and supramundane *jhāna*. The *Dhammasaṅgaṇī*'s exposition of the former begins: "On the occasion when one develops *the path for rebirth in the fine-material sphere* ... one enters and dwells in the first *jhāna*" (my italics). Thus, with this statement, mundane *jhāna* is shown to sustain the round of rebirths; it is a wholesome *kamma* leading to renewed existence. But the supramundane *jhāna* of the path does not promote the continuation of the round. To the contrary, it brings about the round's dismantling and demolition, as the *Atthasālinī* shows with an illustrative simile:

The wholesome states of the three planes are said to lead to accumulation because they build up and increase death and rebirth in the round. But not this. Just as when one man has built up a wall eighteen feet high another might take a club and go along demolishing it, so this goes along demolishing and dismantling the deaths and rebirths built up by the wholesome kammas of the three planes by bringing about a deficiency in their conditions. Thus it leads to demolition.[25]

Supramundane *jhāna* is said to be cultivated "for the abandoning of views." This phrase points to the function of the first path, which is to eradicate the fetters. The supramundane *jhāna* of the first path cuts off the fetter of personality view and all speculative views derived from it. The *Atthasālinī* points out that here we should understand that it abandons not only wrong views but other unwholesome states as well, namely, doubt, clinging to rites and rituals, and greed, hatred and delusion strong enough to lead to the plane of misery. The commentary explicates "for reaching the first plane" as meaning for attaining the fruit of stream-entry.

Besides these, several other differences between mundane and supramundane *jhāna* may be briefly noted. First, with regard to

---

25. Dhs-a 259. See *Expositor*, II 289–90.

their object, the mundane *jhānas* have as object a conceptual entity such as the counterpart sign of the *kasiṇas* or, in the case of the divine abodes, sentient beings. In contrast, for the supramundane *jhāna* of the paths and fruits the object is exclusively Nibbāna. With regard to their predominant tone, in mundane *jhāna* the element of serenity prevails, while the supramundane *jhāna* of the paths and fruits brings serenity and insight into balance. Wisdom is present as right view and serenity as right concentration, both function together in perfect harmony, neither one exceeding the other.

This difference in prevailing tone leads into a difference in function or activity between the two kinds of *jhāna*. Both the mundane and supramundane are *jhānas* in the sense of closely attending (*upanijjhāna*), but in the case of mundane *jhāna* this close attention issues merely in absorption into the object, an absorption that can only suppress the defilement temporarily. In the supramundane *jhāna*, particularly of the four paths, the coupling of close attention with wisdom brings the exercise of four functions at a single moment. These four functions each apply to one of the Four Noble Truths. The path penetrates the First Noble Truth by fully understanding suffering; it penetrates the Second Noble Truth by abandoning craving, the origin of suffering; it penetrates the Third Noble Truth by realising Nibbāna, the cessation of suffering; and it penetrates the fourth Noble Truth by developing the Noble Eightfold Path that leads to the end of suffering. Buddhaghosa illustrates this with the simile of a lamp, which also performs four tasks simultaneously: it burns the wick, dispels darkness, makes light appear, and consumes oil (Vism 690; PP 808).

The Jhānic Level of the Path and Fruit

When the paths and fruits are assigned to the level of the four or five *jhānas*, the question arises as to what factor determines their particular level of jhānic intensity. In other words, why do the path and fruit arise for one meditator at the level of the first *jhāna*, for another at the level of the second *jhāna*, and so forth? The commentaries present three theories concerning the determination of the jhānic level of the path, apparently deriving from the lineages of ancient teachers (Vism 666–67; PP 778–80. Dhs-a 271–

74). The first holds that it is the basic *jhāna*, i.e., the *jhāna* used as a basis for the insight leading to emergence in immediate proximity to the path, that governs the difference in the jhānic level of the path. A second theory says that the difference is governed by the aggregates made the objects of insight on the occasion of insight leading to emergence. A third theory holds that it is the personal inclination of the meditator that governs the difference.

According to the first theory the path arisen in a dry-insight meditator who lacks *jhāna*, and the path arisen in one who possesses a *jhāna* attainment but does not use it as a basis for insight, and the path arisen by comprehending formations after emerging from the first *jhāna*, are all paths of the first *jhāna* only. When the path is produced after emerging from the second, third, fourth and fifth *jhānas* (of the fivefold system) and using these as the basis for insight, then the path pertains to the level of the *jhāna* used as a basis—the second, third, fourth or fifth. For a meditator using an immaterial *jhāna* as basis the path will be a fifth *jhāna* path. Thus in this first theory, when formations are comprehended by insight after emerging from a basic *jhāna*, then it is the *jhāna* attainment emerged from at the point nearest to the path, i.e., just before insight leading to emergence is reached, that makes the path similar in nature to itself.

According to the second theory the path that arises is similar in nature to the states which are being comprehended with insight at the time insight leading to emergence occurs. Thus if the meditator, after emerging from a meditative attainment, is comprehending with insight sense-sphere phenomena or the constituents of the first *jhāna*, then the path produced will occur at the level of the first *jhāna*. On this theory, then, it is the comprehended *jhāna* (*sammasitajjhāna*) that determines the jhānic quality of the path. The one qualification that must be added is that a meditator cannot contemplate with insight a *jhāna* higher than he is capable of attaining.

According to the third theory, the path occurs at the level of whichever *jhāna* the meditator wishes—either at the level of the *jhāna* he has used as the basis for insight or at the level of the *jhāna* he has made the object of insight comprehension. In other words, the jhānic quality of the path accords with his personal inclination. However, mere wish alone is not sufficient. For the path to occur at the jhānic level wished for, the mundane *jhāna* must have been either made the basis for insight or used as the object of insight comprehension.

The difference between the three theories can be understood through a simple example.[26] If a meditator reaches the supramundane path by contemplating with insight the first *jhāna* after emerging from the fifth *jhāna*, then according to the first theory his path will belong to the fifth *jhāna*, while according to the second theory it will belong to the first *jhāna*. Thus these two theories are incompatible when a difference obtains between basic *jhāna* and comprehended *jhāna*. But according to the third theory, the path becomes of whichever *jhāna* the meditator wishes, either the first or the fifth. Thus this doctrine does not necessarily clash with the other two.

Buddhaghosa himself does not make a decision among these three theories. He only points out that in all three doctrines, beneath their disagreements, there is the recognition that the insight immediately preceding the supramundane path determines the jhānic character of the path. For this insight is the proximate and the principal cause for the arising of the path, so whether it be the insight leading to emergence near the basic *jhāna* or that occurring through the contemplated *jhāna* or that fixed by the meditator's wish, it is in all cases this final phase of insight that gives definition to the supramundane path. Since the fruition that occurs immediately after the path has an identical constitution to the path, its own supramundane *jhāna* is determined by the path. Thus a first *jhāna* path produces a first *jhāna* fruit, and so forth for the remaining *jhānas*.

---

26. Dhs-a 274. *See Exposi*tor, II 310.

Jhāna and the Noble Disciples

All noble persons, as we saw, acquire supramundane *jhāna* along with their attainment of the noble paths and fruits. The noble ones at each of the four stages of liberation, moreover, have access to the supramundane *jhāna* of their respective fruition attainments, from the fruition attainment of stream-entry up to the fruition attainments of arahatship. It remains problematic, however to what extent they also enjoy the possession of mundane *jhāna*. To determine an answer to this question we will consult an early typology of seven types of noble disciples, which provides a more psychologically oriented way of classifying the eight noble individuals. A look at the explanation of these seven types will enable us to see the range of jhānic attainment reached by the noble disciples. On this basis we will proceed to assess the place of mundane *jhāna* in the early Buddhist picture of the *arahat*, the perfected individual.

Seven Types of Disciples

The sevenfold typology is originally found in the Kīṭāgiri Sutta of the Majjhima Nikāya (M I 477–79) and is reformulated in the Puggalapaññatti of the Abhidhamma Piṭaka. This typology classifies the noble persons on the paths and fruits into seven types: the faith-devotee (*saddhānusārī*), the one liberated by faith (*saddhāvimutta*), the body-witness (*kāyasakkhi*), the one liberated in both ways (*ubhatobhāgavimutta*), the truth-devotee (*dhammānusārī*), the one attained to understanding (*diṭṭhipatta*), and the one liberated by wisdom (*paññāvimutta*). The seven types may be divided into three general groups, each defined by the predominance of a particular spiritual faculty. The first two types are governed by a predominance of faith, the middle two by a predominance of concentration, and the last three by a predominance of wisdom. To this division, however, certain qualifications will have to made as we go along.

(1) The *faith-devotee* is explained the sutta thus:

> Herein, monks, some person has not reached with his own (mental) body those peaceful immaterial deliverances transcending material form: nor after seeing with wisdom,

have his cankers been destroyed.[27] But he has a certain degree of faith in the Tathāgata, a certain degree of devotion to him, and he has these qualities—the faculties of faith, energy, mindfulness, concentration and wisdom. This person, monks, is called a faith-devotee (M I 479).

The Puggalapaññatti (p. 182) defines the faith-devotee from a different angle as a disciple practising for the fruit of stream-entry in whom the faculty of faith is predominant and who develops the noble path led by faith. It adds that when he is established in the fruit he becomes one liberated by faith. Although the sutta excluded the "peaceful immaterial attainments," i.e., the four immaterial *jhānas*, from the faith-devotee's equipment, this implies nothing with regard to his achievement of the four lower mundane *jhānas*. It would seem that the faith-devotee can have previously attained any of the four fine-material *jhānas* before reaching the path, and can also be a dry-insight worker bereft of mundane *jhāna*.

(2) The one *liberated by faith* is strictly and literally defined as a noble disciple at the six intermediate levels, from the fruit of stream-entry through to the path of arahatship, who lacks the immaterial *jhānas* and has a predominance of the faith faculty.

The Buddha explains the one liberated by faith as follows:

> Herein, monks, some person has not reached with his own (mental) body those peaceful immaterial deliverances transcending material form; but having seen with wisdom, some of his cankers have been destroyed, and his faith in the Tathāgata is settled, deeply rooted, well established. This person, monks, is called one liberated by faith (M I 478).

As in the case of the faith-devotee, the one liberated by faith, while lacking the immaterial *jhānas*, may still be an obtainer of the four mundane *jhānas* as well as a dry insight worker.

The Puggalapaññatti states (pp. 184–85) that the person liberated by faith is one who understands the Four Noble Truths, has seen and verified by means of wisdom the teachings proclaimed by the Tathāgata, and having seen with wisdom has eliminated

---

27. The cankers (*āsava*) are four powerful defilements that sustain saṃsāra: sensual desire, desire for existence, wrong views and ignorance.

some of his cankers. However, he has not done so as easily as the *diṭṭhipatta*, the person attained to understanding, whose progress is easier due to his superior wisdom. The fact that the one liberated by faith has destroyed only some of this cankers implies that he has advanced beyond the first path but not yet reached the final fruit, the fruit of arahatship.[28]

(3) The *body-witness* is a noble disciple at the six intermediate levels, from the fruit of stream-entry to the path of arahatship, who has a predominance of the faculty of concentration and can obtain the immaterial *jhānas*. The sutta explanation reads:

> And what person, monks is a body-witness? Herein, monks, some person has reached with his own (mental) body those peaceful immaterial deliverances transcending material form, and having seen with wisdom, some of his cankers having been destroyed. This person, monks, is called a body-witness (M I 478).

The Puggalapaññatti (p. 184) offers a slight variation in this phrasing, substituting "the eight deliverances" (*aṭṭhavimokkha*) for the sutta's "peaceful immaterial deliverances" (*santa vimokkha āruppa*). These eight deliverances consist of three meditative attainments pertaining to the fine-material sphere (inclusive of all four lower *jhānas*), the four immaterial *jhānas*, and the cessation of perception and feeling (*saññāvedayitanirodha*)—the last a special attainment accessible only to those nonreturners and arahats who have also mastered the eight *jhānas*.[29] The statement of the Puggalapaññatti does not mean either that the achievement of all

---

28. The *Visuddhimagga*, however, says that arahats in whom faith is predominant can also be called "liberated by faith" (Vism 659; PP 770). Its commentary points out that this statement is intended only figuratively, in the sense that those arahats reach their goal after having been liberated by faith in the intermediate stages. Literally, they would be "liberated by wisdom" (Vism-ṭ II 468).

29. The first three emancipations are: one possessing material form sees material forms; one not perceiving material forms internally sees material forms externally; and one is released upon the idea of the beautiful. They are understood to be variations on the jhanas attained with color *kasiṇas*. For the attainment of cessation, see PP 824–833.

eight deliverances is necessary to become a body-witness or that the achievement of the three lower deliverances is sufficient. What is both requisite and sufficient to qualify as a body-witness is the partial destruction of defilements coupled with the attainment of at least the lowest immaterial *jhāna*. Thus the body witness becomes fivefold by way of those who obtain any of the four immaterial *jhānas* and the one who also obtains the cessation of perception and feeling.

(4) One who is *liberated in both ways* is an *arahat* who has completely destroyed the defilements and possesses the immaterial attainments. The commentaries explain the name "liberated in both ways" as meaning "through the immaterial attainment he is liberated from the material body and through the path (of arahatship) he is liberated from the mental body" (MA.II 131). The sutta defines this type of disciple thus:

> And what person, monks, is liberated in both ways? Herein, monks, someone has reached with his own (mental) body those peaceful immaterial deliverances transcending material form, and having seen with wisdom, his cankers are destroyed. This person, monks, is called liberated in both ways (M I 477).

The Puggalapaññatti (p. 184) gives basically the same formula but replaces "immaterial deliverances" with "the eight deliverances." The same principle of interpretation that applied to the body-witness applies here: the attainment of any immaterial *jhāna*, even the lowest, is sufficient to qualify a person as both-ways liberated. As the commentary to the *Visuddhimagga* says: "One who has attained arahatship after gaining even one (immaterial *jhāna*) is liberated both ways" (Vism-ṭ II 466). This type becomes fivefold by way of those who attain arahatship after emerging from one or another of the four immaterial *jhānas* and the one who attains arahatship after emerging from the attainment of cessation (M-a III 131).

(5) The *truth-devotee* is a disciple on the first path in whom the faculty of wisdom is predominant. The Buddha explains the truth-devotee as follows:

> Herein, monks, some person has not reached with his own (mental) body those peaceful immaterial deliverances transcending material form; nor, after seeing with wisdom,

have his cankers been destroyed. But the teachings proclaimed by the Tathāgata are accepted by him through mere reflection, and he has these qualities—the faculties of faith, energy, mindfulness, concentration and wisdom. This person, monks, is called a truth-devotee. (M I 479)

The Puggalapaññatti (p. 185) defines the truth-devotee as one practising for realisation of the fruit of stream-entry in whom the faculty of wisdom is predominant, and who develops the path led by wisdom. It adds that when a truth-devotee is established in the fruit of stream-entry he becomes one attained to understanding, the sixth type. The sutta and Abhidhamma again differ as to emphasis, the one stressing lack of the immaterial *jhānas*, the other the ariyan stature. Presumably, he may have any of the four fine-material *jhānas* or be a bare-insight practitioner without any mundane *jhāna*.

(6) The *one attained to understanding* is a noble disciple at the six intermediate levels who lacks the immaterial *jhānas* and has a predominance of the wisdom faculty. The Buddha explains:

> And what person, monks, is the one attained to understanding? Herein, monks someone has not reached with his own mental body those peaceful immaterial deliverances transcending material form, but having seen with wisdom some of his cankers are destroyed, and the teachings proclaimed by the Tathāgata have been seen and verified by him with wisdom. This person, monks, is called the one attained to understanding. (M I 478)

The Puggalapaññatti (p.185) defines the one attained to understanding as a person who understands the Four Noble Truths, has seen and verified by means of wisdom the teachings proclaimed by the Tathāgata, and having seen with wisdom has eliminated some of his cankers. He is thus the "wisdom counterpart" of the one liberated by faith, but progresses more easily than the latter by virtue of his sharper wisdom. Like his counterpart, he may possess any of the four mundane *jhānas* or may be a dry-insight worker.

(7) The *one liberated by wisdom* is an *arahat* who does not obtain the immaterial attainments. In the words of the sutta:

> And what person, monks, is the one liberated by wisdom? Herein, monks, someone has not reached with his own

(mental) body those peaceful material deliverances transcending material form, but having seen with wisdom his cankers are destroyed. This person, monks, is called one liberated by wisdom. (M I 477–78)

The Puggalapaññatti's definition (p. 185) merely replaces "immaterial deliverance" with "the eight deliverances." Though such arahats do not reach the immaterial *jhānas* it is quite possible for them to attain the lower *jhānas*. The sutta commentary in fact states that the one liberated by wisdom is fivefold by way of the dry-insight worker and the four who attain arahatship after emerging from the four *jhānas*.

It should be noted that the one liberated by wisdom is contrasted not with the one liberated by faith, but with the one liberated in both ways. The issue that divides the two types of *arahat* is the lack or possession of the four immaterial *jhānas* and the attainment of cessation. The person liberated by faith is found at the six intermediate levels of sanctity, not at the level of arahatship. When he obtains arahatship, lacking the immaterial *jhānas*, he becomes one liberated by wisdom even though faith rather than wisdom is his predominant faculty. Similarly, a meditator with predominance of concentration who possesses the immaterial attainments will still be liberated in both ways even if wisdom rather than concentration claims first place among his spiritual endowments, as was the case with the venerable Sāriputta.

Jhāna and the Arahat

From the standpoint of their spiritual stature the seven types of noble persons can be divided into three categories. The first, which includes the faith-devotee and the truth-devotee, consists of those on the path of stream-entry, the first of the eight noble individuals. The second category, comprising the one liberated by faith, the body-witness and the one attained to understanding, consists of those on the six intermediate levels, from the stream-enterer to one on the path of arahatship. The third category, comprising the one liberated in both ways and the one liberated by wisdom, consists only of arahats.[30]

---

30. It should be noted that the Kīṭāgiri Sutta makes no provision in its

The *ubhatobhāgavimutta*, "one liberated in both ways," and the *paññāvimutta* "one liberated by wisdom," thus form the terms of a twofold typology of arahats distinguished on the basis of their accomplishment in *jhāna*. The *ubhatobhāgavimutta arahat* experiences in his own person the "peaceful deliverances" of the immaterial sphere, the *paññāvimutta arahat* lacks this full experience of the immaterial *jhānas*. Each of these two types, according to the commentaries, again becomes fivefold—the *ubhatobhāgavimutta* by way of those who possess the ascending four immaterial *jhānas* and the attainment of cessation, the *paññāvimutta* by way of those who reach arahatship after emerging from one of the four fine-material *jhānas* and the dry-insight meditator whose insight lacks the support of mundane *jhāna*.

The possibility of attaining the supramundane path without possession of a mundane *jhāna* has been questioned by some Theravada scholars, but the *Visuddhimagga* clearly admits this possibility when it distinguishes between the path arisen in a dry-insight meditator and the path arisen in one who possesses a *jhāna* but does not use it as a basis for insight (Vism 666-67; PP 779). Textual evidence that there can be arahats lacking mundane *jhāna* is provided by the Susīma Sutta (S II 199-23) together with is commentaries. When the monks in the sutta are asked how they can be arahats without possessing supernormal powers of the immaterial attainments, they reply: "We are liberated by wisdom" (*paññāvimuttā kho mayaṃ*). The commentary glosses this reply thus: "We are contemplatives, dry-insight meditators, liberated by wisdom alone" (*Mayaṃ nijjhānaka-sukkhavipassaka-paññāmatten'eva vimuttā ti*, S-a II 117). The commentary also states that the Buddha gave his long disquisition on insight in the sutta "to show the arising of knowledge even without concentration" (*vinā pi samādhiṃ evaṃ ñāṇuppattidassanatthaṃ*, S-a II 117). The subcommentary establishes the point by explaining "even without concentration" to mean "even without concentration previously accomplished reaching the mark of serenity" (*samathalakkhaṇappattaṃ purimasiddhaṃ*

---

typology for a disciple on the first path who gains the immaterial jhanas. Vism-ṭ (II 466) holds that he would have to be considered either a faith-devotee or a truth-devotee, and at the final fruition would be one liberated in both ways.

vinā pi samādhin-ti), adding that this is said in reference to one who makes insight his vehicle (S-ṭ II 125).

In contrast to the *paññāvimutta* arahats, those arahats who are *ubhatobhāgavimutta* enjoy a twofold liberation. Through their mastery over the formless attainments they are liberated from the material body (*rūpakāya*), capable of dwelling in this very life in the meditations corresponding to the immaterial planes of existence; through their attainment of arahatship they are liberated from the mental body (*nāmakāya*), presently free from all defilements and sure of final emancipation from future becoming. *Paññāvimutta* arahats only possess the second of these two liberations.

The double liberation of the *ubhatobhāgavimutta arahat* should not be confused with another double liberation frequently mentioned in the suttas in connection with arahatship. This second pair of liberations, called *cetovimutti paññāvimutti*, "liberation of mind, liberation by wisdom," is shared by all arahats. It appears in the stock passage descriptive of arahatship: "With the destruction of the cankers he here and now enters and dwells in the cankerless liberation of mind, liberation by wisdom, having realised it for himself with direct knowledge." That this twofold liberation belongs to *paññāvimutta* arahats as well as those who are *ubhatobhāgavimutta* is made clear by the Putta Sutta, where the stock passage is used for two types of arahats called the "white lotus recluse" and the "red lotus recluse":

> How, monks, is a person a white lotus recluse (*samaṇapuṇḍarīka*)? Here, monks, with the destruction of the cankers a monk here and now enters and dwells in the cankerless liberation of mind, liberation by wisdom, having realised it for himself with direct knowledge. Yet he does not dwell experiencing the eight deliverances with his body. Thus, monks, a person is a white lotus recluse.
>
> And how, monks, is a person a red lotus recluse (*samaṇapaduma*)? Here, monks, with the destruction of the cankers a monk here and now enters and dwells in the cankerless liberation of mind, liberation by wisdom, having realised it for himself with direct knowledge. And he dwells experiencing the eight deliverances with his body. Thus, monks, a person is a red lotus recluse (A II 87).

Since the description of these two types coincides with that of *paññāvimutta* and *ubhatobhāgavimutta* the two pairs may be identified, the white lotus recluse with the *paññāvimutta*, the red lotus recluse with the *ubhatobhāgavimutta*. Yet the *paññāvimutta arahat*, while lacking the experience of the eight deliverances, still has both liberation of mind and liberation by wisdom.

When liberation of mind and liberation by wisdom are joined together and described as "cankerless" (*anāsava*), they can be taken to indicate two aspects of the *arahat*'s deliverance. Liberation of mind signifies the release of his mind from craving and its associated defilements, liberation by wisdom the release from ignorance: "With the fading away of lust there is liberation of mind, with the fading away of ignorance there is liberation by wisdom" (AN I 61). "As he sees and understands thus his mind is liberated from the canker of sensual desire, from the canker of existence, from the canker of ignorance" (M I 183–84)—here release from the first two cankers can be understood as liberation of mind, release from the canker of ignorance as liberation by wisdom. In the commentaries "liberation of mind" is identified with the concentration factor in the fruition attainment of arahatship, "liberation by wisdom" with the wisdom factor.

Since every *arahat* reaches arahatship through the Noble Eightfold Path, he must have attained supramundane *jhāna* in the form of right concentration, the eighth factor of the path, defined as the four *jhānas*. This *jhāna* remains with him as the concentration of the fruition attainment of arahatship, which occurs at the level of supramundane *jhāna* corresponding to that of his path. Thus he always stands in possession of at least the supramundane *jhāna* of fruition, called the "cankerless liberation of mind." However, this consideration does not reflect back on his mundane attainments, requiring that every *arahat* possess mundane *jhāna*.

Although early Buddhism acknowledges the possibility of a dry-visioned arahatship, the attitude prevails that *jhānas* are still desirable attributes in an *arahat*. They are of value not only prior to final attainment, as a foundation for insight, but retain their value even afterwards. The value of *jhāna* in the stage of arahatship, when all spiritual training has been completed, is twofold. One concerns the *arahat*'s inner experience, the other his outer significance as a representative of the Buddha's dispensation.

On the side of inner experience the *jhānas* are valued as providing the *arahat* with a "blissful dwelling here and now" (*diṭṭhadhammasukhavihāra*). The suttas often show arahats attaining to *jhāna* and the Buddha himself declares the four *jhānas* to be figuratively a kind of Nibbāna in this present life (AN IV 453–54). With respect to levels and factors there is no difference between the mundane *jhānas* of an *arahat* and those of a non-*arahat*. The difference concerns their function. For non-arahats the mundane *jhānas* constitute wholesome *kamma*; they are deeds with a potential to produce results, to precipitate rebirth in a corresponding realm of existence. But in the case of an *arahat* mundane *jhāna* no longer generates *kamma*. Since he has eradicated ignorance and craving, the roots of *kamma*, his actions leave no residue; they have no capacity to generate results. For him the jhānic consciousness is a mere functional consciousness which comes and goes and once gone disappears without a trace.

The value of the *jhānas*, however, extends beyond the confines of the *arahat*'s personal experience to testify to the spiritual efficacy of the Buddha's dispensation. The *jhānas* are regarded as ornamentations of the *arahat*, testimonies to the accomplishment of the spiritually perfect person and the effectiveness of the teaching he follows. A worthy monk is able to "gain at will without trouble or difficulty, the four *jhānas* pertaining to the higher consciousness, blissful dwellings here and now." This ability to gain the *jhānas* at will is a "quality that makes a monk an elder." When accompanied by several other spiritual accomplishments it is an essential quality of "a recluse who graces recluses" and of a monk who can move unobstructed in the four directions. Having ready access to the four *jhānas* makes an elder dear and agreeable, respected and esteemed by his fellow monks. Facility in gaining the *jhānas* is one of the eight qualities of a completely inspiring monk (*samantapāsādika bhikkhu*) perfect in all respects; it is also one of the eleven foundations of faith (*saddhāpāda*). It is significant that in all these lists of qualities the last item is always the attainment of arahatship, "the cankerless liberation of mind, liberation by wisdom," showing that all desirable qualities in a bhikkhu culminate in arahatship.[31]

---

31. The references are to: A II 23; III 131,135,114; IV 314–15; V 337.

The higher the degree of his mastery over the meditative attainments, the higher the esteem in which an *arahat* monk is held and the more praiseworthy his achievement is considered. Thus the Buddha says of the *ubhatobhāgavimutta arahat*: "There is no liberation in both ways higher and more excellent than this liberation in both ways" (D II 71).

The highest respect goes to those monks who possess not only liberation in both ways but the six *abhiññās* or "superknowledges": the exercise of psychic powers, the divine ear, the ability to read the minds of others, the recollection of past lives, knowledge of the death and rebirth of beings, and knowledge of final liberation. The Buddha declares that a monk endowed with the six *abhiññās*, is worthy of gifts and hospitality, worthy of offerings and reverential salutations, a supreme field of merit for the world (A III 280–81). In the period after the Buddha's demise, what qualified a monk to give guidance to others was endowment with ten qualities: moral virtue, learning, contentment, mastery over the four *jhānas*, the five mundane *abhiññās* and attainment of the cankerless liberation of mind, liberation by wisdom (M III 11–12). Perhaps it was because he was extolled by the Buddha for his facility in the meditative attainments and the *abhiññās* that the venerable Mahākassapa assumed the presidency of the first great Buddhist council held in Rājagaha after the Buddha's passing away.

The graduation in the veneration given to arahats on the basis of their mundane spiritual achievements implies something about the value system of early Buddhism that is not often recognised. It suggests that while final liberation may be the ultimate and most important value, it is not the sole value even in the spiritual domain. Alongside it, as embellishments rather than alternatives, stand mastery over the range of the mind and mastery over the sphere of the knowable. The first is accomplished by the attainment of the eight mundane *jhānas*, the second by the attainment of the *abhiññās*. Together, final liberation adorned with this twofold mastery is esteemed as the highest and most desirable way of actualizing the ultimate goal.

Buddhist Stories

From the Dhammapada Commentary
Part IV

Translated from the Pāli by
Eugene Watson Burlingame

Selected and revised by
Bhikkhu Khantipālo

Copyright © Kandy; Buddhist Publication Society, (1988)

Publisher's Note

This anthology has been compiled from Eugene Watson Burlingame's classic translation of the background stories from the Dhammapada Commentary, *Buddhist Legends*. Originally published in the Harvard Oriental Series, *Buddhist Legends* has been maintained in print since 1969 by the Pali Text Society. With the latter's permission, the Buddhist Publication Society issues this selection of these stories in booklet form in the Wheel Series, edited and arranged by Bhikkhu Khantipālo. The publisher gratefully acknowledges the kindness of the Pali Text Society for granting permission to publish this anthology. Readers who would like to obtain the complete three-volume collection of Buddhist Legends may contact the Pali Text Society or inquire from bookshops specialising in Asian literature.

PART I
The Attainments of Monks

43. The Elder Nanda

EVEN AS RAIN PENETRATES A HOUSE BADLY THATCHED ... This instruction was given by the Teacher while he was in residence at Jetavana with reference to the Elder Nanda.[1]

Nanda Becomes a Monk in Spite of Himself

For after the Teacher had set in motion the glorious Wheel of Dhamma, he retired to Rājagaha and took up residence at Veḷuvana. Thereupon his father, the great king Suddhodana, sent ten ambassadors to him, one after the other, each with a retinue of a thousand men, saying to them, "Bring my son here and show him to me before my face." After nine ambassadors had gone there, attained arahantship, and failed to return, the Elder Kāḷudāyī went and attained arahantship. And knowing that it was the proper time for the Teacher to go, he described the beauties of the journey and conducted the Teacher with his retinue of twenty thousand arahants to Kapilapura. And there, in the company of his kinsfolk, the Teacher, taking a shower of rain for his text, related the Vessantara Jātaka (Jāt. No. 547). On the following day he entered the city for alms. By the recitation of the stanza, "Be alert! Do not be negligent!" (Dhp. 168) he established his father in the fruit of stream-entry and by the recitation of the stanza: "Live by good and righteous conduct" (Dhp. 169) he established Mahā Pajāpatī in the fruit of stream-entry and his father in the fruit of the second path. And at the end of the meal, with reference to the praise bestowed on him by the Mother of Rāhula, he related the Canda Kinnara Jātaka (Jāt. No. 485).

On the following day, while the ceremonies of Prince Nanda's sprinkling, housewarming, and marriage were in progress, the Teacher entered the house for alms, placed his bowl in Prince

---

1. This story is an elaboration of Udāna III, 2.

Nanda's hands, and told him the things that bring true blessings. Then rising from his seat, he departed without taking his bowl from the hands of the prince. Out of reverence for the Tathāgata, Prince Nanda did not dare say, "Reverend sir, receive your bowl," but thought within himself, "He will take his bowl at the head of the stairs." But even when the Teacher reached the head of the stairs, he did not take his bowl. Thought Nanda, "He will take his bowl at the foot of the stairs." But the Teacher did not take his bowl even there. Thought Nanda, "He will take his bowl in the palace court." But the Teacher did not take his bowl even there. Prince Nanda desired greatly to return to his bride, and followed the Teacher much against his own will. But so great was his reverence for the Teacher that he did not dare say, "Receive your bowl," but continued to follow the Teacher, thinking to himself, "He will take his bowl here! He will take his bowl there! He will take his bowl there!"

At that moment they brought word to his bride Belle-of-the-Country, Janapada-Kalyāṇī, "My lady, the Exalted One has taken Prince Nanda away with him; it is his purpose to deprive you of him." Thereupon Janapada-Kalyāṇī, with tears streaming down her face and hair half-combed, ran after Prince Nanda as fast as she could and said to him, "Noble sir, please return immediately." Her words caused a quaver in Nanda's heart; but the Teacher, without so much as taking his bowl, led him to the monastery and said to him, "Nanda, would you like to become a monk?" So great was Prince Nanda's reverence for the Buddha that he refrained from saying, "I do not wish to become a monk," and said instead, "Yes, I should like to become a monk." Said the Teacher, "Well then, make a monk of Nanda." Thus it happened that on the third day after the Teacher's arrival at Kapilapura he caused Nanda to be made a monk.

On the seventh day the Mother of Rāhula adorned Prince Rāhula and sent him to the Exalted One, saying, "Dear son, go look upon this monk, possessed of a retinue of twenty thousand monks, possessed of a body of the hue of gold, possessed of the beauty of form of Mahā Brahmā. This monk is your father. To him once belonged great stores of treasure. From the time of his Great Renunciation we have not seen him. Ask him for your inheritance, saying, 'Dear father, I am a royal prince, and so soon as I shall receive the ceremonial sprinkling I shall become a Universal Monarch. I have need of wealth; bestow wealth upon me; for to a son belongs the wealth which formerly belonged to his father.'"

Accordingly Prince Rāhula went to the Exalted One. The moment he saw him he conceived a warm affection for his father, and his heart rejoiced within him. And he said, "Monk, pleasant is your shadow," and said much else befitting his own station. When the Exalted One had finished his meal, he pronounced the words of rejoicing, arose from his seat, and departed. Prince Rāhula followed in the footsteps of the Exalted One, saying, "Monk, give me my inheritance; monk, give me my inheritance." The Exalted One did not repel the prince; even the attendants were unable to prevent the prince from accompanying the Exalted One. In this manner the prince accompanied the Exalted One to the grove. Then the thought occurred to the Exalted One, "The paternal wealth which this youth seeks inevitably brings destruction in its train. Behold, I will bestow upon him the seven-fold noble wealth[2] which I received at the foot of the Bodhi Tree; I will make him master of a wealth which transcends the world."

Therefore the Exalted One addressed the Venerable Sāriputta, "Well then, Sāriputta, make a monk of Prince Rāhula." When, however, Prince Rāhula had gone forth into homelessness, the king, his grandfather, was afflicted with great sorrow. Unable to endure his sorrow, he made known his sorrow to the Exalted One and made the following request to him, "It would be good, reverend sir, that the noble monks do not give novice ordination to any youth without the permission of his mother and father." The Exalted One granted him this request. Again one day, as the Exalted One sat in the royal palace after breakfast, the king, sitting respectfully at one side, said to the Exalted One, "Reverend sir, while you were practising your austerities, a certain deity approached me and said to me, 'Your son is dead.' But I refused to believe him and replied, 'My son will not die until he attains Enlightenment.'" Said the Exalted One, "Now will you believe? In a previous existence also, when a brahmin showed you bones

---

2. These seven are: faith, virtue, shame (of evil-doing), fear (of the consequences), learning, generosity, wisdom.

and said to you, 'Your son is dead,' you refused to believe." And with reference to this incident he related the Mahā Dhammapāla Jātaka (Jāt. No. 447). At the conclusion of the story the king was established in the fruit of the third path.

Nanda and the Celestial Nymphs

When the Exalted One had thus established his father in the three fruits, he returned once more to Rājagaha, accompanied by the Order of Monks. Now he had promised Anāthapiṇḍika to visit Sāvatthī as soon as the great monastery of Jetavana should be completed, and receiving word shortly afterwards that the monastery had been completed, he went to Jetavana and took up his residence there. While the Teacher was thus residing at Jetavana, the Venerable Nanda, becoming discontented, told his troubles to the monks, saying, "Brethren, I am dissatisfied. I am now living the holy life, but I cannot endure to live it any longer. I intend to abandon the training and to return to the lower life, the life of a layman."

The Exalted One, hearing of this incident, sent for the Venerable Nanda and said this to him, "Nanda, is the report true that you spoke as follows to a large company of monks, 'Brethren, I am dissatisfied; I am now living the holy life, but I cannot endure to live it any longer; I intend to abandon the training and to return to the lower life, the life of a layman'?"—"It is quite true, reverend sir."—"But, Nanda, why are you dissatisfied with the holy life? Why cannot you endure to live the holy life any longer? Why do you intend to abandon the higher precepts and to return to the lower life, the life of a layman?"—"Reverend sir, when I left my house, my noble bride Janapada-Kalyāṇī, with hair half-combed, took leave of me, saying, 'Noble sir, please return immediately!' Reverend sir, it is because I keep remembering her that I am dissatisfied with the holy life; that I cannot endure to live the holy life any longer; that I intend to abandon the training and to return to the lower life, the life of a layman."

Then the Exalted One took the Venerable Nanda by the arm, and by supernormal power conducted him to the heaven of the Thirty-three. On the way, the Exalted One pointed out to Nanda, in a certain burnt field, seated on a burnt stump, a greedy monkey which had lost her ears and nose and tail in a fire. When they reached the heaven of the Thirty-three, he pointed out five hundred pink-footed celestial nymphs who came to wait upon Sakka, king of the gods. And when the Exalted One had shown the Venerable Nanda these two sights, he asked him this question: "Nanda, which do you regard as being the more beautiful and fair to look upon and handsome, your noble bride Janapada-Kalyāṇī or these five hundred pink-footed celestial nymphs?"

"Reverend sir," replied Nanda, "as far inferior as this greedy monkey which has lost her ears and nose and tail is to Janapada-Kalyāṇī, so is she to these five hundred pink-footed celestial nymphs. In comparison with these nymphs my noble bride does not count; she does not come within a fraction of them; she does not come within a fraction of a fraction of them; on the contrary, these five hundred pink-footed celestial nymphs are infinitely more beautiful and fair to look upon and handsome."

"Cheer up, Nanda!" replied the Exalted One. "I guarantee that you will win these five hundred pink-footed celestial nymphs." Said Venerable Nanda, "If, reverend sir, the Exalted One guarantees that I shall win these five hundred pink-footed celestial nymphs, in that case, reverend sir, I shall take the greatest pleasure in living the exalted life of a monk." Then the Exalted One, taking Nanda with him, disappeared from the heaven of the Thirty-three and reappeared at Jetavana. Now it was not long before the monks heard the following report: "It appears that it is in the hope of winning celestial nymphs that the Venerable Nanda, half-brother of the Exalted One, son of his mother's sister, is living the holy life; it appears that the Exalted One has guaranteed that he shall win five hundred pink-footed celestial nymphs."

As a result the Venerable Nanda's fellow-monks treated him as a hireling and as one bought with a price. And they addressed him accordingly, saying, "It appears that the Venerable Nanda is a hireling; it appears that the Venerable Nanda is one bought with a price. It appears that it is in the hope of winning celestial nymphs that he is living the religious life; it appears that the Exalted One has guaranteed that he shall win five hundred pink-footed celestial nymphs."

Now although his fellow-monks despised him, were ashamed of him, and tormented him by calling him "hireling" and "bought with a price," the Venerable Nanda, living in solitude, withdrawn from the world, heedful, ardent, and resolute, in no long time, even in this life, arrived at the knowledge, realisation, and attainment of that supreme goal of the religious life for the sake of which good youths retire once and for all from the household life to the homeless life. This did he know: "Birth is at an end, lived is the holy life, done is what should be done; there is no more of this to come." And there was yet another venerable elder numbered among the arahants.

Now a certain deity came by night to the Teacher, illuminating the whole Jetavana; and bowing to the Teacher, he thus addressed him, "Reverend sir, the Venerable Nanda, son of the sister of the mother of the Exalted One, by extinction of the taints, even in this life himself abides in the knowledge, realisation, and attainment of freedom from the taints, emancipation of the heart, emancipation by wisdom." And there arose within the Exalted One also knowledge of the following: "By extinction of the taints, Nanda, even in this life, himself abides in the knowledge, realisation, and attainment of freedom from the taints, emancipation of the heart, emancipation by wisdom."

At the end of the same night the Venerable Nanda also approached the Exalted One, bowed to him, and spoke as follows, "Reverend sir, I release the Exalted One from the promise which he made when he guaranteed that I should win five hundred pink-footed celestial nymphs." The Exalted One replied, "Nanda, I myself grasped your mind with my own mind and saw, 'By extinction of the taints, Nanda, even in this life, himself abides in the knowledge, realisation, and attainment of freedom from the taints, emancipation of the heart, emancipation by wisdom.' Likewise a deity informed me of the fact, saying, 'By extinction of the taints, Nanda, even in this life, himself abides in the knowledge, realisation, and attainment of freedom from the taints, emancipation of the heart, emancipation by wisdom.' When, therefore, Nanda, you ceased to cling to the things of the world, and your heart was released from the taints, at that moment I was released from that promise." Then the Exalted One, knowing the meaning of this matter, three times spoke this solemn utterance:

> "He that has crossed the mud and crushed lust's thorn,
> Attained delusion's end, is unmoved in ease or pain."

Now one day the monks approached the Venerable Nanda and asked him, "Friend Nanda, earlier you said, 'I am dissatisfied.' Do you say the same thing now?"—"Brethren, I am in no way inclined to the life of a layman." When the monks heard his answer, they said "Venerable Nanda says that which is not true, utters falsehood. On former days he used to say, 'I am dissatisfied,' but now he says, 'I am in no way inclined to the life of a layman.'" And at once they went and reported the matter to the Exalted One. The Exalted One replied, "Monks, in former days Nanda's personality was like an ill-thatched house, but now it has come to be like a well-thatched house. From the day he saw the celestial nymphs, he has striven to reach the goal of a monk's practice, and now he has reached it." So saying, he pronounced the following stanzas:

13. Even as rain penetrates
    A house badly thatched,
    So likewise lust penetrates
    An uncultivated mind.

14. As rain does not penetrate
    A house well thatched,
    So lust does not penetrate
    A well-cultivated mind.

44. A Certain Monk

HAVING RENOUNCED ALL FORCE ... This instruction was given by the Teacher while he was in residence at Jetavana with reference to a certain monk.

It appears that this monk, upon receiving a subject of meditation from the Teacher, retired to the forest, applied himself diligently to the practice of meditation, and attained arahantship. Thereupon he said to himself, "I will inform the Teacher of the great blessing which I have received," and set out from the forest.

Now a woman living in a certain village through which he passed had just had a quarrel with her husband, and as soon as her husband was out of the house, said to herself, "I will return to the house of my family." So saying, she set out on the road. As she went along the road, she saw the elder. "I'll keep not far from this elder," she thought, and followed close behind him. The elder never looked at her at all.

When her husband returned home and saw his wife nowhere about the house, he concluded to himself, "She must have gone to the village where her family lives," and followed after her. When he saw her, he thought to himself, "It cannot be that this woman would enter this forest all by herself; in whose company is she going?" All of a sudden he saw the elder. He thought, "This monk must have taken her away with him," and went up to the monk and threatened him. Said the woman, "This good monk never so much as looked at me or spoke to me; do not say anything to him." Her husband replied, "Do you mean to tell me that you took yourself off in this fashion? I will treat him as you alone deserve to be treated." And in a burst of rage, out of hatred for the woman, he beat the elder soundly, and having done so, took the woman with him and returned home.

The elder's whole body was covered with weals. After his return to the monastery the monks who massaged his body noticed the weals and asked him, "What does this mean?" He told them the whole story. Then the monks asked him, "Friend, but when this fellow struck you thus, what did you say? Did you get angry?"

"No, friends, I did not get angry." Thereupon the monks went to the Teacher and reported the matter to him, saying, "Reverend sir, when we asked this monk, 'Did you get angry?' he replied, 'No, friends. I did not get angry.' He does not speak the truth, he utters falsehood." The Teacher listened to what they had to say and then replied, "Monks, those who have rid themselves of the defilements have laid aside force; even for those that strike them, they cherish no anger." So saying, he pronounced the following stanza:

405. Having renounced all force
     Against creatures weak and strong,
     Who causes not to kill nor kills—
     That one I call a brāhmaṇa.

45. The Elder Cūḷa Panthaka

By ENERGY AND HEEDFULNESS.... This instruction was given by the Teacher while he was in residence at Veḷuvana with reference to Cūḷa Panthaka, Little Wayman the Elder.

The Birth of Cūḷa Panthaka

We are told that the daughter of a rich merchant of Rājagaha, upon reaching the age of maturity, was provided by her mother and father with quarters on the topmost floor of a seven-storied palace and guarded with excessive care. But in spite of this, maddened with the madness of youth and lusting for a man, she had intercourse with her own slave. Frightened to think that others also might find out about her misconduct, she said to him, "It is out of the question for us to live here any longer. If my mother and father discover my misconduct, they will tear me limb from limb. Let us go live elsewhere."

So taking a few necessary things they could carry in the hand, they left the house by the principal door. "It matters little," said they, "where we go, so long as we go and live where others will know nothing about us." So saying, the two set out together. They took up their residence in a certain place and lived together, with the result that the young wife conceived a child in her womb. When her unborn child reached maturity, she took counsel with her husband, saying, "If I give birth to my child in a place far removed from my family, it will bring suffering to both of us. There is but one place for us to go, and that is home to my parents." But her husband, fearing that if he himself went there he would be killed, kept postponing the day of their departure, saying, "We will go today; we will go tomorrow."

The wife thought to herself, "This simpleton realises the enormity of his offence and therefore dares not go. After all, a mother and a father are one's best friends. Let this fellow go or not; at any rate I intend to go." So while her husband was out of the house, she put the household utensils away, and informing her next-door neighbours that she was going home to her parents, she started out on the road. When her husband returned to the house and failed to see her, he inquired of the neighbours where she had gone. Hearing that she had gone to her parents, he set out after her as fast as he could and overtook her on the road. And right there she gave birth to her child. "What is it, wife?" asked the husband. "Husband, it is a son."—"What shall we do now?"—"That for which we intended to go home to my parents has happened by the way. Why, therefore, should we go there? Let us return to our own home."

Agreeing that this was the best plan, husband and wife returned to their own home. Since their son had been born by the way, they gave him the name Panthaka, Wayman. In no long time the young wife conceived a second child in her womb. (All is to be related in detail precisely as before.) Since this child also was born by the way, they gave him the name Cūḷa Panthaka, Little Wayman, calling the older son Mahā Panthaka, Big Wayman. Taking their two sons, they returned to their own place of residence.

While they were living there, Mahā Panthaka heard other boys speak of their uncles and grandparents. So one day he asked his mother, "Mother, other boys speak of their grandfather and grandmother. Haven't we any relatives?"—"Yes, my son. You have no relatives living here, but you have a grandfather, a rich merchant, living in Rājagaha, and we have many other relatives living there too."—"Why don't we go there, mother?" The mother evaded telling her son why she did not go there. But the children repeated the question time and again. Finally she said to her husband, "These children weary me excessively. Will my mother and father eat us alive when they see us? Come, why not let the children see the family of their grandparents?"—"I should not dare meet them face to face, but I will escort you there."—"Very well; some means must be found by which the children can see their grandparents."

So mother and father took the children, and arriving at Rājagaha in due course, took up their residence in the hall of a certain woman near the gate of the city. Then the mother of the children sent word to her mother and father that she and her children had arrived. When her parents received this message, they said to each other, "As we have passed through the round of existences, perhaps we have not previously had a son or a daughter; but these two have grievously offended against us, and it is out of the question for them to stand in our sight. Let these two take as much money as they need and go and live in some pleasant place. However, let them send the children here." So the two took the money which was sent to them, and giving their children into the hands of the messengers who came, sent them to their grandparents. Thus it happened that the children were brought up in the home of their grandparents.

Of the two children, Cūḷa Panthaka was still very young. Mahā Panthaka, however, used to accompany his grandfather to hear the Buddha teach the Dhamma. And as the result of his frequent visits to the Teacher, his heart inclined to going forth. Accordingly he said to his grandfather, "If you would give me your permission, I should like to go forth as a monk."

"What did you say, dear grandson? There is no one in the whole world whose going forth would give me so much pleasure as your own. If you are able to do so, by all means go forth."

Cūḷa Panthaka as a Monk

Accordingly the grandfather took Mahā Panthaka to the Teacher, who said, "Householder, you have got a boy?"

"Yes, reverend sir, this is a grandson of mine who desires to become a monk under you." The Teacher asked a certain monk to ordain the boy as a novice. The elder assigned to him as a subject of meditation the first five of the constituent parts of the body, and then ordained him. The youth learnt by heart a considerable portion of the Word of the Buddha, kept residence during the season of the rains, obtained acceptance as a monk, and by diligently applying himself to meditation attained arahantship.

As Mahā Panthaka passed his time in the bliss of deep meditation, in the bliss of the fruit of the path, he thought to himself, "Assuredly it is in the power of Cūḷa Panthaka to experience this same bliss." Therefore he went to the treasurer, his grandfather, and said to him, "Great treasurer, if you will give your kind permission, I should like to let Cūḷa Panthaka go forth as a monk."

"By all means let him go forth, reverend sir." We are told that the treasurer was profoundly attached to the dispensation of the Buddha, and that when asked, "Of which daughter of yours are these two children the sons?" he felt ashamed to say, "Of my daughter who ran away," and that for these two reasons he was only too glad to give them permission to go forth as monks.

So the Elder Mahā Panthaka let his brother Cūḷa Panthaka go forth and established him in the precepts. But Cūḷa Panthaka, when he had gone forth, proved a dullard. Indeed in four months he was unable to learn by heart this single stanza:

> Even as the red lotus sweetly scented
> Appears in the morn full blown, replete with scent,
> Behold the Buddha, Angīrasa, resplendent
> Blazing like the sun in the sky.

It seems that in the dispensation of the Buddha Kassapa he had possessed great wisdom, but that, after entering the religious life, he ridiculed and made fun of a certain monk who was a dullard while the latter was trying to learn the Sacred Word; and that this monk, embarrassed by the ridicule to which he was subjected, was unable either to learn the passage by heart or even to repeat it. As the result of that act, Cūḷa Panthaka was reborn as a dullard, and every sentence he learned put the preceding sentence out of his mind; indeed four months passed while he was striving to learn this one stanza.

Thereupon Mahā Panthaka said to his brother, "Cūḷa Panthaka, it is not in your power to master this religion. In four months you have not been able to learn a single stanza. How can you ever hope to reach the goal of the religious life? Leave the monastery at once." So saying he expelled him. But Cūḷa Panthaka was sincerely attached to the dispensation of the Buddha, and the last thing in the world he wished to do was to leave the Order and return to the life of a householder.

Now at that time Jīvaka Komārabhacca, taking an abundant supply of garlands and of various kinds of perfumes, went to his own mango grove, rendered honour to the Teacher, listened to the Dhamma, and then rising from his seat and paying obeisance to the Teacher, approached Mahā Panthaka, who was steward of the Order, and asked him, "Reverend sir, how many monks are living with the Teacher?"—"Five hundred."—"Tomorrow, reverend sir, bring the five hundred monks presided over by the Buddha and take a meal in our house."—"Lay disciple, the bhikkhu Cūḷa Panthaka is a dullard and has made no progress in the Dhamma. I accept the invitation for all except him."

When Cūḷa Panthaka heard that, he thought to himself, "The elder accepts an invitation for all these monks, but in accepting it, deliberately leaves me out. Beyond a doubt my brother's affection for me is gone. Of what profit to me any longer is this religion? I will return to the life of a householder and spend my days giving alms and doing other works of merit." So on the following day, very early in the morning, he set out with the intention of returning to the life of a householder. Very early in the morning also the Teacher surveyed the world, and seeing this incident, preceded Cūḷa Panthaka to the gate and walked back and forth on the same road Cūḷa Panthaka would take.

As Cūḷa Panthaka came along, he saw the Teacher, and approaching him, paid obeisance to him. Said the Teacher, "But, Cūḷa Panthaka, where are you going at this hour of the day?"—"Reverend sir, my brother has expelled me, and therefore I intend to return to the householder's life."—"Cūḷa Panthaka, it was at my hands that you went forth. Therefore when your brother expelled you, why did you not come to me? Come now, what have you to do with the life of a householder? You shall remain with me." So saying, the Teacher stroked him on the head with his hand, the palm of which was marked with the wheel, and taking him with him, went and seated him over against the Perfumed Chamber. And creating by his supernormal power a perfectly clean cloth, he gave it to him, saying, "Cūḷa Panthaka, remain right here, face towards the east, rub this cloth, and say as you do so, 'Dirt-remover! Dirt-remover!'" Just then meal-time was announced, whereupon the Teacher, accompanied by the Order of Monks, went to the house of Jīvaka and sat down on the seat prepared for him.

Cūḷa Panthaka sat down, facing the sun, and rubbed the cloth, saying as he did so, "Dirt-remover! Dirt-remover!" As he rubbed the piece of cloth, it became soiled. Thereupon he thought, "This piece of cloth was perfectly clean before. But through this body of mine it has lost its original character and has become soiled. Impermanent, indeed, are all conditioned things!" And grasping the thought of decay and death, he developed insight. The Teacher, knowing that Cūḷa Panthaka's mind had attained insight, said, "Cūḷa Panthaka, think not that only a piece of cloth has become soiled and dyed with impurity. Indeed within you are lust, impurity, and other defilements; remove them." And sending forth a luminous image of himself, the Teacher, sitting before him, present in bodily form as it were, pronounced the following stanzas:

> "Lust, not dust, is dirt truly called,
> To lust is the term 'dirt' truly given;
> Having abandoned this dirt, O monks,
> Live in the Teaching of one free from dirt.
>
> Hate, not dust, is dirt truly called,
> To hate is the term 'dirt' truly given;
> Having abandoned this dirt, O monks,
> Live in the Teaching of one free from dirt.
>
> Delusion, not dust, is dirt truly called,
> To delusion is the term 'dirt' truly given;
> Having abandoned this dirt, O monks,
> Live in the Teaching of one free from dirt."

At the conclusion of the stanzas, Cūḷa Panthaka attained arahantship together with the supernormal powers, and with the analytical knowledges also a knowledge of the Tipiṭaka.[3]

It appears that in a previous state of existence he had been a king. Once, while making a ceremonial circuit of the city, with sweat pouring down his forehead, he wiped his forehead with a clean cloth, whereupon the cloth became soiled. Thought he: "By reason of this body of mine a cloth so clean as this has lost its former character and become soiled. Impermanent, indeed, are all conditioned things!" Thus did he acquire the concept of impermanence. In consequence of this, in a later existence, a "dirt-remover" became his salvation.

Jīvaka Komārabhacca offered water of donation to the Buddha. The Teacher, covering the bowl with his hand, said, "Jīvaka, are there no monks in the monastery?" Mahā Panthaka replied, "No, reverend sir, there are no monks in the monastery." Said the Teacher, "But, Jīvaka, there are!"

---

3. The supernormal powers (*iddhi*) include such powers as the ability to become invisible, to walk on water, to fly through the sky, etc. The Tipiṭaka is the collection of Buddhist scriptures consisting of the three "baskets": Vinaya, Suttanta, and Abhidhamma.

"Very well," said Jīvaka, and sent a man to find out. Said he, "Go to the monastery and find out whether or not there are any monks there." At that moment Cūḷa Panthaka said to himself, "My brother says, 'There are no monks in the monastery.' I will show him that there are monks in the monastery." And forthwith he filled the whole mango grove with monks. Some of them were making robes, others were dyeing robes, others were repeating the sacred texts. Thus did Cūḷa Panthaka create by supernormal power a thousand monks, each different from every other. So when Jīvaka's messenger saw the numerous monks, he returned and told Jīvaka, "Noble sir, the entire mango grove is full of monks." And right there the Elder Cūḷa Panthaka did as follows:

> Panthaka, multiplying himself a thousandfold,
> Sat in the charming mango grove until he was sent for.

The Teacher said to the man, "Go to the monastery and say, 'The Teacher summons Cūḷa Panthaka.'" The man went and said what he was told to say. Thereupon the cry went up from a thousand throats, "I am Cūḷa Panthaka! I am Cūḷa Panthaka!" The man returned and said, "Reverend sir, they all say they are Cūḷa Panthaka." Said the Teacher, "Well then, go and take by the hand the first monk that says, 'I am Cūḷa Panthaka,' and the rest will disappear." The man did so. Immediately the thousand monks disappeared. The Elder Cūḷa Panthaka returned with the man who came for him.

At the end of the meal the Teacher addressed Jīvaka, "Jīvaka take Cūḷa Panthaka's bowl, and he will pronounce the words of thanksgiving for you." Jīvaka took his bowl. The Elder Cūḷa Panthaka, like a young lion roaring a lion's roar, pronounced the words of thanksgiving, ranging through the whole of the Tipiṭaka. The Teacher arose from his seat, and surrounded by the Order of Monks, went to the monastery. After the monks had shown the Teacher the customary attentions, the Teacher, in front of the Perfumed Chamber, admonished the Order of Monks with an admonition of the Happy One, assigned a subject of meditation, dismissed the Order of Monks, and entered the Perfumed Chamber.

One day in the Hall of Truth the monks began a discussion: "Friends, in four months Cūḷa Panthaka was unable to learn by heart a stanza of four verses; but because he never relaxed his effort he became established in arahantship and has just now become master of the family of Dhamma transcending all worlds." The Teacher came in and asked, "Monks, what is it that you are sitting here now talking about?" When they told him, he said, "Monks, a monk of roused up effort in my Teaching cannot fail to make himself master of the Dhamma that transcends all worlds." So saying, he pronounced the following stanza:

25. By energy and heedfulness,
    By taming and by self-control,
    The wise man should make an isle
    That no flood can overwhelm.

46. Two Fellow-monks

THOUGH OFTEN HE RECITES THE SACRED TEXTS ... This instruction was given by the Teacher while he was in residence at Jetavana with reference to two fellow-monks.

For at Sāvatthī lived two men of good families who were inseparable friends. On a certain occasion they went to the monastery, heard the Teacher teach the Dhamma, renounced the pleasures of the world, gave their hearts to the dispensation of the Buddha, and went forth. When they had kept residence for five years with preceptors and teachers, they approached the Teacher and asked about the duties in his religion. After listening to a detailed description of the duty of meditation and the duty of study, one of them said, "Reverend sir, since I became a monk in old age, I shall not be able to fulfil the duty of study, but I can fulfil the duty of meditation." So he had the Teacher instruct him in the duty of meditation as far as arahantship, and after striving and struggling attained arahantship together with the analytical knowledges. But the other said, "I will fulfil the duty of study." He acquired by degrees the Tipiṭaka, the Word of the Buddha, and wherever he went, taught the Dhamma and chanted it. He went from place to place reciting the Dhamma to five hundred monks and was preceptor of eighteen large communities of monks.

Now a company of monks, having obtained a meditation subject from the Teacher, went to the place of residence of the older monk, and by faithful observance of his admonitions attained arahantship. Thereupon they paid obeisance to the elder and said, "We desire to see the Teacher." Said the elder, "Go, friends, greet the Teacher in my name, and likewise greet the eighty chief elders, and greet my fellow-elder, saying, 'Our teacher greets you.'" So those monks went to the monastery and greeted the Buddha and the elders, saying, "Reverend sir, our teacher greets you." When they greeted their teacher's fellow-elder, he replied, "Who is he?" Said the monks, "He is your fellow-monk, reverend sir."

Said the younger monk, "But what have you learned from him? Of the Dīgha Nikāya (Long Collection) and the other Nikāyas, have you learned a single Nikāya? Of the Three Piṭakas, have you learned a single Piṭaka?" And he thought to himself, "This monk does not know a single stanza containing four verses. Soon after he went forth, he took rags from a dust heap, entered the forest, and gathered a great many pupils about him. When he returns, it behoves me to ask him some questions." Now somewhat later the older monk came to see the Teacher, and leaving his bowl and robe with his fellow-elder, went and greeted the Teacher and the eighty chief elders, afterwards returning to the place of residence of his fellow-elder. The younger monk showed him the customary attentions, provided him with a seat of the same size as his own, and then sat down, thinking to himself, "I will ask him a question."

At that moment the Teacher thought to himself, "Should this monk annoy my son, he is likely to be reborn in hell." So out of compassion for him, pretending to be going the rounds of the monastery, he went to the place where the two monks were sitting and sat down on the seat of the Buddha already prepared. (For wherever the monks sit down, they first prepare the seat of the Buddha, and not until they have so done do they themselves sit down. Therefore the Teacher sat down on a seat already prepared for him.) And when he had sat down, he asked the monk who had taken upon himself the duty of study a question on the first concentration. When the younger monk had answered this question correctly, the Teacher, beginning with the second concentration, asked him questions about the eight attainments and about the form and formless worlds, all of which he answered correctly. Then the Teacher asked him a question about the path of stream-entry, and he was unable to answer it. Thereupon the Teacher asked the monk who was an arahant, and the latter immediately gave the correct answer.

"Well done, well done, monk!" said the Teacher, greatly pleased. The Teacher then asked questions about the remaining paths in order. The monk who had taken upon himself the duty of study was unable to answer a single question, while the monk who had attained to arahantship answered every question he asked. On each of four occasions the Teacher bestowed applause on him. Hearing this, all the deities, from the gods of earth to the gods of the world of Brahmā, including the nāgas and the garuḍas, shouted their applause.

Hearing this applause, the pupils and fellow-residents of the younger monk were offended at the Teacher and said, "Why did the Teacher do this? He bestowed applause on each of four occasions on the old monk who knows nothing at all. But to our own teacher, who has thoroughly learnt everything by heart and is at the head of five hundred monks, he gave no praise at all." The Teacher asked them, "Monks, what is it you are talking about?" When they told him, he said, "Monks, your own teacher is in my dispensation like a man who tends cows for hire. But my son is like a master who enjoys the five products of the cow at his own good pleasure." So saying, he pronounced the following stanzas:

19. Though often he recites the sacred texts,
    The heedless man who does not practise
    Is like a cowherd counting other's cattle:
    He has no share of the holy life.

20. Though little he recites the sacred texts,
    If he practises in accordance with Dhamma,
    Rid of delusion, lust, and hate,
    In wisdom perfect, a heart well-freed,
    One who clings not here or hereafter—
    He has a share of the holy life.

47. The Elder Sappadāsa

THOUGH ONE SHOULD LIVE A HUNDRED YEARS ... This instruction was given by the Teacher while he was in residence at Jetavana with reference to the Elder Sappadāsa.

At Sāvatthī we are told, the son of a good family, after hearing the Teacher teach the Dhamma, went forth and obtained acceptance as a monk. Becoming discontented after a time, he thought to himself, "The life of a layman is not suited to a youth of station like me; but even death would be preferable to remaining a monk." So he went about considering ways of killing himself.

Now one day, very early in the morning, the monks went to the monastery after breakfast, and seeing a snake in the hall where the fire was kept, put it into a jar, closed the jar, and carried it out of the monastery. The discontented monk, after eating his breakfast, drew near, and seeing the monks, asked them, "What's that you've got, friend?"—"A snake, friend."—"What are you going to do with it?"—"Throw it away." The monk thought to himself, "I will commit suicide by letting the snake bite me." So he said to the monks, "Let me take it; I'll throw it away."

He took the jar from their hands, sat down in a certain place, and tried to make the snake bite him. But the snake refused to bite him. Then he put his hand into the jar, waved it this way and that, opened the snake's mouth and stuck his finger in, but the snake still refused to bite him. So he said to himself, "It's not a poisonous snake, but a house-snake," threw it away, and returned to the monastery. The monks asked him, "Did you throw away the snake, friend?"—"Friends, that was not a poisonous snake; it was only a house-snake."—"Friend, that was a poisonous snake all the same; it spread its hood wide, hissed at us, and gave us much trouble to catch. Why do you talk thus?"—"Friends, I tried to make it bite me, and even stuck my finger into its mouth, but I couldn't make it bite." When the monks heard this, they were silent.

Now the discontented monk acted as barber of the monastery; and one day he went to the monastery with two or three razors, and laying one razor on the floor, cut the hair of the monks with the other. When he removed the razor from the floor, the thought occurred to him, "I will cut my throat with this razor and so put myself out of the way." So he went to a certain tree, leaned his neck against a branch, and applied the blade of the razor to his windpipe. Remaining in this position, he reflected upon his conduct from the time of his acceptance as a monk, and perceived that his conduct was flawless, even as the spotless disc of the moon or a cluster of transparent jewels. As he surveyed his conduct, a thrill of joy suffused his whole body. Subduing the feeling of joy and developing insight, he attained arahantship together with the analytical knowledges. Then he took his razor and entered the monastery enclosure.

The monks asked him, "Where did you go, friend?"—"Friends, I went out thinking to myself, 'I will cut my windpipe with this razor and so put myself out of the way.'"—"How did you escape death?"—"I can no longer commit suicide. For I said to myself, 'With this razor I will sever my windpipe.' But instead of so doing, I severed the taints with the razor of knowledge." The monks said to themselves, "This monk speaks falsely, says what is untrue," and reported the matter to the Exalted One. The Exalted One listened to their words and replied, "Monks, those that have rid themselves of the taints are incapable of taking their own life."

"Reverend Sir, you speak of this monk as one who has rid himself of the taints. But how did it come about that this monk, possessed of the faculties requisite for the attainment of arahantship, became discontented? How did he come to possess those faculties? Why didn't that snake bite him?"

"Monks, the simple fact is that snake was his slave in a past life, his third previous existence, and therefore did not dare to bite the body of his own master." Thus briefly did the Teacher explain this cause to them. Thereafter that monk was known as Sappadāsa ("having a snake as his slave").

The monks, after hearing the Exalted One explain the matter, asked him a further question: "Reverend sir, this monk says that he attained arahantship even as he stood with the blade of his razor pressed against his windpipe. Is it possible to gain the path of arahantship in so short a period of time?"

"Yes, monks, a monk who strives with all his might may gain the path of arahantship in raising his foot, in setting his foot on the ground, or even before his foot touches the ground. For it is better for a man who strives with all his might to live but a single instant than for an idle man to live a hundred years." So saying, he pronounced the following stanza:

112. Though one should live a hundred years
 Lazy, of little effort,
 Yet better is life for a single day
 For one who makes a steady effort.

48. The Elder Pūtigatta Tissa

NOT LONG, ALAS, AND IT WILL LIE ... This instruction was given by the Teacher while he was in residence at Sāvatthī with reference to the Elder Pūtigatta Tissa, Tissa with the Putrid Body.

A certain youth of good family who lived at Sāvatthī heard the Teacher teach the Dhamma, gave his heart to the dispensation, and went forth as a monk. After his acceptance into the Order he became known as the Elder Tissa. As time went on, an eruption broke out on his body. At first appeared pustules no bigger than mustard seeds, but as the disease progressed they assumed successively the size of kidney beans, chickpeas, jujube seeds, emblic myrobalans, and vilva fruits. Finally they burst open, and his body became covered with open sores. In this way he came to be called the Elder Pūtigatta Tissa. After a time his bones began to disintegrate, and no one was willing to take care of him. His under and upper robes, which were stained with dried blood, looked like net cakes. His fellow-residents, unable to care for him, cast him out, and he lay down on the ground without a protector.

Now the Buddhas never fail to survey the world twice a day. At dawn they survey the world, looking through the extent of the galaxy towards the Perfumed Chamber, taking cognizance of all they see. In the evening they survey the world, looking from the Perfumed Chamber and taking cognizance of all that is without. Now at this time the Elder Pūtigatta Tissa appeared within the net of the Exalted One's knowledge. The Teacher, knowing that the monk Tissa was ripe for arahantship, thought to himself, "This monk has been abandoned by his associates; at the present time he has no other refuge than me." Accordingly the Teacher departed from the Perfumed Chamber, and pretending to be making the rounds of the monastery, went to the hall where the fire was kept. He washed the boiler, placed it on the brazier, waited in the fire-room for the water to boil, and when he knew it was hot, went and took hold of the end of the bed where that monk was lying.

At that time the monks said to the Teacher, "Please depart, reverend sir; we will carry him in for you." So saying, they took up the bed and carried Tissa into the fire-room. The Teacher caused a measure to be brought and sprinkled hot water. He caused the monks to take Tissa's upper garment, wash it thoroughly in hot water, and lay it in the sunshine to dry. Then he went, and taking his stand near Tissa, moistened his body with hot water and rubbed and bathed him. At the end of his bath his upper robe was dry. The Teacher caused him to be clothed in his upper robe and caused his under robe to be washed thoroughly in hot water and laid in the sun to dry. As soon as the water had evaporated from his body, his under robe was dry. Thereupon Tissa put on one of the yellow robes as an under garment and the other as an upper robe, and with his body refreshed and mind tranquil lay down on the bed. The Teacher took his stand at Tissa's pillow and said to him, "Monk, consciousness will depart from you, your body will become useless and, like a log, will lie on the ground." So saying, he pronounced the following stanza:

41. Not long, alas, and it will lie—
    This body here upon the earth,
    Rejected, void of consciousness,
    And useless as a rotten log.

At the conclusion of the lesson the Elder Pūtigatta Tissa attained arahantship and reached final Nibbāna. The Teacher performed the funeral rites over his body, and, taking the relics, caused a shrine to be erected.

The monks asked the Teacher, "Reverend sir, where was the Elder Pūtigatta Tissa reborn?"—"He has reached final Nibbāna, monks."—"Reverend sir, how did it happen that such a monk, having the supporting tendencies to attain arahantship, came to have a diseased body? Why did his bones disintegrate? Through what deed in a former birth did he obtain the dispositions requisite for the attainment of arahantship?"—"Monks, all these things happened solely because of deeds he committed in a previous existence."—"But, reverend sir, what did he do?"—"Well then, monks, listen.

Story of the Past: The Cruel Fowler

In the dispensation of the Buddha Kassapa, Tissa was a fowler. He used to catch birds in large number, and most of these he served to royalty. Most of those he did not give to royalty he used to sell. Fearing that if he killed and kept the birds he did not sell, they would rot, and desiring to prevent his captive birds from taking flight, he used to break their leg-bones and wing-bones and lay them aside, piling them in a heap. On the following day he would sell them. When he had too many, he would have some cooked also for himself.

One day, when well-flavoured food had been cooked for him, a monk who was an arahant stopped at the door of his house on his round for alms. When Tissa saw the elder, he made his mind serene and thought, "I have killed and eaten many living creatures. A noble elder stands at my door, and an abundance of well-flavoured food is in my house. I will therefore give him alms." So he took the monk's bowl and filled it, and having given him well-flavoured food, saluted the monk respectfully and said: "Reverend sir, may I obtain the highest fruit of the Dhamma you have seen." Said the elder in his words of rejoicing, "So be it." (*End of Story of the Past.*)

"Monks, it was through the meritorious deed Tissa then did that this fruit accrued to him. It was because he broke the bones of birds that his body became diseased and his bones disintegrated. It was because he gave well-flavoured food to the arahant that he attained arahantship."

49. The Elder Vangīsa

WHO, OF BEINGS, KNOWS THEIR DEATH ... This instruction was given by the Teacher while he was in residence at Jetavana with reference to the Elder Vangīsa.[4]

It seems that there lived at Rājagaha a brahmin named Vangīsa who could tell in which of the states of existence men were reborn after death. He would rap on their skulls and say, "This is the

---

4. He was the foremost poet in the Sangha. A collection of his verses is found in the Saṃyutta Nikāya, Chap. 8, and Theragāthā, 1209–79.

skull of a man who has been reborn in hell; this man has been reborn as an animal; this man has been reborn as a ghost; this is the skull of a man who has been reborn in the human world."

The brahmins thought to themselves, "We can use this man to prey upon the world." So clothing him in two red robes, they took him about the country with them, saying to everyone they met, "This brahmin Vangīsa can tell by rapping on the skulls of dead men in which of the states of existence they have been reborn; ask him to tell you in which of the states of existence your own kinsmen have been reborn." People would give him ten pieces of money or twenty or a hundred according to their several means, and would ask him in which of the states of existence their kinsmen had been reborn.

After travelling from place to place, they finally reached Sāvatthī and took up their abode near the Jetavana. After breakfast they saw throngs of people going with perfumes, garlands, and the like in their hands to hear the Dhamma. "Where are you going?" they asked. "To the monastery to hear the Dhamma," was the reply. "What will you gain by going there?" asked the brahmins, "There is nobody like our fellow-brahmin Vangīsa. He can tell by rapping on the skulls of dead men in which of the states of existence they have been reborn. Just ask him in which of the states of existence your own kinsmen have been reborn."

"What does Vangīsa know!" replied the disciples, "There is no one like our teacher." But the brahmins retorted, "There is no one like Vangīsa," and the dispute waxed hot. Finally the disciples said, "Come now, let us go find out which of the two knows the more, your Vangīsa or our teacher." So taking the brahmins with them, they went to the monastery.

The Teacher, knowing that they were on their way, procured and placed in a row five skulls, one each of men who had been reborn in the four states of existence: hell, the animal world, the human world, and the worlds of the gods; and one skull belonging to a man who had attained arahantship. When they arrived, he asked Vangīsa, "Are you the man of whom it is said that by rapping on the skulls of dead men you can tell in which of the states of existence they have been reborn?"—"Yes," said Vangīsa. "Then whose is this skull?" Vangīsa rapped on the skull and said, "This is the skull of a man who has been reborn in hell."—"Good,

good!" exclaimed the Teacher, applauding him. Then the Teacher asked him about the next three skulls, and Vaṅgīsa answered without making a mistake. The Teacher applauded him for each answer he gave and finally showed him the fifth skull. "Whose skull is this?" he asked. Vaṅgīsa rapped on the fifth skull as he had on the others, but confessed that he did not know in which of the states of existence the man had been reborn.

Then said the Teacher, "Vaṅgīsa, don't you know?"—"No," replied Vaṅgīsa, "I don't know."—"I know," said the Teacher. Thereupon Vaṅgīsa asked him, "Teach me this charm."—"I cannot teach it to one who has not gone forth." Thought the brahmin to himself, "If I only knew this charm I should be the foremost man in all India." Accordingly he dismissed his fellow-brahmins, saying, "Remain right here for a few days; I intend to go forth." And he went forth in the presence of the Teacher, obtained acceptance as a monk, and was thereafter known as Elder Vaṅgīsa.

They gave him as his subject of meditation the thirty-two constituent parts of the body and said to him, "Repeat the preliminary words of the formula." He followed their instructions and repeated the preliminary words of the formula. From time to time the brahmins would ask him, "Have you learned the formula?" and the elder would answer, "Just wait a little! I am learning it." In but a few days he attained arahantship. When the brahmins asked him again, he replied, "Friends, I am now unable to learn it." When the monks heard his reply, they said to the Teacher, "Reverend sir, this monk utters what is not true and is guilty of falsehood." The Teacher replied, "Monks, do not say so. Monks, my son now knows all about the passing away and rebirth of beings." So saying, he pronounced the following stanzas:

419. Who, of beings, knows their death,
   Their being born in every way,
   Detached, well-faring, enlightened too—
   That one I call a brāhmaṇa.

420. Him whose bourn men do not know,
   Neither devas nor minstrels divine,
   Pollutions destroyed, an arahant—
   That one I call a brāhmaṇa.

PART II
The Attainments of Nuns

50. Mahā Pajāpatī Gotamī

IN WHOM IS NO WRONG-DOING ... This instruction was given by the Teacher while he was in residence at Jetavana with reference to Mahā Pajāpatī Gotamī (the Buddha's aunt and foster-mother).

When the circumstances requiring the eight important conditions (for admitting nuns) had arisen, the Exalted One proclaimed them and Mahā Pajāpatī Gotamī accepted them by bowing her head, just as a person accustomed to the wearing of ornaments accepts a garland of fragrant flowers by bowing his head. So likewise did all the members of her retinue. She had no preceptor or teacher other than the Exalted One himself. Thus she received acceptance as a nun.

On a subsequent occasion the members of her retinue commented on the manner in which this nun was admitted to full membership in the Order, saying, "Mahā Pajāpatī Gotamī has no teacher or preceptor; by herself alone and with her own hand she received the yellow robes." On hearing this, other nuns were dissatisfied and from then on refused to keep Uposatha day or to celebrate the Pavāraṇā ceremony with her.[5] And going to the Tathāgata, they reported the matter to him. The Teacher listened to what they had to say and then replied, "I myself conferred the eight important conditions on Mahā Pajāpatī Gotamī. I alone am her teacher; I alone am her preceptor. Those who have renounced bad conduct by way of body, speech, and mind, those who have rid themselves of the evil passions, should never entertain feelings of dissatisfaction." And teaching the Dhamma, he pronounced the following stanza:

391. In whom is no wrongdoing
    By body, speech, or mind,

---

5. The ceremony for inviting mutual admonition, held at the end of the rains residence.

In these three ways restrained—
That one I call a brāhmaṇa.

51. The Elder Nun Uppalavaṇṇā

"As sweet as honey" thinks the fool ... This instruction was given by the Teacher while he was in residence at Jetavana with reference to the nun Uppalavaṇṇā.

We are told that Uppalavaṇṇā made her earnest wish at the feet of the Buddha Padumuttara, and that after performing works of merit for a hundred thousand cycles of time, as she passed from birth to birth among gods and humans, she passed from the world of the gods in the dispensation of the present Buddha and was reborn in Sāvatthī as the daughter of a rich merchant. The hue of her skin was like the hue of the calyx of the blue lotus, and therefore they gave her the name Uppalavaṇṇā. When she reached marriageable age, all the princes and merchants in India, without a single exception, sent gifts to the merchant her father, asking him to give them his daughter in marriage.

Thereupon the merchant thought to himself, "I shall not be able to satisfy the wishes of all, but I shall find some way out of the difficulty." So he summoned his daughter and said to her, "You might become a nun." Now she was in her last existence before attaining Nibbāna, and therefore his words were to her, as it were, oil a hundred times refined, sprinkled on her head. Therefore she replied, "Dear father, I will become a nun." So he prepared rich gifts in her honour, and conducting her to the Order of Nuns, had her go forth.

Not long after she had gone forth, her turn came to unlock the Uposatha hall. After she had lighted the lamp and swept the hall, her attention was attracted to the flame of the lamp. And standing there, she looked repeatedly at the flame; and concentrating her attention on the element of fire, she entered into a state of deep concentration. Consummating the deep concentration, she attained arahantship together with the analytical knowledges.

Some time later she went on a pilgrimage for alms in the country, and on her return entered the Dark Forest. At that time it was not forbidden to nuns to reside in a forest. There they built her a hut, set up a bed, and hung curtains round. From the forest she went to Sāvatthī to receive alms, and then set out to return to her hut. Now a cousin of hers, a young brahmin named Ānanda, had been in love with her ever since she lived the household life; and when he heard where she had gone, he went to the forest ahead of the nun, entered the hut, and hid under the bed.

On her return the nun entered the hut, closed the door, and sat down on the bed, unable to see in the dark, because she had just come in out of the sunlight. As soon as she sat down on the bed the youth crawled out from under and climbed on top. The nun cried out, "Fool, do not ruin me! Fool, do not ruin me!" But the youth overcame her resistance, worked his will on her, and went his way. As if unable to endure his wickedness, the great earth burst asunder, and he was swallowed up and reborn in the great hell of Avīci.

The nun told the other nuns what had happened, and the nuns told the monks, and the monks told the Exalted One. Having heard this the Teacher addressed the monks as follows, "Monks, the fool, whoever he may be, whether monk or nun, or lay disciple male or female, who commits an evil act, acts with as much joy and happiness, with as much pleasure and delight, as though he were eating honey or sugar or some other sweet-tasting substance." And joining the connection and instructing them in the Dhamma, he pronounced the following stanza:

69. "As sweet as honey" thinks the fool
So long as the evil is unripe,
But when the evil deed ripens,
Then to the fool comes suffering.

Some time later the throng assembled in the Dhamma hall and began to discuss the incident: "Even those that have rid themselves of taints like the pleasures of love and gratify their passions. Why should they not? They are not kolapa-trees or ant-hills, but are living creatures with bodies of moist flesh. Therefore they also like the pleasures of love and gratify their passions." The Teacher drew near and asked them, "Monks, what are you sitting here now talking about?" They told him. Then he said, "Monks, they that have rid themselves of the taints neither like the pleasures of love nor gratify their passions. For even as a drop of water which has fallen upon a lotus leaf does not cling to it or remain there, but rolls over and falls off; even as a grain of mustard seed does not cling to the point of an awl or remain there, but rolls over and falls off; precisely so sensual love does not cling to the heart of one who has rid himself of the taints nor remain there." And joining the connection, he instructed them in the Dhamma by pronouncing the following stanza, found in the Chapter on the Brāhmaṇa:

401. Who, like water drops on a lotus leaf,
Or mustard seed on a needle point,
Clings not to sensual pleasures—
That one I call a brāhmaṇa.

Now the Teacher summoned King Pasenadi Kosala and said to him, "Your majesty, in this religion young women of good family, as well as young men of good family, renounce many kinsfolk and much wealth, go forth and take up residence in the forest. In case women reside in the forest, it is possible that evil-minded men, inflamed by lust, may conduct themselves towards them with disrespect and arrogance, do them violence, and bring their religious life to naught. Therefore a place of residence for the Order of Nuns should be erected within the city." The king agreed to this and had a place of residence for the Order of Nuns erected on one side of the city. From that time on the nuns resided only within the city.

52. The Elder Nun Kisā Gotamī

THOUGH ONE SHOULD LIVE A HUNDRED YEARS ... This instruction was given by the Teacher at Jetavana, with reference to Kisā Gotamī.

Kisā Gotamī Marries a Rich Merchant's Son

Once upon a time, the story goes, a merchant worth four hundred millions lived at Sāvatthī. Suddenly all of his wealth turned into charcoal. The merchant, overwhelmed with grief, refused to eat and took to his bed. One day a certain friend of his came to see him and asked him, "Sir, why are you so sorrowful?" The merchant told him what had happened. Said his friend, "Sir, do not give yourself over to sorrow. I know a way out of the difficulty, if you will but make use of it."

"Well, sir, what am I to do?"

Said his friend, "Spread matting in your shop, and pile the charcoal on it, and sit down as if you were selling it. People will come along and say to you, 'Most merchants sell such things as clothing and oil and honey and molasses; but you are sitting here selling charcoal.' Then you must say to them, 'If I can't sell what belongs to me, what am I to do?' But again someone may say, 'Most merchants sell such things as clothing and oil and honey and molasses, but you are sitting here selling yellow gold.' Then you must say, 'Where's any yellow gold?' Your customer will say, 'There it is!' Then say, 'Let me have it.' Your customer will bring you a handful of charcoal. Take it, cover it with your hands, and presto! It will turn into yellow gold. Now if your customer should be a maiden, marry her to your son, turn over your four hundred millions to her, and live on what she gives you. But if your customer should be a youth, marry your daughter to him as soon as she reaches marriageable age, turn over your four hundred millions to him, and live on what he gives you."

"A fine plan indeed!" said the merchant. So he piled the charcoal up in his shop, and sat down as if he were selling it. People came along and said to him, "Most merchants sell things such as clothing and oil and honey and molasses; but you are sitting here selling charcoal." To such as asked this question, he replied as follows, "If I can't sell what belongs to me, what am I to do?"

There came one day to the door of his shop a certain maiden, the daughter of a poverty-stricken house. Her name was Gotamī, but by reason of the leanness of her body she was generally known as Kisā Gotamī. She came to buy something for herself; but when she saw the merchant, she said to him, "My good sir, most merchants sell such things as clothing and oil and honey and molasses; but you are sitting here selling yellow gold."—"Maiden, where is there any yellow gold?"—"Right there where you are sitting."—"Let me have some of it, maiden." She took a handful of the charcoal and placed it in his hands. No sooner had it touched his hands than presto! It turned into yellow gold.

Then said the merchant to her, "Which is your house, maiden?" Said she, "Such and such, sir." The merchant, perceiving that she was unmarried, married her to his own son. He then gathered up his wealth (what was previously charcoal turning into yellow gold at his touch), and gave the four hundred millions into her charge. In time she became pregnant, and, after ten lunar months, gave birth to a son. But the child died as soon as he was able to walk.

Kisā Gotamī Seeks Mustard Seed for Her Child

Now Kisā Gotamī had never seen death before. Therefore, when they came to remove the body for burning, she forbade them to do so. She said to herself, "I will seek medicine for my son." Placing the dead child on her hip, she went from house to house inquiring, "Do you know anything that will cure my son?" Everyone said to her, "Woman, you are stark mad that you go from house to house seeking medicine for your dead child." But she went her way, thinking, "Surely I shall find someone who knows medicine for my child."

Now a certain wise man saw her and thought to himself, "This young woman has no doubt borne and lost her first and only child, nor has she seen death before; I must help her." So he said to her, "Woman, I myself do not know how to cure your child, but I know of one who has this knowledge."—"Sir, who is it that knows?"—"Woman, the Teacher knows; go and ask him."—"Good sir, I will go and ask him."

So she went to the Teacher, paid obeisance to him, stood at his side, and asked him, "Venerable sir, is it true, as men say, that you know how to cure my child?"—"Yes, I know that."—"What shall I get?"—"A pinch of white mustard seed."—"I will get that, venerable sir. But in whose house shall I get it?"—"In whose house neither son nor daughter nor any other has yet died."—"Very well, venerable sir," said she, and paid obeisance to him.

Then she placed the dead child on her hip, entered the village, stopped at the door of the very first house, and asked, "Have you here any white mustard seed? They say it will cure my child."—"Yes."—"Well then, give it to me." They brought some grains of white mustard seed and gave them to her. She asked, "Friends, in the house where you dwell has son or daughter yet died?"—"What are you saying, woman? As for the living they are few; only the dead are many."—"Well then, take back your mustard seed; that is no medicine for my child." So saying, she gave back the mustard seed.

After this manner, going from house to house, she plied her quest. There was not a single house where she found the mustard seed she sought; and when the evening came, she thought, "Ah! It's a heavy task I took upon myself. I thought that I alone had lost a child, but in every village the dead are more in number than the living." While she reflected thus her heart, which until then was soft with mother's love, became firm. She took the child and discarded him in the forest. Then she went to the Teacher, paid homage to him, and stood to one side.

Said the Teacher, "Did you get the pinch of mustard seed?"—"No, I did not, venerable sir. In every village the dead are more in number than the living." Said the Teacher, "You imagined vainly that you alone had lost a child. But all living beings are subject to an unchanging law, and it is this: The Prince of Death, like a raging torrent, sweeps away into the sea of ruin all living beings, but still their longings are unfulfilled." And instructing her in the Dhamma, he pronounced the following stanza:

287. In flocks and children finding delight
With a mind clinging—just such a man
Death seizes and carries away,
As a great flood a sleeping village.

As the Teacher uttered the last part of the stanza, Kisā Gotamī was established in the fruit of stream-entry. Likewise did many others also obtain the fruit of stream-entry, and the fruits of the second and third paths. Kisā Gotamī requested the Teacher to let her go forth; accordingly he sent her to the Order of Nuns and directed that they let her go forth. Afterwards she obtained acceptance as a nun and came to be known as the nun Kisā Gotamī.

One day it was her turn to light the lamp in the Uposatha hall. Having lighted the lamp, she sat down and watched the tongues of flame. Some flared up and others flickered out. She took this for her subject of meditation and meditated as follows: "Even as it is with these flames, so also is it with living beings here in the world: some flare up, while others flicker out; only those who have reached Nibbāna are no more seen."

The Teacher, seated in the Perfumed Chamber, sent forth a radiant image of himself, and standing as it were face to face with her, spoke and said: "Even as it is with these flames, so also is it with living beings here in the world: some flare up, while others flicker out; only those who have reached Nibbāna are no more seen. Therefore, better is the life of one who sees Nibbāna, though living but for an instant, than the lives of those who endure for a hundred years and yet do not see Nibbāna." And joining the connection, he instructed her in the Dhamma by pronouncing the following stanza:

114. Though one should live a hundred years,
  Not seeing the Deathless State,
  Yet better is life for a single day
  For one who sees the Deathless State.

At the conclusion of the discourse Kisā Gotamī, even as she sat there, attained arahantship together with the analytical knowledges.

53. The Elder Nun Paṭācārā

THOUGH ONE SHOULD LIVE A HUNDRED YEARS ... This instruction was given by the Teacher, while in residence at Jetavana, with reference to the nun Paṭācārā.

Paṭācārā, we are told, was the daughter of a wealthy merchant of Sāvatthī. Her father was worth four hundred million, and she was exceedingly beautiful. When she was about sixteen years old, her parents provided quarters for her in a palace seven storeys high, and there they kept her, on the topmost floor, surrounded by guards. But in spite of these precautions, she mis-conducted herself, and it was with her own page.[6]

Now it so happened that her father and mother had promised her in marriage to a certain young man who was her social equal, and finally they set the wedding day. When the day was close at hand, she said to the page, "My parents tell me that they intend to give me in marriage to a young man who comes of such and such a family. Now you know very well that when I am once inside my husband's house, you may bring me presents and come to see me all you like, but you will never, never get in. Therefore, if you

---

6. The opening portion of this story closes resembles the opening of story No. 45.

really love me, don't delay an instant, but find some way or other of getting me out of this place."

"Very well, my love, this is what I will do: tomorrow, early in the morning, I will go to the city gate and wait for you at such and such a spot; you manage, somehow or other, to get out of this place and meet me there."

On the following day he went to the appointed place and waited. Paṭācārā got up very early in the morning, put on soiled garments, dishevelled her hair, and smeared her body with red powder. Then, in order to outwit her keepers, she took a waterpot in her hand, surrounded herself with slave-maidens, and set out as if she intended to fetch water. Escaping from the palace, she went to the appointed place and met her lover. Together they went a long way off, and took up their abode in a certain village. The husband tilled the soil, and gathered firewood and leaves in the forest. The wife fetched water in her waterpot, and with her own hand pounded the rice, did the cooking, and performed the other household duties. Thus did Paṭācārā reap the fruit of her own wrongdoing.

By and by, she became pregnant, and when the time for her delivery was near at hand, she made the following request to her husband, "Here I have no one to help me. But a mother and father always have a soft spot in their heart for their child. Therefore take me home to them, that I may give birth to my child in their house." But her husband refused her request, saying to her, "My dear wife, what are you saying? If your mother and father were to see me, they would subject me to all manner of tortures. It is out of the question for me to go." Over and over again she begged him, and each time he refused her.

One day when her husband was away in the forest, she went to the neighbours and said, "Should my husband ask you where I have gone when he returns, tell him that I have gone home to my parents." And having said this she closed the door of her house and went away. When her husband returned and observed that she was not there he inquired of the neighbours and they told him what had happened. "I must persuade her to return," thought he, and set out after her. Finally he caught sight of her, and overtaking her, begged her to return with him. But try as he might, he was unable to persuade her to do so.

When they reached a certain place, the birth pains came upon her. She said to her husband, "Husband, the birth pains have come upon me." So saying, she made her way into a clump of bushes, laid herself upon the ground, and there, with much tossing about and pain, she gave birth to a son. Then she said, "What I set out to go home for is over." So back again to their house she went with him, and once more they lived together.

After a time she became pregnant again. When the time for her delivery was at hand, she made the same request to her husband as before and received the same answer. So she took her child upon her hip and went away just as she had before. Her husband followed her, overtook her, and asked her to return with him. This she refused to do. Now as they went on their way, a fearful storm arose, out of due season. The sky was ablaze with flashes of lightning, and rent asunder, as it were, with thunder claps, and there was an incessant downpour of rain. At that moment the birth pains came upon her. She said to her husband, "Husband, the birth pains are come upon me; I cannot stand it; find me a place out of the rain."

Her husband went here and there, axe in hand, seeking materials for a shelter. Seeing some brushwood growing on the top of an ant-hill, he set about to chop it down. Hardly had he begun his work when a poisonous snake slipped out of the ant-hill and bit him. Instantly his body was burned up, as it were, by flames of fire shooting up within him, his flesh turned purple, and right on the spot he fell down dead.

Paṭācārā, suffering intense pain, watched for her husband to return, but in vain. Finally she gave birth to a second son. The two children, unable to withstand the buffeting of the wind and the rain, screamed at the top of their lungs. The mother took them to her bosom, and crouching upon the ground with her hands and knees pressed together, remained in this posture all night long. Her whole body looked as though there were no blood left in it, and her flesh had the appearance of a sere and yellow leaf.

When the dawn rose, she took her newborn son, his flesh as red as a piece of meat, and placed him on her hip. Then she gave the older boy one of her fingers to hold, and with the words, "Come, dear child, your father has left us," set out along the same path her husband had taken. When she came to the ant-hill, there on top of it she saw her husband lying dead, his flesh purple, his body rigid. "All on account of me," said she, "my husband has died upon the road," and wailing and lamenting, she continued her journey.

When she came to the river Aciravatī, she observed that by reason of the rain, which had lasted all night long, the river was swollen knee-deep, and in places waist-deep. She was too weak to wade across the stream with the two children; therefore she left the older boy on the near bank and carried the younger across to the far side. Breaking off a branch of a tree and spreading it out, she laid the child on it. Then thinking to herself, "I must return to my other child," she took leave of the younger boy and turned to recross the stream. But she could hardly bring herself to leave the little one, and again and again she turned around to look at him.

She had barely reached midstream when a hawk caught sight of the child, and mistaking him for a piece of meat, swooped down from the sky after him. The mother, seeing the eagle swoop down after her child, raised both her hands and screamed with a loud voice, "Begone, begone!" Three times she screamed, but the hawk was so far away that he failed to hear her, and seizing the boy, flew up into the air with him.

When the older boy, who had been left on the near bank, saw his mother stop in the middle of the river and raise her hands, and heard her scream with a loud voice, he thought to himself, "She is calling me." And in his haste he fell into the water. In this way her younger son was carried off by a hawk, and her older son swept away by the river. And she wailed and lamented, saying, "One of my sons has been carried off by a hawk, the other swept away by the water; by the roadside my husband lies dead." And thus wailing and lamenting, she went on her way.

As she proceeded on her way, she met a certain man coming from Sāvatthī. She asked him, "Sir, where do you live?"—"In Sāvatthī, my good woman."—"In the city of Sāvatthī, in such and such a street, lives such and such a family. Do you know them, sir?"—"Yes, my good woman, I know them. But please don't ask me about that family. Ask me about any other family you know."—"Sir, I have no occasion to ask about any other. This is the only family I wish to ask about."—"Woman, you give me no opportunity to avoid telling you. Did you observe that it rained all last night?"

"Indeed I did, sir. In fact, I am the only person the rain fell on all night long. How it came to rain on me, I will tell you by and by. But just tell me what has happened to the family of this wealthy merchant, and I will ask you no further questions."

"My good woman, last night the storm overturned that house, and it fell on the merchant and his wife and his son, and they perished, all three, and their neighbours and kinsmen are even now burning their bodies on one funeral pyre. Look there, my good woman. You can see the smoke now."

Instantly she went mad. Her clothing fell off from her body, but she did not know that she was naked. And naked as at her birth she wandered round and round, weeping and wailing and lamenting, "Both my sons are dead; my husband on the road lies dead; my mother and father and brother burn on one funeral pyre."

Those who saw her yelled, "Crazy fool! Crazy fool!" Some flung rubbish at her, others showered dust on her head, others pelted her with clods of earth.

It so happened that at this time the Teacher was in residence at Jetavana monastery. As he sat there in the midst of his disciples teaching the Dhamma, he saw Paṭācārā approach from afar, and he recognised in her one who for a hundred thousand cycles of time had fulfilled the Perfections, one who had made her earnest wish and attained it.

We are told that in the dispensation of the Buddha Padumuttara she had seen the Teacher Padumuttara assign to an elder nun, an expert in the Vinaya, pre-eminence among those who are versed in the Vinaya. It seemed as if the Teacher were taking her by the arm and admitting the nun to the Garden of Delight. So she formed her resolve and made this aspiration, "May I also obtain from a Buddha like you pre-eminence among nuns versed in the Vinaya." The Buddha Padumuttara, extending his consciousness into the future and perceiving that her aspiration would be fulfilled, made the following prophecy: "In the dispensation of a Buddha to be known as Gotama, this woman will bear the name Paṭācārā, and will obtain pre-eminence among nuns versed in the Vinaya."

So when the Teacher beheld Paṭācārā approaching from afar, her aspiration fulfilled, her earnest wish attained, he said, "There is none other that can be a refuge to this woman, but only I." And he caused her to draw near to the monastery. The moment his disciples saw her, they cried out, "Do not let that crazy woman come here." But he said to them, "Do not hinder her." And when she had come near, he said to her, "Sister, regain your mindfulness!" Instantly, through the power of the Buddha, she regained her mindfulness. At the same moment she became aware that her clothing had fallen off from her body; and recovering at once her shame and fear of wrongdoing, she crouched upon the ground.

A certain man threw her his outer cloak. She put it on, and approaching the Teacher, prostrated herself before his golden feet. Having so done, she said, "Venerable sir, be my refuge, be my support. One of my sons has been carried off by a hawk, the other swept away by the water; by the roadside my husband lies dead; my father's house has been wrecked by the wind, and in it have perished my mother and father and brother, and even now their bodies are burning on one funeral pyre."

The Teacher listened to what she had to say and replied, "Paṭācārā, be troubled no more. You have come to one who is able to be your shelter, your refuge. What you have said is true. One of your sons has been carried off by a hawk, the other swept away by the water; by the roadside your husband lies dead; your father's house has been wrecked by the wind, and in it have perished your mother and father and brother. But just as today, so also all through this round of existences, you have wept over the loss of sons and others dear to you, shedding tears more abundant than the waters of the four oceans." And he uttered the following stanza:

> But little water do the four oceans contain,
> Compared with all the tears that man has shed,
> By sorrow smitten and by suffering distraught.
> Woman, why heedless do you still remain?

In this way the Teacher discoursed on the round of existences without conceivable beginning. As he spoke, the grief which pervaded her body became less intense. Perceiving that her grief had become less intense, he continued his discourse as follows: "Paṭācārā, to one who is on his way to the world beyond, neither sons nor other relatives can ever be a shelter or a refuge. How much less can you expect them to be such to you in this present life! One who is wise should clarify his conduct, and so make clear the path that leads to Nibbāna." So saying, he instructed her in the Dhamma by pronouncing the following stanzas:

288. No sons are there for shelter,
    Nor father, nor related folk;
    For one seized by the Ender
    Kinsmen provide no shelter.

289. Having well understood this fact,
    The wise man well restrained by virtues
    Quickly indeed should clear
    The path going to Nibbāna.

At the conclusion of the discourse, Paṭācāra obtained the fruit of stream-entry and the taints within her, as numerous as the particles of dust on the whole wide earth, were burnt away. Many others likewise obtained the fruit of stream-entry and the fruits of the second and third paths. Paṭācāra, having obtained the fruit of stream-entry, requested the Teacher to let her go forth. The Teacher sent her to the Order of Nuns and directed that she go forth. Afterwards she obtained acceptance as a nun and by reason of her happy demeanour (*paṭitācārattā*) came to be known as Paṭācāra.

One day she filled her waterpot with water, and pouring out water, bathed her feet. As she poured out the water, she spilled some on the ground. The water ran a little way and disappeared. The second time it went a little farther. The third time a little farther yet. So she took this very incident for her subject of meditation, and fixing accurately in her mind the three occurrences, she meditated thus: "Even as the water I spilled the first time ran a little way and disappeared, so also living beings here in the world are dying in youth. Even as the water I spilled the second time ran a little farther, so also living beings here in the world are dying in the prime of life. Even as the water I spilled the third time ran a little farther yet, so also living beings here in the world are dying in old age."

The Teacher, seated in his Perfumed Chamber, sent forth a radiant image of himself, and standing as it were face to face with her, spoke and said: "Paṭācāra, it would be far better to live but a single day, even but a single moment, and see the rise and fall of the five aggregates, than to live a hundred years and not see." And joining the connection, he instructed her in the Dhamma by pronouncing the following stanza:

113. Though one should live a hundred years
 Not seeing rise and fall,
 Yet better is life for a single day
 For one who sees rise and fall.

At the conclusion of the discourse Paṭācāra attained arahantship together with the analytical knowledges.

54. The Elder Nun Bahuputtikā

THOUGH ONE SHOULD LIVE A HUNDRED YEARS ... This instruction was given by the Teacher while he was in residence at Jetavana with reference to Bahuputtikā.

In a certain household at Sāvatthī, we are told, were seven sons and seven daughters. All of them married as soon as they were old enough, and were happy, as was indeed their nature. After a time their father died. But the mother, the eminent female lay disciple, even after the death of her husband, did not relinquish control of his property for some time. One day her sons said to her, "Mother, now that our father is dead, what is the use of your retaining his property? Can we not support you?" She listened to their words, but said nothing. After they had spoken to her several times about the matter, she thought to herself, "My sons will look after me; why do I need to keep the property separate for myself?" So she divided the estate into two parts and distributed them among the children.

After a few days had passed, the wife of her eldest son said to her, "Apparently this is the only house our excellent mother visits; she acts as though she had given both parts of her estate to her eldest son." In like manner did the wives of her other sons address her. So likewise did her daughters address her whenever she entered their houses, from the eldest to the youngest. With such disrespect was she treated that finally she said to herself, "Why should I live with them any longer? I will go forth and live the life of a nun." So she went to the nuns' convent and asked to go forth. They let her go forth and when she had obtained acceptance she went by the name of Bahuputtikā the nun.[7]

"Since I have gone forth in old age," she thought, as she performed the major and minor duties assigned to nuns, "it behoves me to be heedful; I will therefore spend the whole night in meditation. On the lower terrace, putting her hand on a pillar, she guided her steps thereby and meditated. Even as she walked back and forth, fearful that in the dark places she might strike her head against a tree or against some other object, she put her hand on a tree and guided her steps thereby and meditated. Resolved to observe only the Dhamma taught by the Teacher, she considered the Dhamma and pondered the Dhamma and meditated.

The Teacher, seated in the Perfumed Chamber, sent forth a radiant image of himself, and sitting as it were face to face with her, talked with her, saying: "Bahuputtikā, though one should live a hundred years, were one not to behold the Dhamma I have taught and meditate thereon, it would be better for one to live but a moment and behold the Dhamma I have taught." And joining the connection and teaching the Dhamma, he pronounced the following stanza:

115. Though one should live a hundred years
 Not seeing the supreme Dhamma,
 Yet better is life for a single day
 For one who sees the supreme Dhamma.

At the conclusion of the stanza, Bahuputtikā became an arahant possessed of the analytical knowledges.

55. The Elder Nun Dhammadinnā

FOR WHOM THERE IS NO OWNERSHIP ... This instruction was given by the Teacher while he was in residence at Veḷuvana with reference to the nun Dhammadinnā.

For one day, while she was living the household life, her husband Visākha, a lay disciple, heard the Teacher preach the Dhamma and attained the fruit of the third path. Thereupon he thought to himself, "I must now turn over all of my property

---

7. The name means "one with many children."

to Dhammadinnā."[8] Now it had previously been his custom on returning home, in case he saw Dhammadinnā looking out of the window, to smile pleasantly at her. But on this particular day, although she was standing at the window, he passed by without so much as looking at her. "What can this mean?" she thought. "Never mind, when it is meal-time, I shall find out." So when meal-time came, she offered him the usual portion of boiled rice. Now on previous days it had been his custom to say, "Come, let us eat together." But on this particular day he ate in silence, uttering not a word. "He must be angry about something," thought Dhammadinnā.

After the meal Visākha settled himself in a comfortable place, and summoning Dhammadinnā to his side, said to her, "Dhammadinnā, all the wealth that is in this house is yours. Take it!" Thought Dhammadinnā, "Persons who are angry do not offer their property and say, 'Take it!' What can this mean?" After a time, however, she said to her husband, "But, husband, what about you?"—"From this day forth, I shall engage no more in worldly affairs."—"Who will take the spittle you have rejected? In that case permit me also to become a nun."—"Very well, dear wife," replied Visākha, giving her the desired permission. And with rich offerings he escorted her to the nuns' convent and had her go forth. After she had obtained acceptance as a nun she was known as the nun Dhammadinnā.

Dhammadinnā yearned for the life of solitude and so accompanied the nuns to the country. Residing there, in no long time she attained arahantship together with the analytical knowledges. Thereupon she thought to herself, "Now, by reason of me, my kinsfolk will perform works of merit." Accordingly she returned once more to Rājagaha. When the lay disciple Visākha heard that she had returned, he thought to himself, "What can be her reason for returning?" And going to the nuns' convent and seeing the nun, his former wife, he saluted her and seated himself respectfully on one side.

Thought he, "It would be highly improper for me to say to her, 'Noble sister, are you discontented?'[9] I will therefore ask her

---

8. A non-returner has abandoned all greed and possessiveness.
9. Discontented with the holy life of celibacy, implying a desire to return to lay status.

this question." So he asked her a question about the path of stream-entry, and she immediately answered it correctly. Continuing this line of questioning, the lay disciple asked about the remaining paths also. He did not stop, however, at this point, but continuing his questions, asked her about arahantship. "Wonderful, brother Visākha!" exclaimed Dhammadinnā. "But if you desire to know about arahantship, you should approach the Teacher and ask him this question."[10]

Visākha saluted the nun, his former wife, and rising from his seat and going to the Teacher, repeated to the Exalted One their talk and conversation. Said the Teacher, "What my daughter Dhammadinnā said was well said. In answering these questions I also should answer it in the very same way." And expounding the Dhamma, he pronounced the following stanza:

421. For whom there is no ownership
Before or after or midway,
Owing nothing and unattached—
That one I call a brāhmaṇa.

56. The Elder Nun Rūpanandā

THIS IS A CITY MADE OF BONES ... This instruction was given by the Teacher while he was in residence at Jetavana with reference to the nun Janapada-Kalyāṇī Rūpanandā.

The story goes that one day Janapada-Kalyāṇī thought to herself, "My eldest brother has renounced the glory of dominion, has become a monk, and has now become the foremost being in the world, even the Buddha; his son, Rāhula Kumāra, has become a monk; my husband has become a monk; so also has my mother become a nun. Seeing that all these kinsfolk of mine have adopted the holy life, why should I continue any longer to live the household life? I, too, will become a nun." Accordingly she went to the Order of Nuns and became a nun, not at all because of faith, but solely because of love for her kinsfolk. Because of her wondrous beauty, she became known as Rūpanandā ("Beautiful Delight").

---

10. Their conversation is recorded in Majjhima Nikāya No. 44.

One day she heard that the Teacher had said, "Beauty of form is impermanent, involved in suffering, and non-self; so likewise are feeling, perception, the aggregate of mental states, and consciousness, impermanent, involved in suffering, and non-self." Thereupon she said to herself, "In that case he would find fault even with my own form, so beautiful to look upon and so fair to see." Therefore she avoided meeting the Teacher face to face.

Now the residents of Sāvatthī, having given alms early in the morning, took upon themselves the Uposatha precepts. In the evening, clad in spotless upper garments and bearing garlands and flowers in their hands, they assembled at Jetavana to hear the Dhamma. And the Order of Nuns also, desiring to hear the Dhamma, went to the monastery and heard the Dhamma. And having heard the Dhamma, they entered the city, praising the virtues of the Teacher as they entered.

(For there are four standards of judgement prevailing among persons who dwell together in the world. However, there are very few persons in whom the sight of the Tathāgata does not arouse a feeling of satisfaction. Those who judge by what they see, look upon the golden-hued body of the Tathāgata, adorned with the major marks and the minor marks, and are satisfied with what they see. Those who judge by what they hear, listen to the report of the Teacher's virtues through many hundreds of births, and to his voice, endowed with the eight excellences, in the preaching of the Dhamma, and are satisfied with what they hear. Those who judge by austerities are satisfied with his austere robes and so forth. Those whose standard of judgement is the Dhamma reflect: "Such is the virtue of the Master, such is his meditation, such is his wisdom; in virtue and meditation and wisdom the Exalted One is without an equal, is without a peer." Thus they also are satisfied. Indeed those who praise the virtues of the Tathāgata lack words with which to tell their praises.)

Rūpanandā listened to the nuns and the female lay disciples as they recited the praises of the Tathāgata, and having listened, said to herself, "In extravagant terms do they tell the praises of my brother. Suppose he were to find fault with my beauty of form during one single day. How much could he say in that length of time? Suppose I were to go with the nuns, and without letting myself be seen, look upon the Tathāgata, hear him preach the

Dhamma, and then return?" So she said to the nuns, "Today I too will go and hear the Dhamma." Said the nuns, "It has taken a long time to arouse in Rūpanandā a desire to wait upon the Teacher. Today, by reason of her, the Teacher will preach the Dhamma with many and various details." And with delighted hearts, taking her with them, they set out.

From the moment Rūpanandā started out, she kept thinking to herself, "I will not let him see who I am." The Teacher thought to himself, "Today Rūpanandā will come to pay her respects to me; what manner of lesson will do her the most good?" As he considered the matter further, he came to the following conclusion: "This woman thinks a great deal of her beauty of form and is deeply attached to her own person. It will therefore be of advantage to her if I crush out the pride she feels in her beauty of form by means of beauty of form itself, even as one draws out one thorn with another thorn." Accordingly, when it was time for her to enter the monastery, the Teacher put forth his power and created a young woman about sixteen years of age. Surpassing beauty did she possess; she wore crimson garments; she was adorned with all her ornaments, and stood before the Teacher with fan in hand, swinging the fan back and forth.

Now both the Teacher and Rūpanandā beheld this woman. As Rūpanandā entered the monastery with the nuns, she took her place behind the nuns, saluted the Teacher respectfully, and sat down among the nuns. Having done so, she surveyed from head to foot the person of the Teacher, richly brilliant with the major marks, resplendent with the minor marks, surrounded by a halo a fathom in extent. Then she saw the phantom of a woman standing near the Teacher and surveyed her face, glorious as the full moon. Having surveyed this woman, she surveyed her own person and compared herself to a crow standing before a royal goose of golden hue. For from the moment she looked upon this phantom, created by supernatural power, her eyes rolled back and forth. "Oh, how beautiful is her hair! Oh, how beautiful is her forehead!" she exclaimed. She was fascinated by the glorious beauty of every part of her body, and she became possessed with intense desire for equal beauty herself. The Teacher, observing that she was fascinated by the beauty of the woman, proceeded to teach her the Dhamma.

First he transformed the woman from a maiden about sixteen years of age to a woman about twenty years of age. Rūpanandā surveyed her form again, was quickly filled with a feeling of disappointment, and said to herself, "This form is by no means the same as it was before." Gradually the Teacher transformed her, first into a woman who had given birth to one child, then into a woman of middle life, finally into a decrepit old woman. Rūpanandā watched every stage of the transformation saying to herself, "Now this has disappeared, now that has disappeared." When, however, she saw her transformed into a decrepit old woman, and surveyed her standing there, teeth broken, hair grey, body bent, crooked as a curved beam, forced to lean on a cane, trembling in every limb, she was filled with great dispassion.

Then the Teacher caused disease to overmaster the woman. Casting away her cane and her palm-leaf fan, she screamed aloud, fell upon the ground, and rolled over and over, wallowing in her own urine and excrement. Rūpanandā looked upon her and was filled with great dispassion. Then the Teacher showed the death of that woman. Straightaway her body began to bloat. From its nine wound-like openings oozed pus and worms like lamp-wicks. Crows and dogs fell on her and tore her. Rūpanandā looked and thought, "In this very place this woman has come to old age, has come to disease, has come to death. Even so, this body of mine will come to old age, disease, and death." Thus she came to behold her own body in its impermanence; and as a result of doing so, she also saw her body as suffering and as devoid of self.

Straightaway the three modes of existence[11] appeared to her like houses set on fire, or like carrion tied to her neck, and her mind sprang forth to the meditation subject. The Teacher, perceiving that she had beheld her own body in its impermanence, considered within himself, "Will she, or will she not, by herself be able to get a firm footing?" Straightaway he became aware of the following: "She will not be able; she must have support from without." Accordingly, out of consideration for her welfare, he taught her the Dhamma by pronouncing the following stanzas:

---

11. The planes of sensuality, subtle form, and formlessness.

Behold, Nandā, this assemblage of elements
called the body;

It is diseased, impure, putrid; it oozes and leaks;
yet it is desired of simpletons.

As is this body, so also was that; as is that body,
so also will this body be.

Behold the elements in their emptiness;
go not back to the world;

Cast away desire for existence
and you shall go to perfect peace.

Thus, with reference to the nun Nandā, did the Exalted One pronounce these stanzas.

Directing her thought in a way conformable to his teaching, Nandā attained the fruit of stream-entry. Thereupon the Teacher, desiring that she should dwell with insight upon the three paths and the three fruits, and desiring to teach her to meditate upon the void, said to her, "Nandā, think not that there is an essence in this body; for there is not the least essence in this body. This body is but a city of bones, made by building up three hundred bones." So saying, he pronounced the following stanza:

150. This is a city made of bones
　　 Plastered with flesh and blood,
　　 In it are stored decay and death
　　 As well as pride and detraction.

At the conclusion of the lesson the nun Nandā attained arahantship; the multitude also profited by the lesson.

A Taste of Freedom

by
Ven. Ajahn Chah

Copyright © Kandy; Buddhist Publication Society,
(1980, 1988, 2006)

Introduction

The talks translated in this book were all taken from old cassette tape recordings of Venerable Ajahn Chah, some in Thai and some in the northeastern Lao dialect. Most were recorded on poor quality equipment under less than optimum conditions. This presented some difficulty in the work of translation, which was overcome by occasionally omitting very unclear passages and at other times asking for advice from other listeners more familiar with those languages. Nevertheless, there has inevitably been some editing in the process of making this book. Apart from the difficulties presented by the lack of clarity of the tapes, there is also the necessity of editing when one is taking words from the spoken to the written medium. For this, the translator takes full responsibility.

Pali words have occasionally been left as they are, in other cases translated. The criterion here has been readability. Those Pali words which were considered short enough or familiar enough to the reader already conversant with Buddhist terminology have generally been left untranslated. This should present no difficulty, as they are generally explained by the Venerable Ajahn in the course of the talk. Longer words, or words considered to be probably unfamiliar to the average reader, have been translated. Of these, there are two which are particularly noteworthy. They are *masukhallikānuyogo* and *attakilamathānuyogo*, which have been translated as "indulgence in pleasure" and "indulgence in pain" respectively. These two words occur in no less than five of the talks included in this book, and, although the translations provided here are not those generally used for these words, they are, nevertheless, in keeping with the Venerable Ajahn's use of them.

Venerable Ajahn Chah always gave his talks in simple, everyday language. His objective was to clarify the Dhamma, not to confuse his listeners with an overload of information. Consequently, the talks presented here have been rendered into correspondingly simple English. The aim has been to present Ajahn Chah's teaching in both the spirit and the letter.

In this edition of *A Taste of Freedom*, a number of corrections have been made to clumsily worded passages, of which there are now hopefully less than in the first edition. For such inadequacies, the translator must also take responsibility and hopes the reader will bear with any literary shortcomings in order to receive the full benefit of the teachings contained herein.

The translator

A Taste of Freedom

About this Mind

About this mind... in truth there is nothing really wrong with it. It is intrinsically pure. Within itself it's already peaceful. That the mind is not peaceful these days is because it follows moods. The real mind doesn't have anything to it, it is simply (an aspect of) Nature. It becomes peaceful or agitated because moods deceive it. The untrained mind is stupid. Sense impressions come and trick it into happiness, suffering, gladness and sorrow, but the mind's true nature is none of those things. That gladness or sadness is not the mind, but only a mood coming to deceive us. The untrained mind gets lost and follows these things, it forgets itself. Then we think that it is we who are upset or at ease or whatever.

However, really this mind of ours is already unmoving and peaceful ... Really peaceful! Just like a leaf which is still as long as no wind blows. If a wind comes up, the leaf flutters. The fluttering is due to the wind—the "fluttering" is due to those sense impressions; the mind follows them. If it doesn't follow them, it doesn't "flutter." If we know fully the true nature of sense impressions, we will be unmoved. Our practice is simply to see the Original Mind. So we must train the mind to know those sense impressions, and not get lost in them. To make the mind peaceful—just this is the aim of all this difficult practice we put ourselves through.

On Meditation

To calm the mind means to find the right balance. If you try to force your mind too much, it goes too far. If you don't try enough, it doesn't get there; it misses the point of balance.

Normally, the mind isn't still, it's moving all the time, and it lacks strength. Making the mind strong and making the body strong are not the same. To make the body strong we have to exercise it, to push it, in order to make it strong, but to make the mind strong means to make it peaceful, not to go thinking of this and that. For most of us the mind has never been peaceful, it has never had the energy of *samādhi*.[1]

If we force our breath to be too long or too short, we're not balanced; the mind won't become peaceful. It's like when we first start to use a pedal sewing machine. At first we just practise pedalling the machine to get our coordination right, before we actually sew anything. Following the breath is similar. We don't get concerned over how long or short, weak or strong it is—we just note it. We simply let it be, following the natural breathing.

When it's balanced, we take the breathing as our meditation object. When we breathe in, the beginning of the breath is at the nose tip, the middle of the breath at the chest, and the end of the breath at the abdomen. This is the path of the breath. When we breathe out, the beginning of the breath is at the abdomen, the middle at the chest and the end at the nose tip. We simply take note of this path of the breath at the nose tip, the chest, and the abdomen, then at the abdomen, the chest, and the tip of the nose. We take note of these three points in order to make the mind firm, to limit mental activity so that mindfulness and self-awareness can easily arise.

When we are adept at noting these three points, we can let them go and note the in and out breathing, concentrating solely at the tip of the nose or the upper lip where the air passes in and out. We don't have to follow the breath, we just establish mindfulness in front of us at the nose-tip and note the breath at this one point—entering, leaving, entering, leaving. There's no need to think of anything special, just concentrate on this simple task for now, having continuous presence of mind. There's nothing more to do, just breathe in and out.

Soon the mind becomes peaceful, the breath refined. The mind and body become light. This is the right state for the work of meditation.

When sitting in meditation, the mind becomes refined, but whatever the state is that it is in, we should try to be aware of it, to know it. Mental activity is there together with tranquility.

---

1. *Samādhi* is the state of concentrated calm resulting from meditation practice. So we establish it within a boundary. We sit in meditation, staying with the "one who knows."

There is *vitakka*, the action of bringing the mind to the theme of contemplation. If there is not much mindfulness, there will be not much *vitakka*. Then *vicāra*, the contemplation around that theme, follows. Various "weak" mental impressions may arise from time to time, but our self-awareness is the important thing—whatever may be happening we know it continuously. As we go deeper, we are constantly aware of the state of our meditation, knowing whether or not the mind is firmly established. Thus, both concentration and awareness are present.

To have a peaceful mind does not mean that there's nothing happening—mental impressions do arise. For instance, when we talk about the first level of absorption, we say it has five factors. Along with *vitakka* and *vicāra*, *pīti* (rapture) arises with the theme of contemplation and then *sukha* (happiness). These four things all lie together in the mind established in tranquility. They are one state.

The fifth factor is *ekaggatā* or one-pointedness. You may wonder how there can be one-pointedness when there are all these other factors as well. This is because they all become unified on that foundation of tranquility. Together they are called a state of *samādhi*. They are not everyday states of mind; they are factors of absorption. There are these five characteristics, but they do not disturb the basic tranquility. There is *vitakka*, but it does not disturb the mind; *vicāra*, rapture, and happiness arise, but do not disturb the mind. The mind is, therefore, one with these factors. The first level of absorption is like this.

We don't have to call it "first *jhāna*", "second *jhāna*", "third *jhāna*",[2] and so on, let's just call it "a peaceful mind." As the mind becomes progressively calmer, it will dispense with *vitakka* and *vicāra*, leaving only rapture and happiness. Why does the mind discard *vitakka* and *vicāra*? This is because, as the mind becomes more refined, the activity of *vitakka* and *vicāra* is too coarse to remain. At this stage, as the mind leaves off *vitakka* and *vicāra*, feelings of great rapture can arise, tears may gush out. However, as the *samādhi* deepens, rapture, too, is discarded, leaving only

---

2. *Jhāna* is an advanced state of concentration or *samādhi*, wherein the mind becomes absorbed into its meditation subject. It is divided into four levels, each progressively more refined than the previous one.

happiness and one-pointedness, until finally even happiness goes, and the mind reaches its greatest refinement. There is only equanimity and one-pointedness—all else has been left behind. The mind stands unmoving.

Samādhi is the state of concentrated calm resulting from meditation practice. Once the mind is peaceful, this can happen. You don't have to think a lot about it, it just happens by itself. This is called the energy of a peaceful mind. In this state the mind is not drowsy; the five hindrances—sense desire, aversion, restlessness, dullness, and doubt—have all fled.

However, if mental energy is still not strong and mindfulness is weak, there will occasionally arise intruding mental impressions. The mind is peaceful, but it's as if there is "cloudiness" within the calm. It's not a normal sort of drowsiness though, some impressions will manifest—maybe we'll hear a sound or see a dog or something. It's not really clear, but it's not a dream either. This is because these five factors have become unbalanced and weak.

The mind tends to play tricks within these levels of tranquility. Visions will sometimes arise through any of the senses when the mind is in this state, and the meditator may not be able to tell exactly what is happening. "Am I sleeping? No. Is it a dream? No, it's not a dream ..." These impressions arise from a middling sort of tranquility; but if the mind is truly calm and clear, we don't doubt the various mental impressions or visions which arise. Questions like, "Did I drift off then? Was I sleeping? Did I get lost?" don't arise, for they are characteristics of a mind which is still doubting. "Am I asleep or awake? ..." thus the mind is fuzzy. This is the mind getting lost in its moods. It's like the moon going behind a cloud. You can still see the moon, but the clouds covering it render it hazy. It's not like the moon that has emerged from behind the clouds—clear, sharp and bright.

When the mind is peaceful and established firmly in mindfulness and self-awareness, there will be no doubt concerning the various phenomena which we encounter. The mind will truly be beyond the hindrances. We will clearly know as it is everything which arises in the mind. We do not doubt it because the mind is clear and bright. The mind which reaches *samādhi* is like this.

However, some people find it hard to enter *samādhi* because it doesn't suit their tendencies. There is *samādhi*, but it's not strong or firm. However, one can attain peace through the use of wisdom, through contemplating and seeing the truth of things, solving problems that way. This is using wisdom rather than the power of *samādhi*. To attain calm in practice it's not necessary to sit in meditation, for instance. Just ask yourself, "Eh, what is that?" and solve your problem right there! A person with wisdom is like this. Perhaps he can't really attain high levels of *samādhi*, although he develops some, enough to cultivate wisdom. It's like the difference between farming rice and farming corn. One can depend on rice more than on corn for one's livelihood. Our practice can be like this, we depend more on wisdom to solve problems. When we see the truth, peace arises.

The two ways are not the same. Some people have insight and are strong in wisdom, but do not have much *samādhi*. When they sit in meditation, they aren't very peaceful. They tend to think a lot, contemplating this and that, until eventually they contemplate happiness and suffering and see the truth of them. Some incline more towards this than *samādhi*. Whether standing, walking, sitting, or lying,[3] the realisation of the Dhamma can take place. Through seeing, through relinquishing, they attain peace. They attain peace through knowing the truth without doubt, because they have seen it for themselves.

Other people have only a little wisdom, but their *samādhi* is very strong. They can enter very deep *samādhi* quickly, but not having much wisdom, they cannot catch their defilements, they don't know them. They can't solve their problems.

However, regardless of whichever approach we use, we must do away with wrong thinking, leaving only Right View. We must get rid of confusion, leaving only peace. Either way, we end up at the same place. There are these two sides to practice, but these two things, calm and insight, do go together. We can't do away with either of them. They must go together.

That which "looks over" the various factors which arise in meditation is *sati*, mindfulness. This *sati* is a condition which, through practice, can help other factors to arise. Sati is life. Whenever we don't have *sati*, when we are heedless, it's as if we are dead. If we have no *sati*, then our speech and actions have no meaning.

---

3. That is, at all times, in all activities.

This *sati* is simply recollection. It's a cause for the arising of self-awareness and wisdom. Whatever virtues we have cultivated are imperfect if lacking in *sati*. Sati is that which watches over us while standing, walking, sitting, and lying. Even when we are no longer in *samādhi*, *sati* should be present throughout.

Whatever we do, we do carefully. A sense of shame[4] will arise. We will feel ashamed about the things we do which aren't correct. As shame increases, our composure will increase as well. When composure increases, heedlessness will disappear. Even if we don't sit in meditation, these factors will be present in the mind.

These factors arise because of cultivating *sati*. Develop *sati*! This is the quality (*dhamma*) which looks over the work we are doing or have done in the past. It has real value. We should know ourselves at all times. If we know ourselves like this, right will distinguish itself from wrong, the path will become clear, and the cause for all shame will dissolve. Wisdom will arise. We can unify the practice as morality, concentration, and wisdom. To be collected, to be controlled, this is morality. The firm establishing of the mind within that control is concentration. Complete, overall knowledge within the activity in which we are engaged is wisdom. In brief, the practice is just morality, concentration and wisdom, or in other words, the path. There is no other way.

The Path in Harmony

Today I would like to ask you all, "Are you sure yet, are you certain in your meditation practice?" I ask, because these days there are many people teaching meditation, both monks and laypeople, and I'm afraid you may be subject to wavering and doubt. Only if we understand clearly, we will be able to make the mind peaceful and firm.

You should understand "the Eightfold Path" as morality, concentration and wisdom. The path comes together as simply as this. Our practice is to make this path arise within us.

When sitting in meditation, we are told to close the eyes, not to look at anything else, because now we are going to look directly at the mind. When we close our eyes, our attention comes

---

4. This is "shame" based on knowledge of cause and effect, rather than mere emotional guilt.

inwards. We establish our attention on the breath, centre our feelings there, and put our mindfulness there. When the factors of the path are in harmony, we will be able to see the breath, the feelings, the mind, and its mood for what they are. Here we will see the "focus point," where *samādhi* and the other factors of the path converge in harmony.

When you are sitting in meditation, following the breath, think to yourself that you are sitting alone. There is no one sitting around you, there is nothing at all. Develop this feeling that you are sitting alone until the mind lets go of all externals, concentrating solely on the breath. If you are thinking, "This person is sitting over here, that person is sitting over there," there is no peace and the mind doesn't come inwards. Just cast all that aside until you feel there is no one sitting around you, until there is nothing at all, until you have no interest in your surroundings and no wavering.

Let the breath go naturally; don't force it to be short or long or whatever. Just sit and watch it going in and out. When the mind lets go of all external impressions, the sounds of cars and so on will not disturb you. Nothing, whether sights or sounds, will disturb you, because the mind doesn't receive them. Your attention will come together on the breath.

If the mind is confused and won't concentrate on the breath, take a full, deep breath, as deep as you can, and then let it all out till there is none left. Do this three times and then re-establish your attention. The mind will become calm.

It's natural for the mind to be calm for a while, and then restlessness and confusion may arise again. When this happens, concentrate, breathe deeply again, and then reestablish your attention on the breath. Just keep going like this. When this has happened many times you will become adept at it, the mind will let go of all external impressions and they will not reach the mind. Sati will be firmly established. As the mind becomes more refined, so does the breath. Feelings will become finer and finer, the body and mind will be light. Our attention is solely on the inner—we see the in-breaths and out-breaths clearly, and we see all impressions clearly. We will see the coming together of morality, concentration and wisdom. This is called the path in harmony. When there is this harmony, the mind will be free of confusion, it will come together as one. This is known as *samādhi*.

After watching the breath for a long time, it may become very refined; the awareness of the breath will gradually cease, leaving only bare awareness. The breath may become so refined it disappears! Perhaps we are "just sitting," as if there is no breathing at all. Actually, there is breathing, but it seems as if there's none. This is because the mind has reached its most refined state, there is just bare awareness. It has gone beyond the breath. The knowledge that the breath has disappeared becomes established. What will we take as our object of meditation now? We take just this knowledge as our object, that is, the awareness that there's no breath.

Unexpected things may happen at this time; some people experience them, some don't. If they do arise, we should be firm and have strong mindfulness. Some people notice that the breath has disappeared and get fear; they're afraid they might die. Here we should know the situation just as it is. We simply notice that there's no breath and take that as our object of awareness. This, we can say, is the firmest, surest type of *samādhi*. There is only one firm, unmoving state of mind. Perhaps the body will become so light it's as if there is no body at all. We feel like we're sitting in empty space, everything seems empty. Although this may seem very unusual, you should understand that there's nothing to worry about. Firmly establish your mind like this.

When the mind is firmly unified, having no sense impressions to disturb it, one can remain in that state for any length of time. There will be no painful feelings to disturb us. When *samādhi* has reached this level, we can leave it when we choose, but if we come out of this *samādhi*, we do so comfortably, not because we've become bored with it or tired. We come out because we've had enough for now; we feel at ease, we have no problems at all.

If we can develop this type of *samādhi*, then, if we sit, say, thirty minutes or an hour, the mind will be cool and calm for many days. When the mind is cool and calm like this, it is clean. Whatever we experience, the mind will take it up and investigate it. This is a fruit of *samādhi*.

Morality has one function. Concentration has another function, and Wisdom another. These factors are like a cycle. We can see them all within the peaceful mind. When the mind is calm, it has collectedness and restraint because of wisdom and the energy of concentration. As it becomes more collected, it becomes more refined, which in turn gives morality the strength to increase in purity. As our morality becomes purer, it will help in the development of concentration. When concentration is firmly established, it helps in the arising of wisdom. Morality, concentration, and wisdom help each other, they are interrelated like this. In the end, the path becomes one and functions at all times. We should look after the strength which arises from the path, because it is the strength which leads to Insight and Wisdom.

The Benefits and Dangers of Samādhi

Samādhi is capable of bringing much harm or much benefit to the meditator; you can't say it brings only one or the other. For one who has no wisdom it can be harmful, but for one who has wisdom it can bring real benefit, it can lead him to Insight.

That which can be most harmful to the meditator is absorption—*samādhi*, *jhāna*, the *samādhi* with deep, sustained calm. This *samādhi* brings great peace. When there is peace, there is happiness. When there is happiness, attachment and clinging to that happiness arise. The meditator doesn't want to contemplate anything else; he just wants to indulge in that pleasant feeling. When we have been practising for a long time, we may become adept at entering this *samādhi* very quickly. As soon as we start to note our meditation object, the mind enters calm, and we don't want to come out to investigate anything. We just get stuck on that happiness. This is a danger for one who is practising meditation.

We must make use of *upacāra-samādhi*. Here, we enter calm, and then, when the mind is sufficiently calm, we come out and look at outer activity.[5] Looking at the outside with a calm mind gives rise to wisdom. This is hard to understand, because it's almost like ordinary thought and imagining. When thought is there, we may assume that the mind isn't peaceful, but actually that thought is taking place within the calm. There is contemplation, but it doesn't disturb the calm. We may bring thought up in order to contemplate it, to investigate it; it's not that we are aimlessly thinking or guessing away—it's something that arises from a peaceful mind.

---

5. "Outer activity" refers to all manner of sense impressions. It is used in contrast to the "inner activity" of absorption—*samādhi*, *jhāna*, where the mind does not "go out" to external sense impressions.

This is called "awareness within calm, and calm within awareness." If it's simply ordinary thought and imagination, the mind won't be peaceful, it will be disturbed. However, I am not talking about ordinary thought; this is a feeling that arises from the peaceful mind. It's called "contemplation." Wisdom is born right here.

So, there can be right *samādhi* and wrong *samādhi*. Wrong *samādhi* is where the mind enters calm and there's no awareness at all. One could sit for two hours or even all day, but the mind doesn't know where it's been or what's happened. It doesn't know anything. There is calm, but that's all. It's like a well-sharpened knife which we don't bother to put to any use. This is a deluded type of calm, because there is not much self-awareness. The meditator may think he has reached the ultimate already, so he doesn't bother to look for anything else. Samādhi can be an enemy at this level. Wisdom cannot arise because there is no awareness of right and wrong.

With right *samādhi*, no matter what level of calm is reached, there is awareness. There is full mindfulness and clear comprehension. This is the *samādhi* which can give rise to wisdom, one cannot get lost in it. Practitioners should understand this well. You can't do without this awareness; it must be present from beginning to end. This kind of *samādhi* has no danger.

You may wonder, "When does the benefit arise? How does the wisdom arise? From *samādhi*?" When right *samādhi* has been developed, wisdom has the chance to arise at all times. When the eye sees form, the ear hears sound, the nose smells odor, the tongue experiences taste, the body experiences touch, or the mind experiences mental impressions—in all postures—the mind stays with full knowledge of the true nature of those sense impressions, it doesn't "pick and choose." In any posture, we are fully aware of the birth of happiness and unhappiness. We let go of both of these things, we don't cling. This is called Right Practice, which is present in all postures. These words, "all postures," do not refer only to bodily postures, they refer to the mind, which has mindfulness and clear comprehension of the truth at all times. When *samādhi* has been rightly developed, wisdom arises like this. This is called "insight," knowledge of the truth.

There are two kinds of peace—the coarse and the refined. The peace which comes from *samādhi* is the coarse type. When the mind is peaceful there is happiness. The mind then takes this happiness to be peace. However, happiness and unhappiness are becoming and birth. There is no escape from *saṃsāra*[6] here because we still cling to them. So happiness is not peace, peace is not happiness.

The other type of peace is that which comes from wisdom. Here we don't confuse peace with happiness; we know the mind which contemplates and knows happiness and unhappiness as peace. The peace which arises from wisdom is not happiness, but is that which sees the truth of both happiness and unhappiness. Clinging to those states does not arise, the mind rises above them. This is the true goal of all Buddhist practice.

The Middle Way Within

The teaching of Buddhism is about giving up evil and practising good. Then, when evil is given up and goodness is established, we must let go of both good and evil. We have already heard enough about wholesome and unwholesome conditions to understand something about them, so I would like to talk about the Middle Way, that is, the path to escape from both of those things.

All the Dhamma talks and teachings of the Buddha have one aim—to show the way out of suffering to those who have not yet escaped. The teachings are for the purpose of giving us the right understanding. If we don't understand rightly, then we can't arrive at peace.

When the various Buddhas became enlightened and gave their first teachings, they all declared these two extremes—indulgence in pleasure and indulgence in pain.[7] These two ways are the ways of infatuation; they are the ways between which those who indulge in sense pleasures must fluctuate, never arriving at peace. They are the paths which keep us spinning around in *saṃsāra*.

The Enlightened One observed that all beings are stuck in these two extremes, never seeing the Middle Way of Dhamma, so he pointed them out in order to show the penalty involved in

---

6. *Saṃsāra*, the wheel of Birth and Death, is the world of all conditioned phenomena, mental and material, which has the threefold characteristic of Impermanence, Unsatisfactoriness, and Not-self.

7. See Introduction.

both. Because we are still stuck, because we are still wanting, we live repeatedly under their sway. The Buddha declared that these two ways are the ways of intoxication; they are not the ways of a meditator, nor the ways to peace. These ways are indulgence in pleasure and indulgence in pain, or, to put it simply, the way of slackness and the way of tension. If you investigate within, moment by moment, you will see that the tense way is anger, the way of sorrow. Going this way, there is only difficulty and distress. Indulgence in pleasure—if you've escaped from this, it means you've escaped from happiness. These ways, both happiness and unhappiness, are not peaceful states. The Buddha taught to let go of both of them. This is right practice. This is the Middle Way.

These words, "the Middle Way," do not refer to our body and speech, they refer to the mind. When a mental impression which we don't like arises, it affects the mind and there is confusion. When the mind is confused, when it's "shaken up," this is not the right way. When a mental impression arises which we like, the mind goes to indulgence in pleasure—that's not the way either.

We people don't want suffering, we want happiness. However, in fact, happiness is just a refined form of suffering. Suffering itself is the coarse form. You can compare them to a snake. The head of the snake is unhappiness; the tail of the snake is happiness. The head of the snake is really dangerous, it has the poisonous fangs. If you touch it, the snake will bite straight away. However, never mind the head, even if you go and hold onto the tail, it will turn around and bite you just the same, because both the head and the tail belong to the one snake.

In the same way, both happiness and unhappiness, or pleasure and sadness, arise from the same parent—wanting. So when you're happy the mind isn't peaceful. It really isn't! For instance, when we get the things we like, such as wealth, prestige, praise, or happiness, we become pleased as a result. However, the mind still harbors some uneasiness because we're afraid of losing it. That very fear isn't a peaceful state. Later on, we may actually lose that thing and then we really suffer. Thus, if you aren't aware, even if you're happy, suffering is imminent. It's just the same as grabbing the snake's tail—if you don't let go, it will bite. So whether it's the snake's tail or its head, that is, wholesome or unwholesome conditions, they're all just characteristics of the Wheel of Existence, of endless change.

The Buddha established morality, concentration, and wisdom as the path to peace, the way to enlightenment. However, in truth, these things are not the essence of Buddhism. They are merely the path. The Buddha called them *magga*, which means "path." The essence of Buddhism is peace, and that peace arises from truly knowing the nature of all things. If we investigate closely, we can see that peace is neither happiness nor unhappiness. Neither of these is the truth.

The human mind, the mind which the Buddha exhorted us to know and investigate, is something we can only know by its activity. The true "original mind" has nothing to measure it by, there's nothing you can know it by. In its natural state it is unshaken, unmoving. When happiness arises, all that is happening is that this mind is getting lost in a mental impression, there is movement. When the mind moves like this, clinging and attachment to those things come into being.

The Buddha has already laid down the path of practice fully, but we have not yet practised, or if we have, we've practised only in speech. Our minds and our speech are not yet in harmony, we just indulge in empty talk. However, the basis of Buddhism is not something that can be talked about or guessed at. The real basis of Buddhism is full knowledge of the truth of reality. If one knows this truth, then no teaching is necessary. If one doesn't know, then, even if one listens to the teaching, one doesn't really hear. This is why the Buddha said, "The Enlightened One only points the way." He can't do the practice for you; because the truth is something you cannot put into words or give away.

All the teachings are merely similes and comparisons, means to help the mind see the truth. If we haven't seen the truth, we must suffer. For example, we commonly say *saṅkhāras*[8] when referring to the body. Anybody can say it, but, in fact, we have problems simply because we don't know the truth of these *saṅkhāras*, and thus cling to them. Because we don't know the truth of the body, we suffer.

---

8. In the Thai language the word *sungkahn*, from the Pali word *saṅkhāra*—the name given to all conditioned phenomena—is a commonly used term for the body. The Venerable Ajahn uses the word in both ways.

Here is an example. Suppose one morning you're walking to work and a man yells abuse and insults at you from across the street. As soon as you hear this abuse, your mind changes from its usual state. You don't feel so good, you feel angry and hurt. That man walks around abusing you night and day. When you hear the abuse, you get angry, and even when you return home, you're still angry because you feel vindictive; you want to get even. A few days later another man comes to your house and calls out, "Hey! That man who abused you the other day, he's mad, he's crazy! He has been so for years! He abuses everybody like that. Nobody takes any notice of anything he says." As soon as you hear this, you are suddenly relieved. That anger and hurt that you've pent up within you all these days melts away completely. Why? Because you know the truth of the matter now. Before, you didn't know, you thought that man was normal, so you were angry at him. Understanding like that caused you to suffer. As soon as you find out the truth, everything changes: "Oh, he's mad! That explains everything!" When you understand this, you feel fine, because you know for yourself. Having known, then you can let go. If you don't know the truth, you cling right there. When you thought that man who abused you was normal, you could have killed him. However, when you find out the truth, that he's mad, you feel much better. This is knowledge of the truth.

Someone who sees the Dhamma has a similar experience. When attachment, aversion, and delusion disappear, they disappear in the same way. As long as we don't know these things, we think, "What can I do? I have so much greed and aversion." This is not clear knowledge.

It's just the same as when we thought the madman was sane. When we finally see that he was mad all along, we're relieved of worry. No one could show you this. Only when the mind sees for itself, can it uproot and relinquish attachment. It's the same with this body that we call *saṅkhāras*. Although the Buddha has already explained that it's not substantial or a real being as such, we still don't agree, we stubbornly cling to it. If the body could talk, it would be telling us all day long, "You're not my owner, you know." Actually, it's telling us all the time, but it's Dhamma language, so we're unable to understand it. For instance, the sense organs of eye, ear, nose, tongue, and body are continually changing, but I've never seen them ask permission from us even once! Like when we have a headache or a stomach ache—the body never asks permission first, it just goes right ahead, following its natural course. This shows that the body doesn't allow anyone to be its owner, it doesn't have an owner. The Buddha described it as an empty thing.

We don't understand the Dhamma, and so we don't understand these *saṅkhāras*; we take them to be ourselves, as belonging to us or belonging to others. This gives rise to clinging. When clinging arises, "becoming" follows. Once becoming arises, then there is birth. Once there is birth, then old age, sickness, death—the whole mass of suffering—arises. This is *Paṭiccasamuppāda*.[9] We say that ignorance gives rise to volitional activities and that they give rise to consciousness and so on. All these things are simply mental events. When we come into contact with something we don't like, if we don't have mindfulness, ignorance is there and suffering arises straight away. However, the mind passes through these changes so rapidly that we can't keep up with them. It's the same as when you fall from a tree. Before you know it—"Thud!"—you've hit the ground. Actually you've passed many branches and twigs on the way, but you couldn't count them, you couldn't remember them as you passed them. You just fell, and then "Thud!"

The *Paṭiccasamuppāda* is the same as this. If we divide it up as it is in the scriptures, we say ignorance gives rise to volitional activities, volitional activities give rise to consciousness, consciousness gives rise to mind and matter, mind and matter give rise to the six sense bases, the sense bases give rise to sense contact, contact gives rise to feeling, feeling gives rise to wanting, wanting gives rise to clinging, clinging gives rise to becoming, becoming gives rise to birth, birth gives rise to old age, sickness, death, and all forms of sorrow. However, in truth, when you come into contact with something you don't like, there's immediate suffering! That feeling of suffering is actually the result of the whole chain of the *Paṭiccasamuppāda*. This is why the Buddha exhorted his disciples to investigate and know fully their own minds.

---

9. *Paṭiccasamuppāda*—the Chain of Conditioned Arising, one of the central doctrines of Buddhist philosophy.

When people are born into the world, they are without names—once born, we name them. This is convention. We give people names for the sake of convenience, to call each other by. The scriptures are the same. We separate everything up with labels to make studying the reality convenient. In the same way, all things are simply *saṅkhāras*. Their original nature is merely that of things born of conditions. The Buddha said that they are impermanent, unsatisfactory, and not-self. They are unstable. If we don't understand this firmly, our understanding is not straight, and so we have wrong view. This wrong view is that the *saṅkhāras* are ourselves, that we are the *saṅkhāras*, or that happiness and unhappiness are ourselves, that we are happiness and unhappiness. Seeing like this is not full, clear knowledge of the true nature of things. The truth is that we can't force all these things to follow our desires; they follow the way of nature.

A simple comparison is this: suppose you go and sit in the middle of a freeway with the cars and trucks charging down at you. You can't get angry at the cars, shouting, "Don't drive over here! Don't drive over here!" It's a freeway, you can't tell them that! So what can you do? You get off the road! The road is the place where cars run, if you don't want the cars to be there, you suffer.

It's the same with *saṅkhāras*. We say they disturb us, like when we sit in meditation and hear a sound. We think, "Oh, that sound's bothering me." If we understand that the sound bothers us, then we suffer accordingly. If we investigate a little deeper, we will see that it's we who go out and disturb the sound! The sound is simply sound. If we understand like this, then there's nothing more to it, we let it be. We see that the sound is one thing, we are another. One who understands that the sound comes to disturb him is one who doesn't see himself. He really doesn't! Once you see yourself, then you're at ease. The sound is just sound, why should you go and grab it? You see that actually it was you who went out and disturbed the sound. This is real knowledge of the truth. You see both sides, so you have peace. If you see only one side, there is suffering. Once you see both sides, then you follow the Middle Way. This is the right practice of the mind. This is what we call "straightening out our understanding."

In the same way, the nature of all *saṅkhāras* is impermanence and death, but we want to grab them, we carry them about and covet them. We want them to be true. We want to find truth within the things that aren't true! Whenever someone sees like this and clings to the *saṅkhāras* as being himself, he suffers. The Buddha wanted us to consider this.

The practice of Dhamma is not dependent on being a monk, a novice, or a layman; it depends on straightening out your understanding. If our understanding is correct, we arrive at peace. Whether you are a monk or not it's the same, every person has the chance to practise Dhamma, to contemplate it. We all contemplate the same thing. If you attain peace, it's all the same peace; it's the same Path, with the same methods.

Therefore the Buddha didn't discriminate between laymen and monks; he taught all people to practise in order to know the truth of the *saṅkhāras*. When we know this truth, we let them go. If we know the truth there will be no more becoming or birth. How is there no more birth? There is no way for birth to take place because we fully know the truth of *saṅkhāras*. If we fully know the truth, then there is peace. Having or not having, it's all the same. Gain and loss are one. The Buddha taught us to know this. This is peace; peace from happiness, unhappiness, gladness and sorrow.

We must see that there is no reason to be born. Born in what way? Born into gladness. When we get something we like we are glad over it. If there is no clinging to that gladness, then there is no birth; if there is clinging, this is called "birth." So if we get something, we aren't born (into gladness). If we lose, then we aren't born (into sorrow). This is the birthless and the deathless. Birth and death are both founded in clinging to and cherishing the *saṅkhāras*.

So the Buddha said. "There is no more becoming for me, finished is the holy life, this is my last birth." There! He knew the birthless and the deathless! This is what the Buddha constantly exhorted his disciples to know. This is the right practice. If you don't reach it, if you don't reach the Middle Way, then you won't transcend suffering.

The Peace Beyond

It's of great importance that we practise the Dhamma. If we don't practise, then all our knowledge is only superficial knowledge, just the outer shell of it. It's as if we have some sort of fruit, but we haven't eaten it yet. Even though we have that fruit in our hand, we get no benefit from it. Only through the actual eating of the fruit will we really know its taste.

The Buddha didn't praise those who merely believe others; he praised the person who knows within himself. Just as with that fruit, if we have tasted it already, we don't have to ask anyone else if it's sweet or sour. Our problems are over. Why are they over? Because we see according to the Truth. One who has realized the Dhamma is like one who has realized the sweetness or sourness of the fruit. All doubts are ended right here.

When we talk about Dhamma, although we may say a lot, it can usually be brought down to four things, that are simply, to know suffering, to know the cause of suffering, to know the end of suffering, and to know the path of practice leading to the end of suffering. This is all there is. All that we have experienced on the path of practice so far comes down to these four things. When we know these things, our problems are over.

Where are these four things born? They are born just within the body and the mind, nowhere else. So why is the Dhamma of the Buddha so broad and expansive? This is so in order to explain these things in a more refined way, to help us to see them.

When Siddhattha Gotama was born into the world, before he saw the Dhamma, he was an ordinary person just like us. When he knew what he had to know, that is, the truth of suffering, the cause, the end, and the way leading to the end of suffering, he realized the Dhamma and became a perfectly Enlightened Buddha.

When we realize the Dhamma, wherever we sit, we know Dhamma, wherever we are, we hear the Buddha's teaching. When we understand Dhamma, the Buddha is within our minds, the Dhamma is within our minds, and the practice leading to wisdom is within our own minds. Having the Buddha, the Dhamma, and the Sangha within our minds means that whether our actions are good or bad, we know clearly for ourselves their true nature. That is how the Buddha discarded worldly opinions, discarded praise and criticism. When people praised or criticized him, he just accepted it for what it was. These two things are simply worldly conditions, so he wasn't shaken by them. Why not? Because he knew suffering. He knew that if he believed in that praise or criticism, it would cause him to suffer.

When suffering arises, it agitates us, we feel ill at ease. What is the cause of that suffering? It's because we don't know the Truth, this is the cause. When the cause is present, then suffering arises; once arisen we don't know how to stop it. The more we try to stop it, the more it comes on. We say, "Don't criticize me," or "Don't blame me". Trying to stop it like this, suffering really comes on; it won't stop.

The Buddha taught that the way leading to the end of suffering is to make the Dhamma arise as a reality within our own minds. We become one who witnesses the Dhamma for himself. If someone says we are good, we don't get lost in it; if they say we are no good, we don't get lost in it; if they say we are no good, we don't forget ourselves. This way we can be free. "Good" and "evil" are just worldly dhammas; they are just states of mind. If we follow them, our mind becomes the world; we just grope in the darkness and don't know the way out. If it's like this, then we have not yet mastered ourselves. We try to defeat others, but, in doing so, we only defeat ourselves; however, if we have mastery over ourselves, then we have mastery over all—over all mental formations, sights, sounds, smells, tastes, and bodily feelings.

Now, I'm talking about externals, they're like that, but the outside is reflected inside also. Some people only know the outside; they don't know the inside. Like when we say to "see the body in the body."[10] Having seen the outer body is not enough; we must know the body within the body. Then, having investigated the mind, we should know the mind within the mind.

Why should we investigate the body? What is this "body in the body"? When we say "to know the mind," what is this "mind"? If we don't know the mind, then we don't know the things within the mind. This is to be someone who doesn't know suffering,

---

10. Ajahn Chah is referring to a refrain found after each meditation exercise concerning the body, etc, in the Satipaṭṭhānasutta, the Discourse on the Establishment of Mindfulness.

doesn't know the cause, doesn't know the end, and doesn't know the way leading to the end of suffering. The things which should help to extinguish suffering don't help, because we get distracted by the things which aggravate it. It's just as if we have an itch on our head and we scratch our leg! If it's our head that's itchy, then we're obviously not going to get much relief. In the same way, when suffering arises, we don't know how to handle it, we don't know the practice leading to the end of suffering.

For instance, take this body, this body that each of us has brought along to this meeting. If we just see the form of the body, there's no way we can escape suffering. Why not? Because we still don't see the inside of the body, we only see the outside. We only see it as something beautiful, something substantial. The Buddha said that this alone is not enough. We see the outside with our eyes; a child can see it, animals can see it, it's not difficult. The outside of the body is easily seen, but, having seen it, we stick to it, we don't know the truth of it. Having seen it, we grab onto it, and it bites us!

So we should investigate the body within the body. Whatever's in the body, go ahead and look at it. If we just see the outside, it's not clear. We see hair, nails, and so on and they are just pretty things which entice us. Therefore the Buddha taught to see the inside of the body, to see the body within the body. What is in the body? Look closely within! We will see many things inside to surprise us, because even though they are within us, we've never seen them. Wherever we walk, we carry them with us, sitting in a car, we carry them with us, but we still don't know them at all! It's as if we visit some relatives at their house and they give us a present. We take it, put it in our bag, and then leave without opening it to see what is inside. When at last we open it—it's full of poisonous snakes! Our body is like this. If we just see the shell of it, we say it's fine and beautiful. We forget ourselves. We forget impermanence, unsatisfactoriness, and not-self. If we look within this body, it's really repulsive. If we look according to reality, without trying to sugar things over, we'll see that it's really pitiful and wearisome. Dispassion will arise. This feeling of "disinterest" is not that we feel aversion for the world or anything; it's simply our minds clearing up, our minds letting go. We see things as not substantial and dependable and that all things are naturally established just as they are. However we want them to be, they just go their own way. Regardless whether we laugh or cry, they simply are the way they are. Things which are unstable are unstable; things which are not beautiful are not beautiful.

The Buddha said that whenever we experience sights, sounds, tastes, smells, bodily feelings, or mental states, we should release them. When the ear hears sounds, let them go. When the nose smells an odour, let it go. Just leave it at the nose! When bodily feelings arise, let go of the like or dislike that follow, let them go back to their birthplace. The same for mental states. All these things—just let them go their way. This is knowing. Whether it's happiness or unhappiness, it's all the same. This is called meditation.

Meditation means to make the mind peaceful in order to let wisdom arise. This requires that we practise with body and mind in order to see and know the sense impressions of form, sound, taste, smell, touch and mental formations. To put it shortly, it's just a matter of happiness and unhappiness. Happiness is pleasant feeling in the mind, unhappiness is just unpleasant feeling. The Buddha taught to separate this happiness and unhappiness from the mind. The mind is that which knows. Feeling[11] is the characteristic of happiness or unhappiness, like or dislike. When the mind indulges in these things, we say that it clings to or takes that happiness and unhappiness to be worthy of holding. That clinging is an action of mind, that happiness or unhappiness is feeling.

When we say the Buddha told us to separate the mind from feeling, he didn't literally mean to throw them to different places. He meant that the mind must know happiness and know unhappiness. When sitting in *samādhi*, for example, and peace fills the mind, then happiness comes, but it doesn't reach us, unhappiness comes, but doesn't reach us. This is to separate feeling from the mind. We can compare it to oil and water in a bottle. They don't combine. Even if you try to mix them, the oil remains oil, and the water remains water. Why is this so? Because they are of different density.

---

11. Feeling is a translation of the Pali word *vedanā*, and should be understood in the sense Ajahn Chah herein describes it: as the mental states of like, dislike, gladness, sorrow, etc.

The natural state of the mind is neither happiness nor unhappiness. When feeling enters the mind, then happiness or unhappiness is born. If we have mindfulness, then we know pleasant feeling as pleasant feeling. The mind which knows will not pick it up. Happiness is there, but it's "outside" the mind, not buried within the mind. The mind simply knows it clearly.

If we separate unhappiness from the mind, does that mean there is no suffering, that we don't experience it? Yes, we experience it, but we know mind as mind, feeling as feeling. We don't cling to that feeling or carry it around. The Buddha separated these things through knowledge. Did he have suffering? He knew the state of suffering, but he didn't cling to it, so we say that he cut suffering off. And there was happiness too, but he knew that happiness, if it's not known, is like a poison. He didn't hold it to be himself. Happiness was there through knowledge, but it didn't bury itself in his mind. Thus we say that he separated happiness and unhappiness from his mind.

When we say that the Buddha and the Enlightened Ones killed defilements,[12] it's not that they literally killed them. If they had killed all defilements, then we probably wouldn't have any! They didn't literally kill defilements; when they knew them for what they were, they let go of them. Someone who's stupid will grab them, but the Enlightened Ones knew the defilements in their own minds as poison, so they swept them out. They swept out the things which caused them to suffer, they didn't kill them. One who doesn't know this will see some things, such as happiness, as good, and then grab them, but the Buddha just knew them and simply brushed them away.

However, when feeling arises for us, we indulge in it, that is, the mind carries that happiness and unhappiness around. In fact, they are two different things. The activities of mind, pleasant feeling, unpleasant feeling, and so on, are mental impressions, they are the world. If the mind knows this, it can equally do work involving happiness or unhappiness. Why? Because it knows the truth of these things. Someone who doesn't know them sees them as equal. If you cling to happiness, it will be the birthplace of

---

12. Defilements, or *kilesa*, are the habits born of ignorance which infest the minds of all unenlightened beings. and obstruct progress towards liberation.

unhappiness later on, because happiness is unstable, it changes all the time. When happiness disappears, unhappiness arises.

The Buddha knew that because both happiness and unhappiness are unsatisfactory, they have the same value. When happiness arose, he let it go. He had right practice, seeing that both these things have equal values and drawbacks. They come under the Law of Dhamma, that is, they are unstable and unsatisfactory. Once born, they die. When he saw this, Right View arose; the right way of practice became clear. No matter what sort of feeling or thinking arose in his mind, he knew all as simply the continuous play of happiness and unhappiness. He didn't cling to it.

When the Buddha was newly enlightened, he gave a sermon about indulgence in pleasure and indulgence in pain. "Monks! Indulgence in pleasure is the loose way; indulgence in pain is the tense way." These were the two things that disturbed his practice until the day he was enlightened, because at first he didn't let go of them. When he knew them, he let them go, and so was able to give his first sermon. So we say that a meditator should not walk the way of happiness or unhappiness, rather he should know them. Knowing the truth of suffering, he will know the cause of suffering, the end of suffering, and the way leading to the end of suffering. The way out of suffering is meditation itself. To put it simply, we must be mindful.

Mindfulness is knowing, or presence of mind. Right now, what are we thinking; what are we doing? What do we have with us right now? When we observe like this, we are aware of how we are living. When we practise like this, wisdom can arise. We consider and investigate at all times, in all postures. When a mental impression that we like arises, we know it as such; we don't hold it to be anything substantial. It's just happiness. When unhappiness arises, we know that it's indulgence in pain and not the path of a meditator.

This is what we call separating the mind from feeling. If we are clever, we don't attach, we let things be. We become the "one who knows". The mind and feeling are just like oil and water; they are in the same bottle, but they don't mix. Even if we are sick or in pain, we can still know feeling as feeling and the mind as mind. We know painful or comfortable states, but we don't identify with them. We stay only with peace—the peace beyond both comfort and pain.

You should understand it like this, because if there is no permanent self, then there is no refuge. You must live like this, that is, without happiness and without unhappiness. You should stay only with the knowing, you shouldn't carry things around.

As long as we are still unenlightened, all this may sound strange, but it doesn't matter, we just set our goal in this direction. The mind is the mind. It meets happiness and unhappiness, and we see them as merely that; there's nothing more to it. They are divided, not mixed. If they are all mixed up, then we don't know them. It's like living in a house; the house and its occupant are related, but separate. If there is danger in our house, we are distressed because we must protect it, but if the house catches fire, we get out of it. If painful feeling arises, we get out of it, just like we get out of that burning house. When the house is full of fire and we know it, we come running out of it. They are separate things; the house is one thing, the occupant is another.

We say that we separate mind and feeling in this way, but, in fact, they are by nature already separate. Our realization is simply to know this natural separateness according to reality. When we say they are not separated, it's because we're clinging to them through ignorance of the truth.

So the Buddha told us to meditate. This practice of meditation is very important. Merely to know with the intellect is not enough. The knowledge which arises from practice with a peaceful mind and the knowledge which comes from study are really far apart. The knowledge which comes from study is not real knowledge of our minds. The mind tries to hold onto and keep this knowledge. Why do we try to keep it? Just lose it! And then, when it's lost, we cry!

If we really know, then there's letting go, letting things be. We know how things are and don't forget ourselves. If it happens that we are sick, we don't get lost in that. Some people think, "This year I was sick the whole time, I couldn't meditate at all." These are the words of a really foolish person. Someone who's sick and dying should really be diligent in his practice. One may say that one doesn't trust one's body, and so one feels that one can't meditate. If we think like this, then things are difficult. The Buddha didn't teach like that. He said that right here is the place to meditate. When we're sick or almost dying, that's when we can really know and see reality.

Other people say they don't have the chance to meditate because they're too busy. Sometimes school teachers come to see me. They say they have many responsibilities, so there's no time to meditate. I ask them, "When you're teaching, do you have time to breathe?" They answer, "Yes." "So how can you have time to breathe if the work is so hectic and confusing? Here you are far from Dhamma."

Actually, this practice is just about the mind and its feelings. It's not something that you have to run after or struggle for. Breathing continues while working. Nature takes care of the natural processes—all we have to do is try to be aware. Just to keep trying; keep going inwards to see clearly. Meditation is like this.

If we have that presence of mind, then whatever work we do will be the very tool that enables us to know right and wrong continually. There's plenty of time to meditate, we just don't fully understand the practice, that's all. While sleeping we breathe, while eating we breathe, don't we? Why don't we have time to meditate? Wherever we are, we breathe. If we think like this, then our life has as much value as our breath. Wherever we are, we have time.

All modes of thought are mental conditions, not bodily conditions, so we simply need to have presence of mind, then we will know right and wrong at all times. Standing, walking, sitting and lying, there's plenty of time. We just don't know how to use it properly. Please consider this.

We cannot run away from feeling, we must know it. Feeling is just feeling, happiness is just happiness, unhappiness is just unhappiness. They are simply that. So why should we cling to them? If the mind is clever, simply to hear this is enough to enable us to separate feeling from the mind.

If we investigate like this continuously, the mind will find release, but it's not escaping through ignorance. The mind lets go, but it knows. It doesn't let go through stupidity. It doesn't let go because it doesn't want things to be the way they are. It lets go because it knows according to the truth. This is seeing nature, the reality that's all around us.

When we know this, we are skilled with the mind, we are skilled with mental impressions. When we are skilled with mental impressions, we are skilled with the world. This is to be a "Knower of the World." The Buddha was someone who clearly knew the world with all its difficulty. He knew the troublesome, but he also knew that the not troublesome is right here. This world is so confusing, how is it that the Buddha was able to know it? Here we should understand that the Dhamma taught by the Buddha is not beyond our ability. In all postures we should have presence of mind and self-awareness—and when it's time to sit in meditation, we do that.

We sit in meditation to establish peacefulness and cultivate mental energy. We don't do it in order to play around at anything special. Insight meditation is sitting in *samādhi* itself. At some places they say, "Now we are going to sit in *samādhi*, after that we'll do insight meditation." Don't divide them like this! Tranquility is the base which gives rise to wisdom; wisdom is the fruit of tranquility. To say that now we are going to do calm meditation and later we'll do insight—you can't do that! You can only divide them in speech. Just like a knife, the blade is on one side, the back of the blade on the other. You can't divide them. If you pick up one side, you get both sides. Tranquility gives rise to wisdom like this.

Morality is the father and mother of the Dhamma. In the beginning we must have morality. Morality is peace. This means that there are no wrong doings in body or speech. When we don't do wrong, then we don't get agitated; when we don't become agitated, then peace and collectedness arise within the mind. So we say that morality, concentration and wisdom are the path on which all the Noble Ones have walked to enlightenment. They are all one. Morality is concentration, concentration is morality. Concentration is wisdom, wisdom is concentration. It's like a mango. When it's a flower, we call it a flower. When it becomes a fruit, we call it a mango. When it ripens we call it a ripe mango. It's all one mango, but it continually changes. The big mango grows from the small mango; the small mango becomes a big one. You can call them different fruits or all one. Morality, concentration, and wisdom are related like this. In the end, it's the entire path that leads to enlightenment.

The mango, from the moment it first appears as a flower, simply grows to ripeness. This is enough; we should see it like this. Whatever others call it, it doesn't matter. Once it's born, it grows to old age, and then what? We should contemplate this.

Some people don't want to be old. When they get old, they become regretful. These people shouldn't eat ripe mangoes! Why do we want the mangoes to be ripe? If they're not ripe in time, we ripen them artificially, don't we? However, when we become old, we are filled with regret. Some people cry, they're afraid to get old or die. If it's like this, then they shouldn't eat ripe mangoes, better eat just the flowers! If we can see this, then we can see the Dhamma. Everything clears up, we are at peace. Just determine to practice like that.

Today the Chief Privy Councillor and his party have come to hear the Dhamma. You should take what I've said and contemplate it. If anything is not right, please excuse me. However, for you to know whether it's right or wrong depends on your practising and seeing for yourselves. Whatever's wrong, throw it out. If it's right, then take it and use it. However, we actually practise in order to let go of both right and wrong. In the end, we just throw everything out. If it's right, throw it out; wrong, throw it out! Usually, if it's right, we cling to rightness, if it's wrong, we hold it to be wrong, and then arguments follow. However, the Dhamma is the place where there's nothing—nothing at all.

Opening the Dhamma Eye

Some of us start to practise, and even after a year or two, still don't know what's what. We are still unsure of the practice. When we're still unsure, we don't see that everything around us is purely Dhamma, and so we turn to the teachings from the Ajahns. However, when we actually know our own mind, when there is *sati* to look closely at the mind, there is wisdom. All times and all places become occasions for us to hear the Dhamma.

We can learn Dhamma from nature, from trees, for example. A tree is born due to causes, and it grows following the course of nature. Right here, the tree is teaching us Dhamma, but we don't understand this. In due course, it grows until it buds, flowers, and fruits. All we see is the appearance of the flowers and fruit; we're unable to bring this within and contemplate it. Thus, we don't know that the tree is teaching us Dhamma. The fruit appears, and we merely eat it without investigating the nature of the fruit: sweet, sour, or salty. This Dhamma is the teaching of the fruit.

Next, the leaves grow old. They wither, die, and then fall from the tree. All we see is that the leaves have fallen down. We step on them, we sweep them up—that's all. We don't investigate thoroughly, so we don't know that nature is teaching us. Later on, the new leaves sprout, and we merely see that, without taking it further. We don't bring these things into our minds to contemplate. If we can bring all this inwards and investigate it, we will see that the birth of a tree and our own birth are no different. This body of ours is born and exists dependent on conditions, on the elements of earth, water, wind and fire. It has its food, it grows and grows. Every part of the body changes and flows according to its nature. It's no different from the tree; the hair, nails, teeth, and skin—all change. If we know the things of nature, then we will know ourselves.

People are born. In the end they die. Having died, they are born again. Nails, teeth and skin are constantly dying and growing again. If we understand the practice, then we can see that a tree is no different from ourselves. If we understand the teaching of the Ajahns, then we realize that the outside and the inside are comparable. Things with consciousness and those without consciousness do not differ. They are the same. And if we understand this sameness, then when we see the nature of a tree, for example, we will know that it's no different from our own five *khandhas*[13] body, feeling, memory, thinking, and consciousness. If we have this understanding, then we understand Dhamma. If we understand Dhamma, we understand the five *khandhas*, how they constantly shift and change, never stopping.

So, whether standing, walking, sitting, or lying we should have *sati* to watch over and look after the mind. When we see external things, it's like seeing internals. When we see internals, it's the same as seeing externals. If we understand this, then we can hear the teaching of the Buddha. If we understand this, then we can say that Buddha-nature, the "one who knows," has been established. It knows the external. It knows the internal. It understands all things that arise. Understanding like this, then sitting at the foot of a tree we hear the Buddha's teaching. Standing, walking, sitting,

---

13. *Khandhas* are the five "groups" which go to make up what we call "a person."

or lying; we hear the Buddha's teaching. Seeing, hearing, smelling, tasting, touching and thinking; we hear the Buddha's teaching. The Buddha is just this "one who knows" within this very mind. It knows the Dhamma; it investigates the Dhamma. It's not that the Buddha-nature, the "one who knows," arises, rather the mind itself becomes illumined.

If we establish the Buddha within our minds, then we see everything, we contemplate everything, as being no different from ourselves. We see various animals, trees, mountains, and vines as being no different from ourselves. We see poor people and rich people—they're no different! They all have the same characteristics. One who understands like this is content wherever he is. He listens to the Buddha's teaching at all times. If we don't understand this, then even if we spend all our time listening to teachings from the various Ajahns, we still won't understand their meaning.

The Buddha said that the realisation of the Dhamma is just knowing Nature,[14] the reality which is all around us, the Nature which is right here! If we don't understand this Nature we experience disappointment and joy, we get lost in moods, giving rise to sorrow and regret. Getting lost in mental objects is getting lost in Nature. When we get lost in Nature, then we don't know Dhamma. The Enlightened One merely pointed out this Nature. Having arisen, all things change and die. Things we make, such as plates, bowls, and dishes, all have the same characteristic. A bowl is moulded into being due to a cause, man's impulse to create, and as we use it, it gets old, breaks up, and disappears. Trees, mountains, and vines are the same, right up to animals and people.

When Aññā Kondañña, the first disciple, heard the Buddha's teaching for the first time, the realization he had was not very complicated. He simply saw that whatever is born, all that must change and grow old as a natural condition, and eventually must die. Aññā Kondañña had never thought of this before, or, if he had, it wasn't thoroughly clear, so he hadn't yet let go; he still clung to the *khandhas*. As he sat mindfully listening to the Buddha's discourse, Buddha-nature arose in him. He received a

---

14. Nature here refers to all things, mental and physical, not just trees, animals, etc.

sort of Dhamma "transmission," which was the knowledge that all conditioned things are impermanent. Anything which is born must have aging and death as a natural result. This experience was different from anything he'd ever known before. He truly realized his mind, and so "Buddha" arose within him. At that time, the Buddha declared that Añña Kondañña had received the Eye of Dhamma.

What is it that this Eye of Dhamma sees? This Eye sees that whatever is born has aging and death as a natural result. "Whatever is born" means everything! Whether material or immaterial, it all comes under this "whatever is born." It refers to all of Nature. Like this body for instance—it's born and then proceeds to extinction. When it's small it "dies" from smallness to youth. After a while, it "dies" from youth and becomes middle-aged. Then it goes on to "die" from middle age and reach old age, finally reaching the end. Trees, mountains, and vines all have this characteristic.

The vision or understanding of the "one who knows" clearly entered the mind of Añña Kondañña as he sat there. This knowledge of "whatever is born" became deeply embedded in his mind, enabling him to uproot attachment to the body. This attachment was *sakkāyadiṭṭhi*. This means that he didn't take the body to be a self or a being, or in terms of "he" or "me." He didn't cling to it. He saw it clearly, thus uprooting *sakkāyadiṭṭhi*.

And then *vicikicchā* (doubt) was destroyed. Having uprooted attachment to the body, he didn't doubt his realization. *Sīlabbata-parāmāsa*[15] was also uprooted. His practice became firm and straight. Even if his body was in pain or fever, he didn't grasp it, he didn't doubt. He didn't doubt, because he had uprooted clinging. This grasping of the body is called *sīlabbata-parāmāsa*.[16]

---

15. These three things, *sakkāyadiṭṭhi*, *vicikicchā*, and *sīlabbata-parāmāsa*, are, in the scriptures, the first three of the ten "fetters," which are given up on the first glimpse of Enlightenment, known as "Stream Entry." At full Enlightenment all ten fetters are transcended.

16. Thus Ajahn Chah; however, according to the Pali Canon and its exegetical tradition, *sīlabbata-parāmāsa* means "holding on to rules and vows," that is, holding virtues conduct and ascetic practices as the essence of spiritual practice. Ajahn Chah seems to be referring to *kāmupādāna*, "clinging to sensual pleasures," which is only abandoned at the last stage of

When one uproots the view of the body being the self, grasping and doubt are finished with. If just this view of the body as the self arises within the mind, then grasping and doubt begin right there.

As the Buddha expounded the Dhamma, *Aññā Kondañña* opened the Eye of Dhamma. This Eye is just the "one who knows clearly." It sees things differently. It sees this very nature. Seeing Nature clearly, clinging is uprooted and the "one who knows" is born. Previously, he knew, but he still had clinging. You could say that he knew the Dhamma, but he still hadn't seen it, or he had seen the Dhamma, but still wasn't one with it.

At this time the Buddha said, "Kondañña knows." What did he know? He just knew Nature! Usually we get lost in Nature, as with this body of ours. Earth, water, fire, and wind come together to make this body. It's an aspect of Nature, a material object we can see with the eye. It exists depending on food, growing and changing until finally it reaches extinction.

Coming inwards, that which watches over the body is consciousness—just this "one who knows," this single awareness. If it receives through the ear, it's called hearing; through the nose it's called smelling; through the tongue, tasting; through the body, touching; and through the mind, thinking. This consciousness is just one, but when it functions at different places, we call it different things. Through the eye we call it one thing; through the ear we call it another. However, whether it functions at the eye, ear, nose, tongue, body, or mind—it's just one awareness. Following the scriptures, we call it the six consciousnesses, but in reality there is only one consciousness arising at these six different bases. There are six "doors," but a single awareness, which is this very mind.

This mind is capable of knowing the Truth of Nature. If the mind still has obstructions, then we say it knows through ignorance. It knows wrongly and it sees wrongly. Knowing wrongly and seeing wrongly, or knowing and seeing rightly, it's just a single awareness. We say wrong view and right view, but it's just one thing. Right and wrong both arise from this one place. When there is wrong knowledge, we say that ignorance conceals the truth. When there is wrong knowledge, then there is

---

"Non Return." See Majjhima Nikāya sutta 13 (BPS editor).

wrong view, wrong intention, wrong action, wrong livelihood—everything is wrong! And on the other hand, the path of right practice is born in this same place. When there is right, then the wrong disappears.

The Buddha practised enduring many hardships and torturing himself with fasting and so on, but he investigated deeply into his mind until finally he uprooted ignorance. All the Buddhas were enlightened in mind, because the body knows nothing. You can let it eat or not, it doesn't matter, it can die at any time. The Buddhas all practised with the mind. They were enlightened in mind.

Having contemplated his mind, the Buddha gave up the two extremes of practice—indulgence in pleasure and indulgence in pain. In his first discourse he expounded the Middle Way between these two. However, we hear his teaching and it grates against our desires. We're infatuated with pleasure and comfort, infatuated with happiness, thinking we are good, we are fine—this is indulgence in pleasure. It's not the right path. Dissatisfaction, displeasure, dislike, and anger—this is indulgence in pain. These are the extreme ways which one on the path of practice should avoid.

These "ways" are simply the happiness and unhappiness which arise. The "one on the path" is this very mind, the "one who knows." If a good mood arises, we cling to it as good; this is indulgence in pleasure. If an unpleasant mood arises, we cling to it through dislike; this is indulgence in pain. These are the wrong paths; they aren't the ways of a meditator. They're the ways of the worldly, those who look for fun and happiness and shun unpleasantness and suffering.

The wise know the wrong paths, but they relinquish them, they give them up. They are unmoved by pleasure and displeasure, happiness and unhappiness. These things arise, but those who know don't cling to them, they let them go according to their nature. This is Right View. When one knows this fully, there is liberation. Happiness and unhappiness have no meaning for an Enlightened One.

The Buddha said that the Enlightened Ones were far from defilements. This doesn't mean that they ran away from defilements, they didn't run away anywhere. Defilements were there. He compared it to a lotus leaf in a pond of water. The leaf and the water exist together, they are in contact, but the leaf doesn't become damp. The water is like defilements, and the lotus leaf is the Enlightened Mind.

The mind of one who practices is the same; it doesn't run away anywhere, it stays right there. Good, evil, happiness, and unhappiness, right and wrong, arise, and he knows them all. The meditator simply knows them, they don't enter his mind. That is, he has no clinging. He is simply the experiencer. To say he simply experiences is our common language. In the language of Dhamma, we say he lets his mind follow the Middle Way.

These activities of happiness, unhappiness, and so on are constantly arising because they are characteristics of the world. The Buddha was enlightened in the world, he contemplated the world. If he hadn't contemplated the world, if he hadn't seen the world, he couldn't have risen above it. The Buddha's Enlightenment was simply enlightenment of this very world. The world was still there: gain and loss, praise and criticism, fame and disrepute, happiness and unhappiness were still there. If there weren't these things, there would be nothing to become enlightened to! What he knew was just the world, that which surrounds the hearts of people. If people follow these things, seeking praise and fame, gain and happiness, and trying to avoid their opposites, they sink under the weight of the world.

Gain and loss, praise and criticism, fame and disrepute, happiness and unhappiness—this is the world. The person who is lost in the world has no path of escape; the world overwhelms him. This world follows the Law of Dhamma; so we call it worldly dhamma. He who lives within the worldly dhamma is called a worldly being. He lives surrounded by confusion.

Therefore, the Buddha taught us to develop the path. We can divide it up into morality, concentration, and wisdom—develop them to completion! This is the path of practice which destroys the world. Where is this world? It is just in the minds of beings infatuated with it! The action of clinging to praise, gain, fame, happiness, and unhappiness is called "world." When it is there in the mind, then the world arises, the worldly being is born. The world is born because of desire. Desire is the birthplace of all worlds. To put an end to desire is to put an end to the world.

Our practice of morality, concentration, and wisdom is otherwise called the Eightfold Path. This Eightfold Path and the eight worldly dhammas are a pair. How is it that they are a pair? If we speak according to the scriptures, we say that gain and loss, praise and criticism, fame and disrepute, happiness and unhappiness are the eight worldly dhammas. Right View, Right Intention, Right Speech, Right Action, Right Livelihood, Right Effort, Right Mindfulness, and Right Concentration, this is the Eightfold Path. These two eightfold ways exist in the same place. The eight worldly dhammas are right here in this very mind, with the "one who knows," but this "one who knows" has obstructions, so it knows wrongly and thus becomes the world. It's just this one "one who knows," no other! The Buddha-nature has not yet arisen in this mind; it has not yet extracted itself from the world. The mind like this is the world.

When we practise the path, when we train our body and speech, it's all done in that very same mind. It's the same place, so they see each other; the path sees the world. If we practise with this mind of ours, we encounter this clinging to praise, fame, pleasure, and happiness, we see the attachment to the world. The Buddha said, "You should know the world. It dazzles like a king's royal carriage. Fools are entranced, but the wise are not deceived." It's not that he wanted us to go all over the world looking at everything, studying everything about it. He simply wanted us to watch this mind that is attached to it. When the Buddha told us to look at the world, he didn't want us to get stuck in it; he wanted us to investigate it, because the world is born just in this mind. Sitting in the shade of a tree you can look at the world. When there is desire, the world comes into being right there. Wanting is the birth place of the world. To extinguish wanting is to extinguish the world.

When we sit in meditation, we want the mind to become peaceful, but it's not peaceful. Why is this? We don't want to think, but we think. It's like a person who goes to sit on an ant's nest: the ants just keep on biting him. When the mind is the world, then even while sitting still with our eyes closed, all we see is the world. Pleasure, sorrow, anxiety, confusion—it all arises. Why is this? It's because we still haven't realized Dhamma. If the mind is like this, the meditator can't endure the worldly dhammas, he doesn't investigate. It's just the same as if he were sitting on an ants' nest. The ants are going to bite because he's right on their home! So what should he do? He should look for some poison or use fire to drive them out.

However, most Dhamma practitioners don't see it like that. If they feel content, they just follow contentment, feeling discontent, they just follow that. Following the worldly dhammas, the mind becomes the world. Sometimes we may think, "Oh, I can't do it, it's beyond me ...," so we don't even try! This is because the mind is full of defilements; the worldly dhammas prevent the path from arising. We can't endure in the development of morality, concentration, and wisdom. It's just like that man sitting on the ants' nest. He can't do anything, the ants are biting and crawling all over him, he's immersed in confusion and agitation. He can't rid his sitting place of the danger, so he just sits there, suffering.

Just so it is with our practice. The worldly dhammas exist in the minds of worldly beings. When those beings wish to find peace, the worldly dhammas arise right there. When the mind is ignorant, there is only darkness. When knowledge arises, the mind is illumined, because ignorance and knowledge are born in the same place. When ignorance has arisen, knowledge can't enter, because the mind has accepted ignorance. When knowledge has arisen, ignorance cannot stay. Therefore, the Buddha exhorted his disciples to practise with the mind, because the world is born in this mind, the eight worldly dhammas are there.

The Eightfold Path, that is, investigation through calm and insight meditation, our diligent effort, and the wisdom we develop, all these things loosen the grip of the world. Attachment, aversion, and delusion become lighter, and being lighter, we know them as such. If we experience fame, material gain, praise, happiness, or suffering, we're aware of it. We must know these things before we can transcend the world, because the world is within us.

When we're free of these things, it's just like leaving a house. When we enter a house, what sort of feeling do we have? We feel that we've come through the door and entered the house. When we leave the house, we feel that we've left it, we come into the bright sunlight; it's not dark like it was inside. The action of the mind entering the worldly dhammas is like entering the house. The mind which has destroyed the worldly dhammas is like one who has left the house.

So the Dhamma practitioner must become one who witnesses the Dhamma for himself. He knows for himself whether the worldly dhammas have left or not, whether or not the path has been developed. When the path has been well developed, it purges the worldly dhammas. It becomes stronger and stronger. Right view grows as wrong view decreases, until finally the path destroys defilements—either that or defilements will destroy the path!

Right view and wrong view, there are only these two ways. Wrong view has its tricks as well, you know, it has its wisdom—but it's wisdom that's misguided. The meditator who begins to develop the path experiences a separation. Eventually, it's as if one is two people—one in the world and the other on the path. They divide, they pull apart. Whenever one's investigating, there's this separation, and it continues on and on until the mind reaches insight, *vipassanā*.

However, maybe it's *vipassanā* defilement![17] Having tried to establish wholesome results in our practice, seeing them, we attach to them. This type of clinging comes from our wanting to get something from the practice. This is *vipassanā* defilement; the wisdom of defilements (i.e., "defiled wisdom"). Some people develop goodness and cling to it, they develop purity and cling to that, or they develop knowledge and cling to that. The action of clinging to that goodness or knowledge is *vipassanā* defilement infiltrating our practice.

So when you develop *vipassanā*, be careful! Watch out for *vipassanā* defilement, because they're so close that sometimes you can't tell them apart. However, with right view we can see them both clearly. If it's *vipassanā* defilement, there will be suffering arising at times as a result. If it's really *vipassanā*, there's no suffering. There is peace. Both happiness and unhappiness are silenced. This you can see for yourself.

This practice requires endurance. Some people, when they come to practise, don't want to be bothered by anything, they don't want friction. However, there's friction the same as before. We must try to find an end to friction through friction itself! So, if there's friction in your practice, then it's right. If there's no friction,

---

17. That is, *vipassanā-upakkilesa*—the subtle defilements arising from meditation practice.

it's not right, you just eat and sleep as much as you want. When you want to go anywhere or say anything, you just follow your desires. The teaching of the Buddha grates. The supermundane goes against the worldly. Right view opposes wrong view, purity opposes impurity. The teaching grates against our desires.

There's a story in the scriptures about the Buddha before he was enlightened. At that time, having received a plate of rice, he floated that plate on a stream of water, determining in his mind, "If I am to be enlightened, may this plate float against the current of the water." The plate floated upstream! That plate was the Buddha's Right View, or the Buddha-nature that he became awakened to. It didn't follow the desires of ordinary beings. It floated against the flow of his mind; it was contrary in every way.

These days, in the same way, the Buddha's teaching is contrary to our hearts. People want to indulge in greed and hatred, but the Buddha won't let them. They want to be deluded, but the Buddha destroys delusion. So the mind of the Buddha is contrary to that of worldly beings. The world calls the body beautiful; the Buddha says it's not beautiful. They say the body belongs to us, he says not so. They say it's substantial, he says it's not. Right view is above the world. Worldly beings merely follow the flow of the stream.

Continuing on, when the Buddha got up from there, he received eight handfuls of grass from a brahmin. The real meaning of this is that the eight handfuls of grass were the eight worldly dhammas—gain and loss, praise and criticism, fame and disrepute, happiness and unhappiness. The Buddha, having received this grass, determined to sit on it and enter *samādhi*. The action of sitting on the grass was itself *samādhi*, that is, his mind was above the worldly dhammas, subduing the world until it realized the transcendent. The worldly dhammas became like refuse for him, they lost all meaning. He sat over them, but they didn't obstruct his mind in any way. The various *māras* came to try to overcome him, but he just sat there in *samādhi*, subduing the world, until finally he became enlightened to the Dhamma and completely defeated *Māra*.[18] That is, he defeated the world. So the practice of developing the path is that which kills defilements.

---

18. Māra (the Tempter), the Buddhist personification of evil. To the meditator it represents all that obstructs the quest for enlightenment.

People these days have little faith. Having practised a year or two, they want to get there, and they want to go fast. They don't consider that the Buddha, our Teacher, had left home a full six years before he became enlightened. This is why we have "freedom from dependence."[19] According to the scriptures, a monk must have at least five rains[20] before he is considered able to live on his own. By this time he has studied and practised sufficiently, he has adequate knowledge, he has faith and his conduct is good. If someone who practises for five years, I say he's competent. However, he must really practise, not just "hang out" in the robes for five years. He must really look after the practice; really do it!

Until you reach five rains you may wonder, "What is this 'freedom from dependence' that the Buddha talked about?" You must really try to practise for five years, and then you'll know for yourself the qualities he was referring to. After that time, you should be competent, competent in mind, one who is certain. At the very least, after five rains, one should be at the first stage of enlightenment. This is not just five rains in body, but five rains in mind as well. That monk has fear of blame, a sense of shame and modesty. He doesn't dare to do wrong either in front of people or behind their backs, in the light or in the dark. Why not? Because he has reached the Buddha, the "one who knows". He takes refuge in the Buddha, the Dhamma, and the Sangha.

To depend truly on the Buddha, the Dhamma, and the Sangha, we must see the Buddha. What use would it be to take refuge without knowing the Buddha? If we don't yet know the Buddha, the Dhamma, and the Sangha, our taking refuge in them is just an act of body and speech, the mind still hasn't reached them. Once the mind reaches them we know what the Buddha, the Dhamma, and the Sangha are like. Then we can really take refuge in them, because these things arise in our minds. Wherever we are, we will have the Buddha, the Dhamma and the Sangha within us.

One who is like this doesn't dare to commit evil acts. This is why we say that one who has reached the first stage

---

19. "Freedom from dependence," that is, he lives under the guidance of a senior monk, for the first five years.

20. "Rains" refers to the yearly three-month rains retreat by which monks count their age. Thus, a monk of five rains has been monk for five years.

of enlightenment will no longer be born in the woeful states. His mind is certain, he has entered the Stream, and there is no doubt for him. If he doesn't reach full enlightenment today, it will certainly be some time in the future. He may do wrong, but not enough to send him to Hell, that is, he doesn't regress to evil bodily and verbal actions—he is incapable of it. So we say that person has entered the Noble Birth. He cannot return. This is something you should see and know for yourselves in this very life.

These days, those of us who still have doubts about the practice hear these things and say, "Oh, how can I do that?" Sometimes we feel happy, sometimes troubled, pleased or displeased. For what reason? Because we don't know Dhamma. What Dhamma? Just the Dhamma of Nature, the reality around us, the body and the mind.

The Buddha said, "Don't cling to the five *khandhas*, let them go, give them up!" Why can't we let them go? Just because we don't see them or know them fully. We see them as ourselves, we see ourselves in the *khandhas*. Happiness and suffering, we see as ourselves, we see ourselves in happiness and suffering. We can't separate ourselves from them. When we can't separate them, it means we can't see Dhamma, we can't see Nature.

Happiness, unhappiness, pleasure, and sadness—none of them is us, but we take them to be so. These things come into contact with us, and we see a lump of *attā*, or self. Wherever there is self, there you will find happiness, unhappiness, and everything else. So the Buddha said to destroy this "lump" of self, that is, to destroy *sakkayādiṭṭhi*, identity view. When the view of *attā* (self) is destroyed, the view of *anattā* (non-self) naturally arises.

We take Nature to be us and ourselves to be Nature, so we don't know Nature truly. If it's good, we laugh with it, if it's bad, we cry over it. However, Nature is simply *saṅkhāras*. As we say in the funeral chanting, *"tesaṃ vūpasamo sukho,"*—pacifying the *saṅkhāras* (conditioned phenomena) is real happiness. How do we pacify them? We simply remove clinging and see them as they really are.

So, there is truth in this world. Trees, mountains, and vines all live according to their own truth, they are born and die following their nature. It's just we people who aren't true! We see it and make a fuss over it, but Nature is impassive—it just is as it is. We laugh, we cry, we kill, but Nature remains in truth, it is truth. No matter how happy or sad we are, this body just follows its own nature. It's born, it grows up and ages, changing and getting older all the time. It follows Nature in this way. Whoever takes the body to be himself and carries it around with him, will suffer.

Añña Kondañña recognized this "whatever is born" in everything, be it material or immaterial. His view of the world changed. He saw the truth. Having got up from his sitting place, he took that truth with him. The activity of birth and death continued, but he simply looked on. Happiness and unhappiness were arising and passing away, but he merely noted them. His mind was constant. He no longer fell into the woeful states. He didn't get overpleased or unduly upset about these things. His mind was firmly established in the activity of contemplation.

There! Añña Kondañña had received the Eye of Dhamma. He saw Nature, which we call *saṅkhāras*, according to truth. Wisdom is that which knows the truth of *saṅkhāras*. This is the mind which knows and sees Dhamma, which has surrendered.

Until we have seen the Dhamma, we must have patience and restraint. We must endure, we must renounce! We must cultivate diligence and endurance. Why must we cultivate diligence? Because we're lazy! Why must we develop endurance? Because we don't endure! That's the way it is. However, when we are already established in our practice, have finished with laziness, then we don't need to use diligence. If we already know the truth of all mental states, if we don't get happy or unhappy over them, we don't need to exercise endurance, because the mind is already Dhamma. The "one who knows" has seen the Dhamma, it is the Dhamma.

When the mind is Dhamma, it stops. It has attained peace. There's no longer a need to do anything special, because the mind is Dhamma already. The outside is Dhamma, the inside is Dhamma. The "one who knows" is Dhamma. The state is Dhamma, and that which knows the state is Dhamma. It is one. It is free.

This Nature is not born; it does not age nor sicken. This Nature does not die. This Nature is neither happy nor sad, neither big nor small, heavy nor light; neither short nor long, black nor white. There's nothing you can compare it to. No convention can reach it. This is why we say Nibbāna has no colour. All colors are merely conventions. The state which is beyond the world is beyond the reach of worldly conventions.

The Dhamma is that which is beyond the world. It is that which each person should see for himself. It is beyond language. You can't put it into words; you can only talk about ways and means of realizing it. The person who has seen it for himself has finished his work.

Convention and Liberation

The things of this world are merely conventions of our own making. Having established them, we get lost in them, and refuse to let go, giving rise to clinging to our personal views and opinions. This clinging never ends; it is *saṃsāra*, flowing endlessly on. It has no completion. Now, if we know conventional reality, then we'll know Liberation. If we clearly know Liberation, then we'll know convention. This is to know the Dhamma. Here there is completion.

Take people, for instance. In reality, people don't have any names; we are simply born naked into the world. If we have names, they arise only through convention. I've contemplated this and have seen that if you don't know the truth of this convention, it can be really harmful. It's simply something we use for convenience. Without it, we couldn't communicate, there would be nothing to say, no language.

I've seen Westerners when they sit in meditation together in the West. When they get up after sitting, men and women together, sometimes they go and touch each other on the head![21] When I saw this I thought, "Eh, if we cling to convention, it gives rise to defilements right here." If we can let go of convention, give up our opinions, we are at peace.

Take the generals and colonels, men of rank and position, who come to see me. When they come, they say, "Oh, please touch my

---

21. The head is regarded as sacred in Thailand, and to touch a person's head is considered an insult. Also, according to tradition, men and women do not touch each other in public. On the other hand, sitting in meditation is regarded as a "holy" activity. The Venerable Ajahn was here using an example of Western behavior that would particularly shock the Thai audience.

head."[22] If they ask like this, there's nothing wrong with it, they're glad to have their heads touched. However, if you tapped their heads in the middle of the street, it would be a different story! This is because of clinging. So I feel that letting go is really the way of peace. Touching a head is against our customs, but in reality it is nothing. When they agree to having it touched, there's nothing wrong with it, just like touching a cabbage or a potato.

Accepting, giving up, letting go—this is the way of lightness. Wherever you're clinging, there's becoming and birth right there. There's danger right there. The Buddha taught about convention, he taught about undoing convention in the right way, and so to reach Liberation. This is freedom, not to cling to conventions. All things in this world have a conventional reality. Having established them, we should not be fooled by them, because getting lost in them really leads to suffering. This point concerning rules and conventions is of utmost importance. One who can get beyond them is beyond suffering.

However, they are a characteristic of our world. Take Mr. Boonmah, for instance; he used to be just one of the crowd, but now he's been appointed the District Commissioner. It's just a convention, but it's a convention we should respect. It's part of the world of people. If you think, "Oh, before we were friends, we used to work at the tailor's together," and then you go and pat him on the head in public, he'll get angry. It's not right, he'll resent it. So we should follow the conventions in order to avoid giving rise to resentment. It's useful to understand convention; living in the world is just about this. Know the right time and place, know the person.

Why is it wrong to go against conventions? It's wrong because of people! You should be clever, knowing both convention and Liberation. Know the right time for each. If we know how to use rules and conventions comfortably, then we are skilled. However, if we try to behave according to the higher level of reality in the wrong situation, this is wrong. Where is it wrong? It's wrong with people's defilements, nothing else! People all have defilements. In one situation we behave in one way, in another situation we must

---

22. It is considered auspicious in Thailand to have one's head touched by a highly esteemed monk.

behave in another way. We should know the ins and outs because we live within conventions. Problems occur because people cling to them. If we suppose something to be, then it is. It's there because we suppose it to be there. However, if you look closely, in the absolute sense, these things don't really exist.

As I have often said, before we were laymen and now we are monks. We lived within the convention of "layman," and now we live within the convention of "monk." We are monks by convention, not monks through Liberation. In the beginning we establish conventions like this, but if a person merely becomes a monk, this doesn't mean he overcomes defilements. If we take a handful of sand and agree to call it salt, does this make it salt? It is salt, but only in name, not in reality. You couldn't use it to cook with. It's only use is within the realm of that agreement, because there's really no salt there, only sand. It becomes salt only through our supposing it to be so.

This word "Liberation" is itself just a convention, but it refers to that beyond conventions. Having achieved freedom, having reached liberation, we still have to use convention in order to refer to it as liberation. If we didn't have convention, we couldn't communicate, so it does have its use.

For example, people have different names, but they are all people just the same. If we didn't have names to differentiate between them, and we wanted to call out to somebody standing in a crowd, saying, "Hey, Person! Person!", it would be useless. You couldn't say who would answer you because they're all "person." However, if you called, "Hey, John!", then John would come, the others wouldn't answer. Names fulfill just this need. Through them we can communicate, they provide the basis for social behavior.

You should know both convention and liberation. Conventions have a use, but in reality there really isn't anything there. Even people are non-existent! They are merely groups of elements, born of causal conditions, growing dependent on conditions, existing for a while then disappearing in the natural way. No one can oppose or control it. However, without conventions we would have nothing to say, we'd have no names, no practice, no work. Rules and conventions are established to give us a language, to make things convenient, and that's all.

Take money, for example. In olden times, there weren't any coins or notes, they had no value. People used to barter goods, but those things were difficult to keep, so they created money, using coins and notes. Perhaps in the future we'll have a new king decree that we don't have to use paper money, we should use wax, melting it down and pressing it into lumps. We say this is money and use it throughout the country. Let alone wax, it may even happen that they decide to make chicken dung the local currency—all the other things can't be money, just chicken dung! Then people would fight and kill each other over chicken dung! This is the way it is. You could use many examples to illustrate convention. What we use for money is simply a convention that we have set up; it has its use within that convention. Having decreed it to be money, it becomes money. However, in reality, what is money? Nobody can say. When there is a popular agreement about something, then a convention comes about to fulfill the need. The world is just this.

This is convention, but to get ordinary people to understand liberation is really difficult. Our money, our house, our family, our children, and our relatives are simply conventions that we have invented, but, really, seen in the light of Dhamma, they don't belong to us. Maybe if we hear this, we don't feel so good, but reality is like that. These things have value only through the established conventions. If we establish that it doesn't have value, then it doesn't have value. This is the way it is; we bring convention into the world to fulfill a need.

Even this body is not really ours; we just suppose it to be so. It's truly just a supposition. If you try to find a real, substantial self within it, you can't. There are merely elements which are born, continue for a while, and then die. Everything is like this. There's no real, true substance to it, but it's proper that we use it. It's like a cup. At some time that cup must break, but while it is there you should use it and look after it well. It's a tool for your use. If it breaks, there is trouble, so even though it must break, you should try your utmost to preserve it. Just so we have the four supports[23] which the Buddha taught us again and again to contemplate. They are the supports on which a monk depends

---

23. The four basic supports or requisites of a monk—robes, alms food, lodgings, and medicines.

to continue his practice. As long as you live, you will depend on them, however, you should understand them. Don't cling to them, giving rise to craving in your mind.

Convention and liberation are related like this continually. Even though we use convention, don't place your trust in it as being the truth. If you cling to it, suffering will arise. The case of right and wrong is a good example. Some people see wrong as being right and right as being wrong, but, in the end, who really knows what is right and what is wrong? We don't know. Different people establish different conventions about what's right and what's wrong, but the Buddha took suffering as his guideline. If you want to argue about it, there's no end to it. One says, "right," another says, "wrong." One says, "wrong," another says, "right." In truth we don't really know right and wrong at all! However, at a useful, practical level, we can say that right is not to harm oneself and not to harm others. In this way, it fulfils a use.

So, after all, both rules and conventions and liberation are simply dhammas. One is higher than the other, but they go hand in hand. There is no way that we can guarantee that anything is definitely like this or like that, so the Buddha said to just let it be. Let it be as uncertain. However much you like it or dislike it, you should understand it as uncertain.

Regardless of time and place, the whole practice of Dhamma comes to completion at the place where there is nothing. It's the place of surrender, of emptiness, of laying down the burden. This is the finish. It's not like the person who says, "Why is the flag fluttering in the wind? I say it's because of the wind." Another person says it's because of the flag. The other retorts that it's because of the wind. There's no end to this! The same as the old riddle, "Which came first, the chicken or the egg?" There's no way to reach a conclusion, this is just Nature. All these things we say are merely conventions, we establish them ourselves. If you know these things with wisdom, then you'll know impermanence, unsatisfactoriness, and not self. This is the outlook which leads to enlightenment.

You know, training and teaching people with varying levels of understanding is really difficult. Some people have certain ideas, you tell them something, and they don't believe you. You tell them the truth, and they say it's not true. "I'm right, you're wrong ..." There's no end to this. If you don't let go, there will be suffering. I've told you before about the four men who go into the forest. They hear a chicken crowing, "Kak-ka-dehhh!" One of them wonders, "Is that a rooster or a hen?" Three of them say together, "It's a hen," but the other doesn't agree, he insists it's a rooster. "How could a hen crow like that?", he asks. They retort, "Well, it has a mouth, hasn't it?" They argue till the tears fall, really getting upset over it, but in the end they're all wrong. Whether you say a hen or a rooster, they're only names. We establish these conventions, saying a rooster is like this, a hen is like that; a rooster cries like this, a hen cries like that ... This is how we get stuck in the world! Remember this! Actually, if you just say that really there's no hen and no rooster, then that's the end of it. In the field of conventional reality one side is right and the other side is wrong, but there will never be complete agreement. Arguing till the tears fall has no use!

The Buddha taught us not to cling. How do we practise non-clinging? We practise simply to give up clinging, but this non-clinging is very difficult to understand. It takes keen wisdom to investigate and penetrate this, to really achieve non-clinging. When you think about it, whether people are happy or sad, content or discontent, doesn't depend on their having little or having much—it depends on wisdom. All distress can be transcended only through wisdom, through seeing the truth of things.

The Buddha exhorted us to investigate, to contemplate. This "contemplation" means simply to try to solve these problems correctly. This is our practice. Like birth, old age, sickness, and death—they are the most natural and common of occurrences. The Buddha taught us to contemplate birth, old age, sickness, and death, but some people don't understand this. "What is there to contemplate?", they say. They were born, but they don't know birth. They will die, but they don't know death.

A person who investigates these things repeatedly, will see Truth. Having seen Truth, he will gradually solve his problems. Even if he still has clinging, if he has wisdom and sees that old age, sickness and death are the way of Nature, then he will be able to relieve suffering. We study the Dhamma simply for this—to cure suffering. There isn't really much as the basis of Buddhism, there's just the birth and death of suffering, the Buddha called this the

Truth. Birth is suffering, old age is suffering, sickness is suffering, and death is suffering. People don't see this suffering as the Truth, however, if we know Truth, then we know suffering.

This pride in personal opinions, in these arguments, has no end. In order to put our minds at rest, to find peace, we should contemplate our past, the present, and the things which are in store for us, such as birth, old age, sickness, and death. What can we do to avoid being plagued by these? Even though we may still have a little worry, if we investigate till we know according to the Truth, all suffering will abate, because we will no longer cling to birth, old age, sickness, and death.

No Abiding

We hear some parts of the teachings that we can't really understand. We think they shouldn't be the way they are, so we don't follow them, but really there is a reason to all the teachings. Maybe it seems that things shouldn't be that way, but they are. At first I didn't even believe in sitting meditation. I couldn't see what use it would be to just sit with your eyes closed. Walking meditation ... Walk from this tree, turn around and walk back again ... I thought, "Why bother? What's the use of all that walking?" However, walking and sitting meditation are actually of great use.

Some people's tendencies make them prefer walking meditation, others prefer sitting, but you can't do without either of them. In the scriptures the Buddha talks about the four postures: standing, walking, sitting, and lying. We live with these four postures. We may prefer one to the other, but we must use all four

They say to make these four postures even, to make the practice even in all postures. At first I couldn't figure out what this "making them even" meant, "Maybe it means that we sleep for two hours, then stand for two hours, and then walk for two hours ... Maybe that's it?" I tried it, but couldn't do it; it was impossible! That's not what it means to make the postures even. "Making the postures even" refers to the mind, to our awareness. That is, to make the mind give rise to wisdom, to illumine the mind. This wisdom of ours must be present in all postures; we must know, or understand, constantly. Standing, walking, sitting, or lying, we must know all mental states as impermanent, unsatisfactory, and not-self. Making the postures even in this way can be done, it is possible. Whether like or dislike is present in the mind, we don't forget our practice, we are aware.

If we just focus our attention on the mind constantly, then we have the gist of the practice. Whether we experience mental states that the world knows as good or bad, we don't forget ourselves, we don't get lost in good or bad. We just go straight. Making the postures constant in this way is possible. If we have constancy in our practice and we are praised, then it's simply praise; if we are blamed, then it's just blame. We don't get high or low over it, we stay right here. Why? Because we see the danger in all those things, we see their results. We are constantly aware of the danger in both praise and blame. Normally, if we have a good mood, the mind is good too, we see them as the same thing; if we have a bad mood, the mind goes bad as well, and we don't like it. This is the way it is; this is uneven practice.

If we have constancy just to the extent of knowing our moods, and knowing we're clinging to them, this is better already. That is, we have awareness, we know what's going on, but we still can't let go. We see ourselves clinging to good and bad, and we know it. We cling to good and know it's still not right practice, but we still can't let go. This is 50% or 70% of the practice already. There still isn't release, but we know that, if we could let go, that would be the way to peace. We keep going like that, seeing the equally harmful consequences of all our likes and dislikes, of praise and blame, continuously. Whatever there is, the mind is constant in this way.

However, for worldly people, if they get blamed or criticized, they get really upset. If they get praised, it cheers them up; they say it's good and get really happy over it. If we know the truth of our various moods, if we know the consequences of clinging to praise and blame, the danger of clinging to anything at all, we will become sensitive to our moods. We will know that clinging to them really causes suffering. We see this suffering, and we see our very clinging as the cause of that suffering. We begin to see the consequences of grabbing and clinging to good and bad, because we've grasped them and seen the result before—no real happiness. So now we look for the way to let go.

Where is this "way to let go?" In Buddhism we say, "Don't cling to anything." We never stop hearing about this, "Don't cling to anything!" This means to hold, but not to cling. Like this flashlight. We think, "What is this?" So we pick it up, "Oh, it's a flashlight," then we put it down again. We hold things in this way. If we didn't hold anything at all, what could we do? We couldn't walk in meditation or do anything, so we must hold things first. It's wanting, yes, that's true, but later on it leads to *pāramī* (perfection). Like wanting to come here, for instance ... Venerable Jagaro[24] came to Wat Pah Pong. He had to want first in order to come. If he hadn't felt that he wanted to come he wouldn't have come. For anybody it's the same, they come here because of wanting. However, when wanting arises don't cling to it! So you come, and then you go back ... What is this? We pick it up, look at it and see, "Oh, it's a flashlight," then we put it down. This is called holding, but not clinging, we let go. We know, and then we let go. To put it simply, we say just this, "Know, then let go." Keep looking and letting go. "This, they say, is good; this, they say, is not good," know, and then let go. Good and bad, we know it all, but we let it go. We don't foolishly cling to things, but we "hold" them with wisdom. Practising in this "posture" can be constant. You must be constant like this. Make the mind know in this way, let wisdom arise. When the mind has wisdom, what else is there to look for?

We should reflect on what we are doing here. For what reason are we living here, what are we working for? In the world they work for this or that reward, but the monks teach something a little deeper than that. Whatever we do, we ask for no return. We work for no rewards. Worldly people work because they want this or that, because they want some gain or other, but the Buddha taught to work just in order to work; we don't ask for anything beyond that. If you do something just to get some return, it'll cause suffering. Try it out for yourself! You want to make your mind peaceful, so you sit down and try to make it peaceful—you'll suffer! Try it. Our way is more refined. We do, and then let go; do, and then let go.

Look at the brahmin who makes a sacrifice: he has some desire in mind, so he makes a sacrifice. Those actions of his won't

---

24. Venerable Jagaro, the Australian second Abbot of Wat Pah Nanachat at that time, who brought his party of monks and laypeople to see Ajahn Chah.

help him transcend suffering because he's acting on desire. In the beginning we practise with some desire in mind; we practise on and on, but we don't attain our desire. So we practise until we reach a point where we're practising for no return, we're practising in order to let go. This is something we must see for ourselves, it's very deep. Maybe we practise because we want to go to Nibbāna—right there, you won't get to Nibbāna! It's natural to want peace, but it's not really correct. We must practise without wanting anything at all. If we don't want anything at all, what will we get? We won't get anything! Whatever you get is just a cause for suffering, so we practise not getting anything.

Just this is called "making the mind empty." It's empty, but there is still doing. This emptiness is something people don't usually understand, but those who reach it see the value of knowing it. It's not the emptiness of not having anything; it's the emptiness within the things that are here like this flashlight. We should see this flashlight as empty, because within the flashlight there is emptiness. It's not the emptiness where we can't see anything, it's not like that. People who understand like that have got it all wrong. You must understand emptiness within the things that are here.

Those who are still practising because of some idea of gain are like the brahmin who makes a sacrifice just to fulfill some wish. Like the people who come to see me in order to be sprinkled with "holy water." When I ask them, "Why do you want this 'holy water?'" they say, "We want to live happily and comfortably and not get sick." There! They'll never transcend suffering that way. The worldly way is to do things for a reason, to get some return, but in Buddhism we do things without any idea of gain. The world has to understand things in terms of cause and effect, but the Buddha teaches us to go above cause, beyond effect; to go above birth and beyond death; to go above happiness and beyond suffering. Think about it ... There's nowhere to stay. We people live in a "home." To leave home and go where there is no home, we don't know how to do it, because we've always lived with becoming, with clinging. If we can't cling, we don't know what to do.

Most people don't want to go to Nibbāna, there's nothing there; nothing at all. Look at the roof and the floor here. The upper extreme is the roof, that's an "abiding." The lower extreme is the floor, and that's another "abiding." However, in the empty space between the floor and the roof there's nowhere to stand. One could stand on the roof, or stand on the floor, but not on that empty space. Where there is no abiding, that's where there's emptiness, and, to put it bluntly, we say that Nibbāna is this emptiness. People hear this, and they back up a bit, they don't want to go. They're afraid they won't see their children or relatives. This is why, when we bless the laypeople, we chant, "May you have long life, beauty, happiness, and strength." This makes them really happy. "*Sādhu!*,"[25] they all say. They like these things. If you start talking about emptiness, they don't want it, they're attached to abiding. However, have you ever seen a very old person with a beautiful complexion? Have you ever seen an old person with a lot of strength, or a lot of happiness? No ... However, we chant, "Long life, beauty, happiness, and strength" and they're all really pleased, every single one says, "*Sādhu!*" This is like the brahmin who makes oblations to achieve some wish. In our practice we don't "make oblations," we don't practise in order to get some return. We don't want anything. If we still want something then there is still something there. Just make the mind peaceful and have done with it! However, if I talk like this you may not be very comfortable, because you want to be "born" again.

All you lay practitioners should get close to the monks and see their practice. To be close to the monks means to be close to the Buddha, to be close to his Dhamma. The Buddha said, "Ānanda, practise a lot, develop your practice! Whoever sees the Dhamma sees me, and whoever sees me sees the Dhamma." Where is the Buddha? We may think the Buddha has been and gone, but the Buddha is the Dhamma, the Truth. Some people like to say, "Oh, if I was born in the time of the Buddha I would go to Nibbāna." Here, stupid people talk like this. The Buddha is still here. The Buddha is Truth. Regardless of whoever is born or dies, the Truth is still here. The Truth never departs from the world; it's there all the time. Whether a Buddha is born or not, whether someone

---

25. *Sādhu* is the traditional Pali word used to acknowledge a blessing, dhamma teaching, etc. It means "it is well."

knows it or not, the truth is still there. So we should get close to the Buddha, we should come within and find the Dhamma. When we reach the Dhamma we will reach the Buddha; seeing the Dhamma we will see the Buddha and all doubts will dissolve.

To put it simply, it's like Teacher Choo.[26] At first he wasn't a teacher, he was just Mr. Choo. When he studied and passed the necessary grades, he became a teacher and became known as Teacher Choo. How did he become a teacher? Through studying the required things, thus allowing Mr. Choo to become Teacher Choo. When Teacher Choo dies, the study to become a teacher still remains, and whoever studies it will become a teacher. That course of study to become a teacher doesn't disappear anywhere, just like the Truth, the knowing of which enabled the Buddha to become the Buddha. So the Buddha is still here. Whoever practises and sees the Dhamma, sees the Buddha.

These days people have got it all wrong; they don't know where the Buddha is. They say, "If I had been born in the time of the Buddha, I would have become a disciple of his and become enlightened." That's just foolishness. You should understand this. Don't go thinking like that at the end of the rains retreat, because you'll disrobe. Don't think like that! In an instant an evil thought can arise in the mind, and you could kill somebody. In the same way, it only takes a split second for good to flash into the mind, and you're there already. Don't think that you have to be a monk for a long time to be able to meditate. Where the right practice lies is in the instant we make *kamma*. In a flash an evil thought arises, and before you know it you've committed some really heavy kamma. In the same way, all the disciples of the Buddha practised for a long time, but the time they attained enlightenment was merely one thought instant. So don't be heedless, even in minor things. Try hard, try to get close to the monks, contemplate things, and then you'll know about monks. Well, that's enough, huh? It must be getting late now, some people are getting sleepy. The Buddha said not to teach Dhamma to sleepy people.

---

26. In Thailand the word "Teacher" is used as a title of address much like "Doctor" is used in English. "Teacher Choo" was one of four elderly local residents who came to spend the rains retreat at Wat Pah Nanachat and to whom the latter part of this talk was addressed.

Right View—The Place of Coolness

The practice of Dhamma goes against our habits, the Truth goes against our desires, and so there is difficulty in the practice. Some things which we understand as wrong may be right, while the things we take to be right may be wrong. Why is this? Because our minds are in darkness, we don't clearly see the Truth. We don't really know anything, and so are fooled by people's lies. They point out what is right as being wrong, and we believe it; that which is wrong, they say is right, and we believe that. This is because we are not yet our own masters. Our moods lie to us constantly. We shouldn't take this mind and its opinions as our guide, because it doesn't know the truth.

Some people don't want to listen to others at all, but this is not the way of a man of wisdom. A wise man listens to everything. One who listens to Dhamma must listen just the same, whether he likes it or not, and must not blindly believe or disbelieve. He must stay at the halfway mark, the middle point, and not be heedless. He just listens and then contemplates, giving rise to the right results accordingly. A wise man should contemplate and see the cause and effect for himself before he believes what he hears. Even if the teacher speaks the truth, don't just believe it, because you don't yet know the truth of it for yourself.

It's the same for all of us, including myself. I've practised before you; I've seen through many lies before. For instance, "This practice is really difficult, really hard." Why is the practice difficult? It's just because we think wrongly, we have wrong view.

Previously I lived together with other monks, but I didn't feel right. I ran away to the forests and mountains, fleeing the crowd, the monks, and novices. I thought that they weren't like me; they didn't practise as hard as I did. They were sloppy. That person was like this, this person was like that. This was something that really put me in turmoil; it was the cause for my continually running away. However, whether I lived alone or with others I still had no peace. On my own I wasn't content; in a large group I wasn't content. I thought this discontent was due to my companions, due to my moods, due to my living place, the food, the weather, due to this and that. I was constantly searching for something to suit my mind.

As a *dhutaṅga*[27] monk, I went traveling, but things still weren't right. So I contemplated, "What can I do to make things right? What can I do?" Living with a lot of people I was dissatisfied; with few people I was dissatisfied. For what reason? I just couldn't see it. Why was I dissatisfied? Because I had wrong view, just that; because I still clung to the wrong Dhamma. Wherever I went, I was discontented, thinking, "Here it is no good, there it is is no good ..." on and on like that. I blamed others. I blamed the weather, the heat and cold, I blamed everything! Just like a mad dog. It bites whatever it meets, because it's mad. When the mind is like this, our practice is never settled. Today we feel good, tomorrow no good. It's like that all the time. We don't attain contentment or peace.

The Buddha once saw a jackal, a wild dog, run out of the forest where he was staying. It stood still for a while, then it ran into the underbrush, and then out again. Then it ran into a tree hollow, then out again. Then it went into a cave, only to run out again. One minute it stood, the next it ran, then it lay down, then it jumped up ... That jackal had mange. When it stood, the mange would eat into its skin, so it would run. Running, it was still uncomfortable, so it would lie down. Then it would jump up again, running into the underbrush, a tree hollow, never staying still. The Buddha said, "Monks, did you see that jackal this afternoon? Standing, it suffered, running, it suffered, sitting, it suffered, lying, down it suffered. In the underbrush, a tree hollow or a cave, it suffered. It blamed standing for its discomfort, it blamed sitting, it blamed running, and lying down; it blamed the tree hollow, the underbrush, and the cave. In fact, the problem was with none of those things. That jackal had mange. The problem was with the mange."

We monks are just the same as that jackal. Our discontent is due to wrong view. Because we don't exercise sense restraint, we blame our suffering on externals. Whether we live at Wat Pah Pong, in America, or in London we aren't satisfied. Going to live at Bung Wai or any of the other branch monasteries, we're still

---

27. *Dhutaṅga* properly means "ascetic." A *dhutaṅga* monk is one who keeps some or all of the thirteen ascetic practices allowed by the Buddha. *Dhutaṅga* monks traditionally spend time traveling (often on foot) in search of quiet places for meditation, teachers, or simply as a practice in itself.

not satisfied. Why not? Because we still have wrong view within us, just that! Wherever we go, we aren't content. However, just as that dog, if the mange is cured, is content wherever it goes, so it is for us. I reflect on this often, and I teach you this often, because it's very important.

If we know the truth of our various moods, we arrive at contentment. Whether it's hot or cold, we are satisfied, with many people or with few people, we are satisfied. Contentment doesn't depend on how many people we are with; it comes only from right view. If we have right view, then, wherever we stay, we are content. However, most of us have wrong view. It's just like a maggot! A maggot's living place is filthy, its food is filthy, but it suits the maggot. If you take a stick and brush it away from its lump of dung, it'll struggle to crawl back into it. It's the same when the Ajahn teaches us to see rightly. We resist, it makes us feel uneasy. We run back to our "lump of dung" because that's where we feel at home. We're all like this. If we don't see the harmful consequences of all our wrong views, then we can't leave them and the practice is difficult. So we should listen. There's nothing else to the practice.

If we have right view, wherever we go we are content. I have practised and seen this already. These days there are many monks, novices, and laypeople coming to see me. If I still didn't know, if I still had wrong view, I'd be dead by now! The right abiding place for monks, the place of coolness, is just Right View itself. We shouldn't look for anything else. So even though you may be unhappy, it doesn't matter, that unhappiness is uncertain. Is that unhappiness your "self"? Is there any substance to it? Is it real? I don't see it as being real at all. Unhappiness is merely a flash of feeling that appears and then is gone. Happiness is the same. Is there a consistency to happiness? Is it truly an entity? It's simply a feeling that flashes suddenly and is gone. There! It's born, and then it dies. Love just flashes up for a moment, and then disappears. Where is the consistency in love or hate or resentment? In truth, there is no substantial entity in them, they are merely impressions that flare up in the mind and then die. They deceive us constantly, we find no certainty anywhere. Just as the Buddha said, when unhappiness arises, it stays for a while, and then disappears. When unhappiness disappears, happiness arises and lingers for a while and then dies. When happiness disappears, unhappiness arises again ... on and on like this.

In the end we can say only this—apart from the birth, the life, and the death of suffering, there is nothing. There is just this. However, we who are ignorant run and grab it constantly. We never see the truth of it, that there's simply this continual change. If we understand this, then we don't need to think very much, but we have much wisdom. If we don't know it, then we will have more thinking than wisdom—and maybe no wisdom at all! It's not until we truly see the harmful results of our actions, that we can give them up. Likewise, it's not until we see the real benefits of practice, that we can follow it and begin working to make the mind "good."

If we cut a log of wood and throw it into the river, and that log doesn't sink or rot or run aground on either of the banks of the river, that log will definitely reach the sea. Our practice is comparable to this. If you practise according to the path laid down by the Buddha, following it straight, you will transcend two things. What two things? Just those two extremes that the Buddha said were not the path of a true meditator—indulgence in pleasure and indulgence in pain. These are the two banks of the river. One of the banks of that river is hate, the other is love. Or else, one can say that one bank is happiness, the other unhappiness. The "log" is this mind. As it "flows down the river," it will experience happiness and unhappiness. If the mind doesn't cling to that happiness or unhappiness it will reach the "ocean" of Nibbāna. You should see that there is nothing other than happiness and unhappiness arising and disappearing. If you don't "run aground" on these things, then you are on the path of a true meditator.

This is the teaching of the Buddha. Happiness, unhappiness, love, and hate are simply established in Nature according to the constant law of Nature. The wise person doesn't follow or encourage these states, he doesn't cling to them. This is the mind which lets go of indulgence in pleasure and indulgence in pain. It is the right practice. Just as that log of wood will eventually flow to the sea, so will the mind which doesn't attach to these two extremes inevitably attain peace.

Epilogue

Do you know where it will end? Or will you just keep on learning like this? Or is there an end to it? That's okay, but it's the external study, not the internal study. For the internal study you have to study these eyes, these ears, this nose, this tongue, this body and this mind. This is the real study. The study of books is just the external study; it's really hard to get it finished.

When the eye sees form, what sort of things happens? When ear, nose, and tongue experience sounds, smells, and tastes, what takes place? When the body and mind come into contact with touches and mental states, what reactions take place? Are there still greed, aversion and delusion there? Do we get lost in forms, sounds, smells, tastes, textures, and moods? This is the internal study. It has a point of completion.

If we study, but don't practise, we won't get any results. It's like a person who raises cows. In the morning he takes the cow out to eat grass, in the evening he brings it back to its pen—but he never drinks the cow's milk. Study is alright, but don't let it be like this. You should raise the cow and drink its milk too. You must study and practise as well to get the best results.

Here, I'll explain it further. It's like a person who raises chickens, but doesn't get the eggs. All he gets is the chicken dung! This is what I tell people who raise chickens back home! Watch out you don't become like that! This means we study the scriptures, but we don't know how to let go of defilements, we don't know how to "push" greed, aversion and delusion from our minds. Study without practice, without this "giving up," brings no results. This is why I compare it to someone who raises chickens, but doesn't collect the eggs, he just collects the dung. It's the same thing.

The Buddha wanted us to study the scriptures because of this, and then to give up evil actions through body, speech and mind; to develop goodness in our deeds, speech, and thoughts. The real worth of mankind will come to fruition through our deeds, speech, and thoughts. However, if we only talk well, without acting accordingly, it's not yet complete. If we do good deeds, but the mind is still not good, this is still not complete. The Buddha taught to develop fine deeds, fine speech, and fine thoughts. This is the treasure of mankind. The study and the practice must both be good.

The Noble Eightfold Path of the Buddha, the path of practice, has eight factors. These eight factors are nothing other than this very body: two eyes, two ears, two nostrils, one tongue, and one body. This is the path. And the mind is the one who follows the path. Therefore both the study and the practice exist in our body, speech, and mind.

Have you ever seen scriptures which teach about anything other than the body, the speech, and the mind? The scriptures only teach about this; nothing else. Defilements are born here. If you know them, they die right here. So you should understand that the practice and the study both exist right here. If we study just this much, we can know everything. It's like our speech: to speak one word of Truth is better than a lifetime of wrong speech. Do you understand? One who studies and doesn't practise is like a ladle in a soup pot. The ladle is in the pot every day, but it doesn't know the flavor of the soup. If you don't practise, even if you study till the day you die, you won't know the taste of Freedom!

Occasion of the talks

On Meditation is an informal talk given in the northeastern dialect, taken from an unidentified tape.

The Path in Harmony and *The Benefits and Dangers of Samādhi* are a composite of two talks given in England in 1979 and 1977, respectively.

The Middle Way Within was given in the northeastern dialect to an assembly of monks and laypeople in 1970.

The Peace Beyond is a condensed version of a talk given to the Chief Privy Councillor of Thailand, Mr. Sanya Dharmasakti, at Wat Nong Pah Pong, 1978.

Opening the Dhamma Eye was given at Wat Nong Pah Pong to the assembly of monks and novices in October, 1968.

Convention & Liberation is an informal talk given in the northeastern dialect, taken from an unidentified tape.

No Abiding is a talk given to the monks, novices and laypeople of Wat Pah Nanachat on a visit to Wat Nong Pah Pong during the rains of 1980.

A Biographical Sketch of Venerable Ajahn Chah

Venerable Ajahn Chah (Pra Bodhinyāna Thera) was born into a typical farming family in Bahn Gor village, in the province of Ubol Rachathani, northeast Thailand, in 1917. He lived the first part of his life as any other youngster in rural Thailand, and, following the custom, took ordination as a novice in the local village Wat (temple) for a number of years, where he learned to read and write, in addition to some basic Buddhist teachings.

After a number of years, he returned to the lay life to help his parents, but, feeling an attraction to the monastic life, he again entered a Wat at the age of twenty, this time obtaining the higher acceptance as a *bhikkhu*, or Buddhist monk. He spent the first few years of his bhikkhu life studying scriptures and learning Pali, but the death of his father awakened him to the transience of life and instilled in him a desire to find the real essence of the Buddha's teaching.

He began to travel to other monasteries, studying the monastic discipline in detail and spending a very brief, but significant time with Venerable Ajahn Mun, the most outstanding meditation Master of the ascetic, forest-dwelling tradition. Following his time with Venerable Ajahn Mun, he spent a number of years traveling around Thailand, spending his time in forests and charnel grounds, ideal places for developing meditation practice.

At length he came within the vicinity of the village of his birth, and when word got around that he was in the area, he was invited to set up a monastery in the Pah Pong forest, a place at that time reputed to be the habitat of wild animals and ghosts. Venerable Ajahn Chah's impeccable approach to meditation, the Dhamma practice, and his simple, direct style of teaching, with the emphasis on practical application and a balanced attitude, began to attract a large following of monks and laypeople.

In 1966 the first Westerner came to stay at Wat Pah Pong, the American Venerable Sumedho Bhikkhu. From that time on, the number of foreign people who came to Ajahn Chah began to steadily increase, until in 1975, the first branch monastery for

Western and other non-Thai nationals, Wat Pah Nanachat, was set up with Ajahn Sumedho as the abbot.

Venerable Ajahn Chah was invited to England together with Ajahn Sumedho in 1976, the outcome of which was eventually the establishment of the first branch monastery of Wat Pah Pong outside of Thailand. Since then, further branch monasteries have been established in England, Switzerland, Australia, America, New Zealand, and Italy.

In 1980 Venerable Ajahn Chah began to feel more acutely the symptoms of dizziness and memory lapse which he had been feeling for some years. This led to an operation in 1981, which, however, failed to reverse the onset of the paralysis that eventually rendered him completely bedridden and unable to speak. However, this did not stop the growing number of monks and laypeople coming to practise at his monastery, for whom the teachings of Ajahn Chah are a constant guide and inspiration.

After remaining bedridden and silent for an astonishing ten years, being carefully tended by his monks and novices, Venerable Ajahn Chah passed away on the 16th of January, 1992, at the age of 74. He left behind him a thriving community of monastics and layfollowers living in monasteries all over the world. They continue the practice of the Buddha's teachings under the inspiration of this great meditation teacher.

Mātṛceṭa's Hymn to the Buddha

An English Rendering of the Śatapañcāśatka

by
Ven. S. Dhammika

WHEEL PUBLICATION NO. 360/361

Copyright © Kandy; Buddhist Publication Society, (1989)

Notes

All references to the Pali Nikāyas are to volume and page number of the Pali Text Society editions.

Introduction

For centuries people have stood in awe of the Buddha and his attainments and have strived to express their feelings in stone and bronze and with brush and ink. Some have been moved by what the Buddha said, its logical consistency, its scope and its humanism. Others have been inspired by the personality of the Lord himself, his manner and conduct, and even his physical form. The joyful faith and appreciation that is evoked on recollecting the Buddha's personality and singing his praise gives such people the strength they need to walk the Path. For them the Dhamma comes alive through the life and example of the Buddha.

Such a person was the poet Mātṛceṭa. He was born in India in about the first century A.D., and was converted from Hinduism to Buddhism by the great philosopher Āryadeva. He wrote about a dozen works, some of such beauty that he came to be regarded as one of India's greatest poets.[1] I-tsing, the Chinese pilgrim who travelled through India in the seventh century A.D., says of Mātṛceṭa's poems:

"These charming compositions are equal in beauty to the heavenly flowers and the high principles which they contain rival in dignity the lofty peaks of a mountain. Consequently in India all who compose hymns imitate his style, considering him the father of literature. Even men like the Bodhisattvas Asaṅga and Vasubandhu admire him greatly. Throughout India everyone who becomes a monk is taught Mātṛceṭa's two hymns as soon as they can recite the five and ten precepts."

I-tsing also recounts a beautiful legend that was told about the poet indicating his wide popularity:

While the Buddha was living, he was once, while instructing his followers, wandering in a wood among the people. A nightingale in the wood, seeing the Buddha, ... began to utter its melodious notes, as if to praise him. The Buddha, looking back at his disciples, said:

---

1. A. K. Warder, *Indian Kāvya Literature* (Delhi, 1974), Vol. II, Chapter 7, contains a detailed and informative analysis of the style, contents and alliterations in Mātṛceṭa's works and of their place in the Indian Kavya tradition.

"That bird transported with joy at the sight of me unconsciously utters its melodious notes. On account of this good deed, after my passing away this bird shall be born in human form, and named Mātṛceṭa, shall praise my virtues with true appreciation."

Other than these few scraps of information we know nothing of Mātṛceṭa and today his name is remembered only for its association with his greatest work, the Śatapañcāśatka.

The name Śatapañcāśatka literally means "Hymn in a Hundred and Fifty Verses," although there are actually a hundred and fifty-two, or in some versions, a hundred and fifty-three verses in the work. It lies very much within the *bhakti* or devotional genre of Indian literature but is refreshingly free from the florid style that so often characterises such works. Shackleton-Bailey notes that the "style of the Hymn is simple and direct, free from swollen compounds and elaborate conceits."[2] Warder says that "the restraint of these verses is that of complete mastery of the medium, able to express rich meaning with a few carefully chosen words and without the support of outward display." He goes on to say that the verses "are handled with a kind of reticence suggestive of the poet's humility and detachment, both of which are probably sincere."[3] Certainly all who are familiar with the Hymn in its original Sanskrit acknowledge the great beauty of both its language and meaning. In ancient India numerous commentaries were written on the Hymn. It was popular with the followers of all schools of Buddhism and was translated into several different languages. Tāranātha, the great Tibetan historian, says the Hymn had an important part to play in the spread of Buddhism outside India, and should it become as well known as it once was it may continue to create an interest in the Buddha and his teachings.[4]

Centuries before Mātṛceṭa, the householder Upāli was so inspired by the Buddha's presence that he too composed a hymn of praise. When asked why he had done so he replied:

"It is as if there were a great heap of different flowers which a clever garland maker or his apprentice might string into a

---

2. D.R. Shackleton-Bailey, *The Śatapañcāśatka of Mātśceṭa* (Cambridge, 1951).

3. Indian Kāvya Literature, Vol. II, p. 234.

4. Lama Chimpa and Alaka Chattopadhayaya, Taraṇatha's History of Buddhism in India (Calcutta, 1980), Chapter 18.

variegated garland. Likewise the Lord has many splendid qualities. And who would not give praise to one worthy of praise?"[5]

There can be no doubt that Mātṛceṭa's hymn likewise is an expression of a deep devotion to the Buddha and an admiration of his qualities. But quite apart from the author's motive in writing it, the value and indeed the purpose of the Hymn to the Buddha is twofold. First it is meant to awaken our faith. Mātṛceṭa recognised as did the Lord himself that faith has the power to arouse a tremendous amount of positive zeal and energy. Long before we have directly experienced it, faith keeps our eyes fixed firmly on the goal. When we stumble and fall, faith picks us up; when doubt causes us to falter, it urges us on; and when we get side-tracked, it brings us back to the Path. Without faith in the Buddha and the efficacy of his Dharma we would never even bother to try to put the teachings into practice. As Nāgārjuna says:

"One associates with the Dharma out of faith, but one knows truly out of understanding; understanding is the chief of the two, but faith precedes."[6]

The Buddha's qualities are worthy of respect in themselves, but when they are described so fully and so beautifully in verses like those of Mātṛceṭa, our faith can only be strengthened and grow.

The other purpose of the Hymn is to urge us into action. Mātṛceṭa highlights the Buddha's gentleness, his non-retaliation, his patience and his other qualities, knowing that when we have a deep admiration for someone it is natural to try to emulate him. One feels that he used his poetic skills to the full in the hope that we would be inspired enough to make the Buddha our model and follow his example. When we read that the Buddha extended the hand of friendship to all without exception we feel we should try to do the same. On being reminded that the Buddha endured abuse and hardship without complaint we find the strength to be a little more forbearing. When brooding over our imperfections casts us down, nothing fills us with new determination and vigour more than calling to mind the Buddha's attainments. The receptive mind will transform admiration into action.

---

5. Majjhima Nikāya, II:387.
6. Ratnavalī 5.

The Hymn may have another value as well: as an aid to meditation. In concentration meditation thoughts are silenced, in mindfulness meditation they are observed with detachment, but in recollection meditation thoughts are directed to a specific subject which is then carefully pondered upon. The Buddha says: "Monks, whatever a monk ponders on and thinks about often the mind in consequence gets a leaning in that way," and this is certainly true.[7] Any type of thought that is prominent in our mind will have an influence upon our personality and behaviour. To consciously and intentionally think positive thoughts will, in time, allow such thoughts to arise quite naturally, and from that will spring deeds associated with such positive thoughts. In practising the Recollection of the Buddha, *Buddhānussati*, one sits silently, and having made the mind receptive, thinks about the Buddha's many deeds and qualities. In time, faith and devotion, both of which are important spiritual faculties, begin to gain in strength, thus adding energy and even fervour to our practice. Those who do this meditation usually either read or recite the well-known *Iti pi so* formula to help guide their thoughts. But they may find that reading extracts from the Hymn to the Buddha can be used together with this formula, or at times as a substitute for it, with very positive results.

D.R. Shackleton-Bailey has done a complete English translation of the Hymn to the Buddha and Edward Conze has translated parts of it.[8] Both these translations are literal and scholarly but do not give sufficient regard to the spirit of the work and the author's intention in writing it—to inspire and to uplift. By reworking these two translations and occasionally referring to the Sanskrit text with the help of my friend, Ven. Hippola Paññakitti, I have attempted to produce a readable rendering of this beautiful and important work. Those interested in a scholarly version of the Hymn are advised to read Shackleton-Bailey's translation with its copious notes on language, manuscript variations and textual difficulties.

---

7. Majjhima Nikāya, II:115.

8. Edward Conze, *Buddhist Texts Through the Ages* (New York, 1954).

Hymn to the Buddha

1. Invocation

1 No faults in any way are found in him;
   All virtues in every way dwell in him.

2 To go to him for refuge, to sing his praise,
   to do him honour and to abide in his Dharma
   is proper for one with understanding.

3 The only Protector,
   his faults are gone without residue.
   The All-knowing One,
   his virtues are present without fail.

4 Even the most spiteful man
   cannot with justice find fault
   in the thoughts, words or deeds of the Lord.

5 To be born human and encounter the great joy
   of the good Dharma is a chance rarer than
   a turtle thrusting its neck through a yoke
   floating freely in the great ocean.

6 So how could I not put voice to good use now,
   for it is impermanent and may soon be liable to change.

7 Though I know that the Sage's virtues
   are beyond all human calculation,
   still I will recount a portion of them,
   if only for my own delight.

8 Homage to you, O Self-developed One
   whose good works are many and wondrous,
   whose virtues are too numerous and awesome to define.

9 Their number? They are infinite.
   Their nature? Words must fail.

But to speak of them bestows great good, so I shall speak much.

* * *

2. In Praise of Causes

10   Having brushed aside doubts
     about whether or not it could be done,
     of your own free will you took
     this helpless world under your protection.

11   You were kind without being asked,
     you were loving without reason,
     you were a friend to the stranger
     and a kinsman to those without kin.

12   You gave even your own flesh
     not to mention your wealth and possessions.
     Even your own life's breath, O Kindly One,
     you gave to those who wished for it.[9]

13   A hundred times you ransomed your own body and life
     for the bodies and lives of living beings
     in the grip of their would-be slayers.

14   It was not fear of hell or desire for heaven
     but utter purity of heart
     that made you practise the good.

15   By always avoiding the crooked
     and adhering to the straight,
     you became the highest receptacle for purity.

16   When attacked you used your fiery power
     against the defilements, but in your noble heart
     felt only sympathy for those who were defiled.

---

9.   Here and in verses 13, 17 and 18 reference is to the Buddha sacrificing his life in former births as recounted in the Jātaka Stories.

17 The joy beings feel on saving their lives
equals not the joy you experienced
when you gave your life for others.

18 No matter how often murderers cut you to pieces,
regardless of the pain
you felt only compassion for them.

19 That seed of perfect enlightenment,
that jewel-like mind of yours,
only you, Great Hero, know its essence.
Others are far from understanding it.

20 "Nirvana is not won without perseverance":
thinking thus you roused great energy
without a thought for yourself.

21 Your progress towards excellence never faltered
and now you have attained
the state that cannot be bettered.

22 But you did not practise in order to experience
the pleasant and fruitful results of meditation.
Always in your heart the motive was compassion.

23 For the happiness which, though sublime,
cannot be shared with others,
pains rather than pleases
those like you, O Righteous One.

24 You imbibed good speech, bad speech you shunned like poison,
from mixed speech you extracted what was sweet.[10]

25 Purchasing words of wisdom even with your own life,
in birth after birth, O Knower of Gems,
you were zealous for enlightenment.

---

10. A mixture of truth and falsehood, useful and useless.

26 Thus striving through the three incalculable aeons
    accompanied only by your resolution,
    you gained the highest state.[11]

* * *

3. In Praise of Incomparability

27 By not envying the superior,
    despising the inferior,
    or competing with equals,
    you attained pre-eminence in the world.

28 You were devoted to virtues for their own sake,
    not for the rewards that come from them,
    and thus due to your right progress
    they have all come to completion within you.

29 So much good have you gathered by your deeds
    that even the dust on your feet
    has become a source of merit.

30 You dissolved and uprooted your faults,
    you purified and brought to completion your virtues,
    and by this wise procedure
    you reached the highest attainment.

31 You struck at faults with your might
    so that not even their shadow
    lingers in the depths of your mind.[12]

32 Step by step you nurtured the virtues
    and established them in yourself, so that now
    not even their likeness is found elsewhere.

---

11. It is said to take a bodhisattva at least three incalculable aeons to attain full enlightenment. See Har Dayal, *The Bodhisattva Doctrine in Buddhist Sanskrit Literature* (London, 1932).

12. *Ātmasaṃtāne*: literally, "the flow (of consciousness) that makes up the self." Pali, *cittasantati*.

33 All worldly objects of comparison
    can be damaged or obstructed,
    limited by time and space, easily acquired.

34 How can they be compared with your virtues—
    virtues unrivalled, unapproachable,
    stable, unceasing, unsurpassed?

35 When measured against the unfathomable
    and boundless depth of your understanding,
    the ocean becomes as if a mere puddle.

36 When matched with your calm equanimity,
    the firmness of the earth
    seems like the quivering of a flower petal.

37 Beside the radiance of your wisdom,
    which destroys the darkness of ignorance,
    the sun does not attain even the brightness of a firefly.

38 The purity of the moon, the sky or a pool in autumn
    appears clouded when compared
    with the purity of your words, thoughts and deeds.

39 I have compared you with all that is admired in the world,
    but still how far are those miserable things
    from the qualities of a Buddha.

40 For there is only one thing that resembles you,
    O Kindly One, and that is the jewel of the Dharma
    through which you attained the highest.

41 But if something were to be found comparable to you,
    to make such comparison
    would be the act of a foolish and disrespectful man.

* * *

4. In Praise of Wonders

42 Your victory over Māra evokes wonder in people
    but considering your great virtues
    I think this is but a minor thing.[13]

43 Even those who lash out in fury to assault you
    are not a heavy burden for your patience to bear
    housed as it is in such a worthy vessel.

44 What is truly wondrous is this:
    after you conquered Māra, on that same night
    you were able to conquer your own defilements.

45 He who is amazed at your victory over opponents,
    might well be amazed at the sun for dispelling the darkness
    with its garland of a thousand rays.

46 You have overcome three things with three things:
    passion with passionlessness,
    anger with love,
    and ignorance with wisdom.

47 Good deeds you praise, bad deeds you blame,
    but towards those who act thus
    you are free from any "for" or "against."

48 Is any praise high enough for you
    whose mind transcends
    attachment to the noble and dislike for the ignoble?[14]

49 You did not cling to virtue
    nor yearn for those who were virtuous.
    Ah! See the purity of this most tranquil being!

50 How permanently calm your mind is can be known
    by seeing how unalterably calm your senses are.

---

13. *Māra*: evil personified, the Tempter in Buddhism.
14. *Arahant*: literally, a saint. *Tīrthika*: an adherent of a non-Buddhist sect.

51 Even the foolish acknowledge the purity of your mind.
    The goodness of your words and deeds
    reflects your pure thoughts.

* * *

5. In Praise of Form

52 Lovely yet calming, bright but not blinding, gentle
    yet strong. Who would not be inspired just to see you?

53 The joy one feels on beholding you for the first time
    does not diminish even after seeing you a hundred times.

54 Each time it is seen, your form gives joy;
    its beauty is such that one is never satisfied.

55 Your body is worthy as a receptacle
    and your virtues are worthy as occupants.
    Both are excellent in themselves
    and both complement each other perfectly.

56 Where else could the virtues of a Tathāgata
    be so well housed as in your body,
    shining as it does with auspicious marks and signs?[15]

57 Your body seems to say to your virtues:
    "I am blessed to have you,"
    and your virtues seem to respond:
    "Where better could we dwell?"

* * *

---

15. *Tathāgata*: An epithet of the Buddha meaning the "Thus Come One" or the "Thus Gone One." The thirty-two major marks and the eighty minor signs are special features of a Buddha's physical body.

6. In Praise of Compassion

58 You long bound yourself to compassion in order to free
all those in the world who were bound by defilements.

59 Which shall I praise first, you or the great compassion
by which you were long held in saṃsāra
though well you knew its faults?[16]

60 Although you preferred the delights of solitude,
compassion led you to spend your time among the crowd.

61 Like a mighty dragon drawn from its lake by a spell,
compassion led you from forest to town
for the sake of those to be taught.

62 Though abiding in deep tranquillity, the development of
compassion made you take up even the musical art.[17]

63 Your powers, your lion's roar
and the manifestation of virtues are but glitter
rubbed off the nugget of your innate compassion.[18]

64 Your compassion was kind only towards others,
but was cruel towards her own master.
Towards you alone, O Lord, compassion was pitiless.[19]

65 That same compassion
had you cut into a hundred pieces

---

16. *Saṃsāra*: the beginningless round of birth and death.

17. In one of his former lives the Buddha was born as a musician and used his skills to convert the gods. See Guttila Jātaka.

18. On the ten psychic powers, see Nyanatiloka, *Buddhist Dictionary* (Colombo, 1972) under *Iddhi*. The "lion's roar" is the Buddha's bold and confident claim to enlightenment. The meaning of this verse is that compassion, the nugget, is the most important thing while the powers, etc., "the glitter," are just a by-product of that compassion.

19. Here and in verses 65 and 66 compassion is personified as one who acts for the sake of others even to the extent of causing discomfort to the Buddha.

and cast you like an offering to the four quarters,
all for the sake of others.

66 But clearly compassion always acted in accordance
with your will. For although she oppressed you,
he did not transgress against your desires.

* * *

7. In Praise of Speech

67-8 Well worded and significant, true and sweet,
deep or plain or both together, condensed or copious.
Hearing such words of yours, would not even an opponent
be convinced that you were all-knowing?

69 Generally your speech was wholly sweet
but when necessary it would be otherwise.
But either way, every word was well spoken
because it always achieved its purpose.

70 Soft or hard or possessing both qualities,
all your words when distilled had but one taste.[20]

71 Ah! How pure, perfect and excellent your actions are,
that you employed these jewel-like words in such a way.

72 From your mouth pleasing to the eye, drop words
pleasing to the ear, like nectar from the moon.[21]

73 Your sayings are like a spring shower settling the dust of
passions, like a garuḍa killing the serpent of hatred.[22]

---

20. The taste of liberation (*vimuttirasa*)—Udāna 56.
21. The ancient Indians believed that nectar fell from the moon.
22. The *garuḍa* is a mythological bird, the natural enemy of the serpent.

74 They are like the sun again and again
dispelling the darkness of ignorance,
like Śakra's sceptre splitting the mountain of pride.[23]

75 Your speech is excellent in three ways:
based on fact it is truthful,
because its motive is pure it causes no confusion,
and being relevant it is easily understood.

76 When first heard your words excite the mind
but when their meaning is pondered over
they wash away all ignorance and passion.

77 They go to the hearts of all.
While comforting the grieving they alarm the heedless
and rouse those preoccupied with pleasures.

78 Truly your words are for all: they delight the wise,
strengthen those of middling intelligence
and illuminate the minds of the dull.

79 Your sayings coax men from false views
and draw them towards Nirvana.
They remove faults and rain down virtues.

80 Your knowledge embraces all things,
your mindfulness is ever present
and thus what you say will always come to pass.

81 Because you never speak at the wrong time
or in the wrong place or towards the wrong person,
your words, like energy rightly applied, are never wasted.

* * *

---

23. Śakra is the king of the gods in Vedic mythology. He has a sceptre of unbreakable hardness.

8. In Praise of Teaching

82 Your dispensation and only yours is the true path:
its methods are pleasant, its fruits good,
it is free from faults and lovely
in the beginning, the middle and the end.[24]

83 If fools, because of their attachment to deluded views,
condemn your wonderful teaching,
then deluded views are their own worst enemy.

84 Remembering the suffering which you endured
for the sake of others, it would be good
to listen to your teachings even if they were wrong.

85 But coming from one so kind in words and deeds,
how much more should your teachings be practised
with all the vigour one would use to remove
a blazing turban from one's head.

86 Freedom, the joy of enlightenment,
praiseworthy virtues and peace:
these four benefits are all gained from your teaching.

87 O Great Hero, your teachings brought trembling to sectarians,
misery to Namuci, but rejoicing to both gods and men.[25]

88 Even the rule of Death, which extends
without impediment or obstacle over the triple world,
has been crushed by your teaching.[26]

89 For those who fathom your teachings can live an aeon
if they so desire, but freely they depart
to the realm where death cannot tread.[27]

---

24. *Ekāyanam*: literally, the one way, thus "the true path."

25. *Namuci*: another name for Māra.

26. The triple world: the world of desire, the world of form and the formless world. See *Buddhist Dictionary* under *Loka*.

27. For the notion that those who have mastered the teaching can live for an

90 Only in your dispensation is time divided
    for studying the scriptures, pondering their meaning
    and practising meditation.

91 What is more distressful than this, Great Sage,
    that some people do not revere your teaching,
    full of goodness as it is?

* * *

9. In Praise of Benefits Conferred

92 Just to hear you brings joy;
    just to look upon you calms the heart;
    your speech refreshes and your teaching frees.

93 People rejoice at your birth,
    they celebrate as you grow,
    they benefit from your presence
    and sorrow in your absence.

94 To praise you removes faults,
    to recollect you brings joy,
    to follow you gives understanding,
    to know you purifies the heart.

95 To approach you brings good fortune,
    to serve you gives wisdom,
    to worship you dispels fear,
    to wait upon you bestows prosperity.

96 You are a great lake of goodness,
    with waters purified by virtue,
    surface calmed by meditation
    and depths stilled by wisdom.

97 Your form is a jewel to see,
    your speech is a jewel to hear,

---

aeon, see Dīgha Nikāya, II: 103,118.

your teachings are a jewel to reflect upon.
Truly, you are a mine bearing the jewels of goodness.

98 You are an island for those swept along by the flood,
a shelter for the stricken,
a refuge for those in fear of becoming,
a resort for those who aspire to liberation.

99 To all living beings
you are a useful vessel because of your virtue,
a fertile field because of your perfect fruit,
a true friend because of the benefits you confer.

100 You are admired for your altruism,
charming for your tenderness,
beloved for your gentleness
and honoured for your many virtues.

101 You are cherished because of your flawlessness,
delightful because of the goodness of your form and speech,
opulent because you promote the good of all,
and blessed because you are the abode of virtues.

* * *

10. In Praise of Guidance

102–3 You admonish the stubborn,
restrain the hasty and straighten the crooked.
You encourage the slow and harness the tamed.
Truly, you are the unsurpassed guide of men.

104 You have pity for the suffering, good-will for the happy,
compassion for the distressed, benevolence for all.

105 The hostile evoke your warmth,
the immoral receive your help, the fierce find you tender.
How wonderful is your noble heart!

106 If father and mother are to be honoured
    because of concern for their children,
    what reverence should you receive whose love has no limits?

107 You are a wall of safety
    for those hovering at the edge of the cliff,
    those blind to their own welfare,
    those who are their own worst enemy.

108 For the welfare of the two worlds
    and to help beings transcend them,
    you lit the lamp of wisdom
    among those who dwell in darkness.[28]

109 When worldly enjoyments are at stake,
    men and gods act at variance with each other.
    But because they can enjoy the Dharma in harmony,
    they are reconciled in you.

110 O Blessed One, you have given the comfort
    of the Dharma unstintingly to all,
    regardless of birth, age or caste,
    regardless of time or place.

111 As if amazed and envious
    the gods honour with joined palms even your disciples,
    who unlike them are free from amazement and envy.

112 Ah! How brilliant is the arising of a Buddha,
    that cream of saṃsāra.
    Because of him the gods envy mankind.

* * *

---

28. The "two worlds" are the world of gods and the world of humans.

11. In Praise of Arduous Deeds

113 Fatigue, loss of the joy of solitude,
the company of fools, the press of the crowd
and the pairs of opposites: all these discomforts
you endure as if they were blessings.[29]

114 With mind detached, you quietly work
for the welfare of the world.
How awesome is the Buddha-nature of the Buddha![30]

115 You ate poor food, sometimes you went hungry.
You walked rough paths and slept on the ground
trampled hard by the hooves of cattle.[31]

116 Though you are the Master, in order to serve others
you endured insults and adapted your clothes and words,
out of love for those whom you taught.

117 You are the Lord, but you never lord over others.
All may use you as a servant to obtain the help they need.

118 No matter who provoked you,
where or how, never did you transgress
your own path of fair conduct.

119 You help those who wish you ill
more than most men
help those who wish them well.

120 To an enemy intent on evil
you are a friend intent on good.
To one who gleefully seeks faults
you respond by seeking virtues.

---

29. The pairs of opposites are praise and blame, cold and heat, sickness and health, ease and discomfort, etc.

30. *Buddhadharmatā.* See *Encyclopaedia of Buddhism,* Vol. III (Colombo, 1973), p. 435.

31. For a description of the hardships and simplicity of the Buddha's life similar to those mentioned here, see Aṅguttara Nikāya, 1:34.

121 Those who sought to give you poison and fire
you approached with compassion and nectar.

122 You conquered revilers with patience,
the malicious with blessings,
slanderers with truth and the cruel with kindness.

123 You reversed in an instant
the manifold natures and evil destinies
of those depraved from beginningless time.

* * *

12. In Praise of Skill

124 Through your skill in teaching the rough became gentle,
the mean became generous and the cruel became kind.

125 A Nanda became serene, a Mānastabdha[32] humble,
an Aṅgulimāla compassionate.
Who would not be amazed?[33]

126 Delighted with the flavour of your teaching,
many wise ones left their beds of gold
to sleep on beds of straw.

127 Because you knew time and temperaments,
sometimes you remained silent when questioned,
sometimes you spoke first, and at other times you aroused
their interest and then spoke.

128 Having first scrubbed clean the garment of the mind
with talk on generosity and other virtues,
you then applied the dye of the Dharma.

---

32. *Mānastabdha* means "stiff with pride."
33. Nanda was so distracted by sensual thoughts that he was unable to meditate—Udāna 21. Mānastabdha was so proud that he would not even respect his parents—Saṃyutta Nikāya, I:177. Aṅgulimāla was a terrible murderer—Majjhima Nikāya, II: 98–103. All were skillfully transformed by the Buddha.

129 There is no expedient or opportunity
which you did not use
in order to rescue this pitiful world
from the fearful abyss of saṃsāra.

130 To train people in different situations,
according to their state of mind,
many and various were the words and deeds you used.

131 They were pure and friendly, honoured and praised,
saluted and acclaimed by both gods and men.

132 Difficult it is to speak well and then do good.
But for you, O Truthful One, both these things come easily.

133 By your purity alone you could have cleansed the whole universe.
In the triple world no one is to be found like you.

134 You rose up for the welfare of all beings
lost in the beginningless and fearful straits of becoming.

* * *

13. In Praise of Freedom from Debt

135 I know not how to repay you
for what you have done;
even those who have attained Nirvana
are still in your debt.

136 Established in the Dharma by you,
they accomplished their own welfare only.
But you worked by yourself for the welfare of all,
so how can you be repaid for that?

137 You look upon those who slumber and gently awaken them.
You are a kind and heedful friend to those who are heedless.

138 You have declared the destruction of the defilements,
you have exposed Māra's delusions,
you have taught the evils of saṃsāra,
you have revealed the place without fear.

139 Those who work for the welfare of the world
and those of compassionate heart, what could they do
wherein you have not already led the way?

140 If your good qualities could be given to others,
surely you would have shared them with all, even with
Devadatta.[34]

141 Out of compassion for the world
you promoted the good Dharma for so long on earth.
Many disciples have you raised
capable of working for the welfare of the world.[35]

142 Many personal converts have you trained,
Subhadra being the last.
What still remains of your debt to living beings?[36]

143 Powdering your bones into tiny pieces
with the diamond of concentration,
even in the end you continued to do what was hard to do.

144 "My Dharma body and my physical body both exist
only for the sake of others." Speaking thus
even in Nirvana you taught this reluctant world.[37]

---

34. Devadatta was the Buddha's evil cousin who caused a schism in the monastic community and even tried to kill the Buddha.

35. Shackleton-Bailey includes, prior to this verse, a verse of which he notes that its grammatical peculiarities and exclusion from early texts are "sufficiently strong grounds for doubting its authenticity." I have therefore decided to omit it.

36. As he lay on his death-bed the Buddha taught and made a disciple of Subhadra. See Dīgha Nikāya, II:149, 153.

37. Here and in verse 145 the Buddha's teaching or Dharma body, which lasts as long as people understand and practise his teachings, is compared with

145 Having given your entire Dharma body to the virtuous,
you broke your physical body into fragments
and attained final Nirvana.

146 What steadfastness! What conduct!
What form! What virtue!
Truly there is nothing about the Buddha's qualities
that is not wonderful.

147 Yet even to you whose speech and actions are so helpful
are some men hostile. Behold the ferocity of delusion!

148 O ocean of good, treasury of gems,
heap of merit, mine of virtues!
Those who honour you are themselves worthy of honour.

149 Your virtues are limitless
but my capacity to praise them is not.
Therefore I shall finish, not because I am satisfied
but for fear of running out of words.

150 Only you can measure your own qualities
being as they are beyond measure,
beyond number, thought and comparison.

151 I have hardly begun to sing your praise
and yet already my heart is filled with joy.
But need a lake be drained before one's thirst be quenched?

152 Through the merit arising from my good deed,
born of faith in the Sage,
may the minds of beings now tossed by evil thoughts
be free from distress and come to peace.

---

his physical body which disintegrates at death. See I.B. Horner's discussion on *dhammakāya* in *Milinda's Questions* (London, 1963), p.xl.

ABOUT PARIYATTI

Pariyatti is dedicated to providing affordable access to authentic teachings of the Buddha about the Dhamma theory (*pariyatti*) and practice (*paṭipatti*) of Vipassana meditation. A 501(c)(3) nonprofit charitable organization since 2002, Pariyatti is sustained by contributions from individuals who appreciate and want to share the incalculable value of the Dhamma teachings. We invite you to visit www.pariyatti.org to learn about our programs, services, and ways to support publishing and other undertakings.

Pariyatti Publishing Imprints

Vipassana Research Publications (focus on Vipassana as taught by S.N. Goenka in the tradition of Sayagyi U Ba Khin)

BPS Pariyatti Editions (selected titles from the Buddhist Publication Society, copublished by Pariyatti)

MPA Pariyatti Editions (selected titles from the Myanmar Pitaka Association, copublished by Pariyatti)

Pariyatti Digital Editions (audio and video titles, including discourses)

Pariyatti Press (classic titles returned to print and inspirational writing by contemporary authors)

Pariyatti enriches the world by

- disseminating the words of the Buddha,
- providing sustenance for the seeker's journey,
- illuminating the meditator's path.

www.ingramcontent.com/pod-product-compliance
Lightning Source LLC
Chambersburg PA
CBHW020348170426
43200CB00005B/98